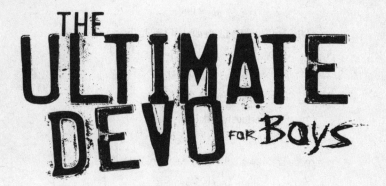

ALSO IN THE 2:52 SERIES

2:52 Boys' Bible

How to Draw Good, Bad & Ugly Bible Guys

How to Draw Big Bad Bible Beasts

Big Bad Bible Giants

Bible Heroes & Bad Guys

Seriously Sick Bible Stuff

Weird & Gross Bible Stuff

Creepy Creatures & Bizarre Beasts from the Bible

Bible Angels & Demons

Bible Freaks & Geeks

Bible Wars & Weapons

365 DAILY DEVOTIONS

THE ULTIMATE DEVO for Boys

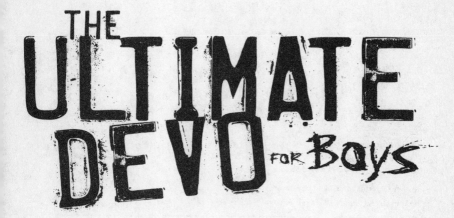

AND JESUS GREW IN WISDOM AND IN STATURE,
AND IN FAVOR WITH GOD AND MEN
LUKE 2:52 –NIV

ED STRAUSS

ZONDER**kidz**

ZONDERVAN.com/
AUTHOR**TRACKER**
follow your favorite authors

ZONDERKIDZ

2:52 Ultimate Devo for Boys
Copyright © 2007, 2009 by Edward Strauss

Requests for information should be addressed to:

Zonderkidz, *Grand Rapids, Michigan 49530*

Library of Congress Cataloging-in-Publication Data

Strauss, Ed, 1953-
    2:52 ultimate devo for boys / by Ed Strauss.
      p. cm.
    ISBN 978-0-310-71314-2 (softcover)
     1. Boys—Prayers and devotions. 2. Preteens—Prayers and devotions.
  3. Bible—Meditations. I. Title.
  BV4855.S758 2009
  242'.62—dc22
                                     2009013980

Cover design: *Cindy Davis*
Interior design: *Carlos Eluetrio Estrada and Luke Daab*

Printed in the United States of America

09 10 11 12 13 14 15 16 17 18 • 24 23 22 21 20 19 18 17 16 15 14 13 12 11 10 9 8 7 6 5 4 3 2 1

YOUNG AND FUN LOVING

Don't let anyone look down on you because you are young, but set an example for the believers in speech, in life, in love, in faith and in purity.
— 1 Timothy 4:12

Timothy was a young man when he joined Paul's team. Timothy was timid, but God saw that he had the right stuff and later made him a leader of the churches. Only problem was, Timothy was still so young. Many older Christians thought young meant immature, so Paul told Timothy to prove that this wasn't true by setting an example of living as a Christian.

What does this mean for you? Does it mean that being a Christian is super-serious business and that you should never laugh, never have goofy moments and never enjoy any wild, energetic fun? Does it mean you have to try to be perfect? No, it doesn't mean any of that. But being young and fun loving does not equal being foolish and out-of-control.

Live for the truth and give careful thought to how you speak and behave. You may be full of energy and jokes, but don't let go completely so that you become outrageously foolish and disrespectful like a baboon that's throwing stuff at the crowds watching him. Yes, have fun, but remember how God expects all Christians—young and old—to behave.

More people are watching your life than you imagine. Don't give them any reason to look down on you or the faith you believe in.

SEEING THAT GOD IS REAL

"God's invisible qualities — his eternal power and divine nature — have been clearly seen, being understood from what has been made."
— Romans 1:20

God is a spiritual being. He lives in another dimension, and human eyes just aren't made for seeing spiritual things. That whole realm is invisible to us. But there is a way to clearly understand what he's like. How's that? By looking at the world that God made.

When you play a super cool computer game with cutting-edge graphics, you just know that some awesome programmer designed the thing, right? Even if the programmer's not around for you to actually see, you know he or she exists. If you walk into your friend's house and see a million-piece Lego castle, you might ask, "Whoa! Did you build this?" If your friend says, "Nah. The dog sneezed, and this all fell into place," you'd say, "Yeah, riiight."

It's the same with God. Study the awesome way that nature works and how complex living things are, and it hits you that you're looking at the work of an invisible, intelligent Creator. And this Creator's not just super smart, he has awesome power. When people examine things like DNA or the human brain, even if they don't know God they figure there had to be an intelligent designer behind it. It's far too amazing to be an accident.

Do you want to see evidence of God? Look at the things he created. They tell you a lot about what he's like and give you a glimpse of how powerful he is.

JESUS' POWERFUL RESURRECTION

"He was not abandoned to the grave, nor did his body see decay. God has raised this Jesus to life, and we are all witnesses of the fact."
—Acts 2:31–32

Jesus was nailed to a cross on a Friday morning, and he died that afternoon. His friends buried him just before sunset, and Jesus' lifeless body lay in a cold, dark tomb all that night, all the next day, and all the next night. Then at dawn Sunday morning, there was a violent earthquake, the stone door of his tomb rolled aside, and Jesus walked out. He appeared to his disciples, proving that he was alive again.

You may say, "Okay, I saw a program on TV about a guy whose heart stopped. He was dead for two minutes, and then the doctors gave him an electric shock, and he came back to life." Yeah, but that guy wasn't nearly beaten to death by Roman soldiers and then nailed to a cross. And he didn't lay dead in a tomb for about forty hours. When people are dead like Jesus was dead, they stay dead.

Another thing: when Jesus' body came back to life, his flesh-and-blood corpse was transformed into a powerful, eternal body that could walk through walls or appear and disappear. His body had been utterly changed. This was a supernatural miracle.

Jesus is the only person who ever actually died, rose from the dead, and now lives forever! His resurrection was huge, convincing proof that he was who he claimed to be—God's Son.

LOOKS AREN'T EVERYTHING

"In all Israel there was not a man so highly praised for his handsome appearance as Absalom."
—2 Samuel 14:25

King David was a very handsome guy, and he married Maacah, the drop-dead gorgeous Princess of Geshur. Well, no big surprise that their son Absalom was so good-looking! From the top of his head to the end of his big toe, there wasn't a blemish on him. There wasn't even one freckle out of place. Problem was Absalom was in love with how he looked. He thought his hair was so cool, he let it grow down past his waist. He had five pounds of curly locks!

Absalom's outside might have been picture-perfect, but his heart was seriously messed up. This is the guy who killed his older brother, tried to murder his father, and took advantage of ten women up on the palace roof where everyone could see them. Whoa! Talk about a mess! If you think that Absalom sounds like a Hollywood star with his life out of control, you got that one right! Some dudes don't make good role models no matter what kind of celebrity they are.

It's nice if you're good-looking, but that really isn't the important thing. If you don't know right from wrong, looks don't count for much. Are you ready for this one? The Bible says that a good-looking person with no morals is like a gold ring stuck through the snotty snout of a pig! (Proverbs 11:22)

You can be plain, or you can be a looker; it really doesn't matter. What's important is to have godly character.

THE HOLY SPIRIT'S POWER

"You will receive power when the Holy Spirit comes on you."
—Acts 1:8

What's this? Receiving power? That sounds good—like a superpower! But who is this Holy Spirit? The Holy Spirit is also called the Spirit of God, and Jesus promised his disciples that after he went to heaven he'd send the Spirit of God himself into their hearts—to live inside them! Wow! No wonder you get power! When God's Spirit enters you, you admit the most powerful being in the universe into your life.

There are lots of movies and cartoons about kids receiving superpowers. Someone gets bombarded with radiation, or a genetically altered spider bites him, and the next thing you know he can walk up walls, bend steel bars, or surround himself with a force field. Of course, on top of going to school and doing homework, these superheroes have to wear colorful costumes and go out and save the world!

Although superheroes aren't real, what the Bible says about God filling you with the power of his Holy Spirit is real. Of course, God probably won't give you the ability to climb up skyscrapers. God gives his Spirit so that you'll have power to live like a Christian. His Spirit also comforts you when you're afraid or sad. The Holy Spirit teaches you how to pray and guides you in your choices. The Spirit also helps you tell others about Jesus.

God's Spirit can give you power, and you need that power. So, pray and ask God to help you access the power of the Holy Spirit, so you can begin to live a stronger Christian life.

TRACKING DOWN TREASURE

If you look for it as for silver and search for it as for hidden treasure, then you will ... find the knowledge of God. For the Lord gives wisdom.

—Proverbs 2:4–6

King Solomon wrote this proverb, and he knew all about searching for treasure. Once a year his ships sailed south to a mysterious African land called Ophir and came back loaded down with gold. Solomon took in more than twenty-five tons of gold a year! For centuries, people have wondered where those gold mines were, but the secret's lost now.

What would you do if you found a genuine treasure map that led to King Solomon's mines or some other buried treasure? You'd be mighty interested in tracking down that treasure, right? Even if you had to crawl up mountains and hack through jungles, you'd keep at it. It's worth it for riches like that! Think how much you get into searching for treasure when it's just graphics in a computer game.

There's treasure in the Bible too — real treasure. The knowledge of God is worth more than buried treasure ... and definitely more than computer-animated jewels. How does that figure? Simple. Having faith in Jesus guarantees you'll have eternal life in a paradise beyond your wildest dreams. Obeying God's Word gives you heavenly rewards that'll still glow like the sun a million years after diamonds have turned to dust.

Those are good reasons to read your Bible. Dig in, and you'll come out with your mind full of wisdom and your heart full of spiritual treasure.

BUFF ISN'T ENOUGH

"Let not ... the strong man boast of his strength ... but let him who boasts boast about this: that he understands and knows me, that I am the Lord."
—Jeremiah 9:23, 24

God had just finished telling the Israelites that disaster was going to hit their land and there was nothing they could do to stop it. The enemy was going to invade their land and smash into their fortresses. The Israelites could boast till they were blue in the face about how strong they were, but they weren't anywhere near strong enough to stop what was coming. Only God could protect them.

If you're tough, don't lie and say, "Oh man, look at me! I'm a pitiful weakling." If you're strong and you know that you're strong, have a healthy self-confidence. Know that kids can't push you around. If tough situations come up, be confident that you can face them. There's nothing wrong with that. God wants you to be strong.

But don't go around boasting about how strong you are, because no matter how tough you are you can't handle all the heavy stuff life sends your way. A lot of things are so big that you can't protect yourself from them. If you depend on your muscles alone, you'll go under. But realize that you have your limits and that you need God to protect you, and you'll make it.

God is strongest of all. When you can't handle stuff, trust him to take care of it.

THE ULAM FAMILY REUNION

The sons of Ulam were brave warriors who could handle the bow. They had many sons and grandsons — 150 in all.

—1 Chronicles 8:40

Imagine going to an Ulam family reunion! Guess what they talked about? Bows and arrows. Guess what activities they had? Archery contests. Now, Ulam's great-great-great-great-great grandfather was Prince Jonathan. Jonathan was such a top archer that when David wrote a song about him, he called it *The Lament of the Bow* and talked about Jonathan's archery skill. You see, archery had been in Ulam's family for generations.

Different families are into different things. Wait till the next family reunion or get-together and listen to what the men talk about: maybe they're big into football or antique cars or computer games. Some families are into movies or horses or chess or camping, and well ... some are into archery. If no one's into the same thing as anyone else, don't sweat it. But usually families have some kind of common interest—at least eating.

Maybe your family's pet hobbies bore you to tears. Or maybe other kids wonder about your family traditions. Don't let it bother you. Whether you're totally into the family thing or not, it's part of your heritage. It's part of who you are and shows that you have roots that go back for generations. Roots are good.

As you get older, you start asking, "Who am I?" A big part of the answer to that question is who your family is and what your family traditions are.

A WISE MAN'S ATTITUDE

Do not rebuke a mocker or he will hate you; rebuke a wise man and he will love you.

— Proverbs 9:8

Why, when you think of a certain kid, would you describe him as a mocker? Well, these days you probably wouldn't. Instead, you'd say, "Man, does that kid have a mouth on him!" Or, "What a know-it-all!" Back in Bible days they had a simple name for a kid like that—mocker. No matter what you tried to tell this kid, he'd mock you.

Try to set him straight on something, and he just hates you. Why should he listen? He knows it all already. Of course he doesn't, but he's so defensive and proud that he can't bear to listen to any kind of correction. So he tries to act smart and uses sarcastic humor to attack anyone who tries to straighten him out. You learn quickly not to try to tell him anything.

A know-it-all is a pain to be around. So be wise. When your friends try to teach you how not to goof up, or your parents rebuke you after you've blown it, listen to what they say and learn from it. It'll keep you from making the same mistake again. When someone goes to the trouble to correct you, it shows they care about you.

Don't get into it with a mocker, and don't be a mocker yourself. You'll learn a lot more and be a lot easier to live with if you're willing to listen to correction.

DON'T LET THE BULL LOOSE!

Do not do anything that endangers your neighbor's life.
—Leviticus 19:16

Now, there's a commonsense law that makes sense, huh? It's simple and to the point. But God didn't stop there. Most people really need things spelled out, so God spelled them out: If you have a mean bull that has a bad habit of goring people with its horns, keep el toro locked up in a pen (Exodus 21:29). Do not let the bull loose, whatever you do!

Some kids can't stand rules. They just wanna cut loose and go out and have fun. Yeah, but if you don't obey common sense rules, you endanger other people's lives. You might leap off the diving board right on top of another swimmer. Ignore the maximum-number-of-kids-on-a-trampoline rule, and you'll bounce some kid off the trampoline onto his head. Every summer, lots of kids are rushed from pools and trampolines to the hospital. Rules are there for a reason.

You may wonder why God put so many laws in the Bible—especially in the Old Testament. He did it because he loves people and doesn't want to see them hurt. That's why he wrote laws to protect people's property—so someone couldn't just come along and take what didn't belong to them. That's why he wrote laws against stealing and lying and cheating others. That's why he made laws about being kind to other people.

You're smart to obey God's laws. It's great if you understand why the rules exist. But even if you don't understand, remember, God put rules there to protect you and others.

CHECKING YOUR MOTIVES

The Lord searches every heart and understands every motive behind
the thoughts.

— 1 Chronicles 28:9

God hears every word you speak. He knows every thought you think. And get this: he knows the motives behind every thought you think. God shines a light into your heart, checking out what motivates you, what makes you do what you do. You can't hide anything from him! No wonder King David said, "Before a word is on my tongue you know it completely" (Psalm 139:4). You bet God does! He knew what you were going to say before you even thought it.

At the end of your life when you stand before the judgment seat of Christ, you'll be rewarded for all the good you've done, and all the garbage will be burned away. At that time, you'll be asked to give an account to God for every thoughtless word you've said. Jesus said that if you even think of sinning, it's as if you've already done the deed.

What effect does it have on you to know that God knows the motives behind your actions? Don't let it worry you. Sure, you should have a healthy respect for God, but more than anything, double-check your motives. Ask God to forgive you when you slip up. He loves you, and he's on your side!

God knows absolutely everything you do, say, think, or think about thinking. That's a good reason to do good, speak good, and even think good.

DEVOTION 12

TALKING TO GOD ALL DAY LONG

"Pray continually; give thanks in all circumstances, for this is God's will for you."

—1 Thessalonians 5:17,18

P ray continually? Does that mean I'm supposed to stumble around on my knees with my eyes shut? Nice try, buddy. You won't even make it across the street if you try that stunt. Praying continually means that you can talk to God no matter what you're doing. And prayer isn't just asking God for stuff. Often it's a quick thank you to God. Sometimes it simply means being aware of God and wanting to obey him.

When you hear the words "prayer time," what comes to your mind? Saying twenty seconds worth of grace over leftover pasta? Yawning bedside prayers for forty seconds? Those things are prayer, true, but with 1,440 minutes in a day, don't you have more time for God than one minute? God is your best friend, and he's with you all day long. If you spent all day with one of your friends, you'd talk to him a lot, right?

So communicate with God. He wants to hear from you. Prayer is talking honestly and respectfully to God, and you should do that no matter what else you're doing—whether you're lying down to sleep, making a tough decision, or white-water rafting with your eyes wide open. Yes, it's okay to pray with your eyes open.

God is always here listening, and he has the power to answer your prayers. So stay in close communication with him.

ONE GOD - ONE WAY TO HEAVEN

"Salvation is found in no one else, for there is no other name under heaven given to men by which we must be saved."
—Acts 4:12

If you want to please God and live forever in heaven, first you have to figure out who God is. So, who is the true god? Were the ancient Greeks right when they said that when you leave this life you will live in Elysium with Zeus? Nope. Well then, how about the ancient Scandinavians who said that you will live in Valhalla with Thor? No. This verse tells us that there's only one God who brings salvation—the God of the Bible. All other so-called gods are imposters.

Now, how do you find salvation with the one true God? What do you have to do to make sure that you end up in heaven? If you brush your teeth faithfully four hundred times a day, rake leaves off every driveway in your city, and rescue at least forty cats from trees, will that do it? No. Those things will wear you out, but they won't get you into heaven. So what's the way?

Jesus said, "I am the way." He added, "No one comes to the Father except through me" (John 14:6). Okay, now we're zeroing in on how to find salvation. You have to go through Jesus! In fact, the Bible makes it very clear: "If you confess with your mouth, 'Jesus is Lord,' and believe in your heart that God raised him from the dead, you will be saved" (Romans 10:9).

Praying to Zeus won't save you. Being the best Boy Scout on the block won't save you. Only believing in Jesus gives you eternal life.

CONTROLLING THE HEAT VENTS

A fool gives full vent to his anger, but a wise man keeps himself under control.
—Proverbs 29:11

H ave you ever heard the phrase "give full vent"? What does it mean to give "full vent" to our anger? Giving full vent means to really let'r rip—tell 'em what's on your mind with as much direct honesty as you can manage. Not advised. A wise man deals with problems, yes, but he keeps his anger under control so no one gets burned.

Maybe you have a short fuse and you're easily angered. Or maybe it's only certain kids that get under your skin and annoy you.

Even when we've been provoked, the Bible says, "Everyone should be … slow to become angry" (James 1:19). Don't give full vent to your anger. Here's an interesting test to help you see what a big deal self-control is in the Bible. If you or someone you know has a thing in their Bible called a concordance (it's sort of like an index) look up "self control" and count how many verses use those exact words.

A wise man keeps himself under control. He keeps his lungs and his tongue under control. He keeps his fists under control. He deals with tough circumstances without hurting others.

DEVOTION 15

ALIEN FUNGI

"I have seen something that looks like mildew in my house."
—Leviticus 14:35

You know what mildew is? It's a whitish growth that sometimes appears on walls and ceilings inside houses. You sometimes see black mold moving in too. Mildews and molds were a problem in ancient Israel, and they're still a pain—especially if your room is warm and humid and you never open the window to air the place out. Your bedroom is private, of course, but it shouldn't smell private.

Not only do mildew and mold look yucky, but they can cause health risks. If you have asthma, they can make you seriously ill. Even if you don't have asthma, they can sicken you. And mold growing on plates of half-eaten food under your bed? That stuff can be deadly. Sweaty, dirty socks can give you athlete's foot, and the itch can nearly drive you crazy. The list goes on and on.

If you see something strange, tell your parents. It could be alien fungus taking over the world, beginning with your bedroom (just kidding). Check stuff out, and you can solve problems before they even start. And while you're at it, take those dishes to the kitchen and dump your dirty jeans in the laundry. If your socks are grimy and slimy, change them.

If you get in the habit of taking care of details, good things will start happening, and bad things will stop happening. One thing for sure: at least the mildew and mold won't get you.

BURST OF POWER

"The Spirit of the Lord came upon him in power so that he tore the lion apart with his bare hands."
—Judges 14:6

You've heard of Samson, the super strong guy—rippling muscles, flowing long hair. Well, one day he was walking along the road when this ferocious roaring lion leaped out. Then it was like King Kong wrestling T. Rex, only Samson didn't just snap its jaw, he ripped the cat apart! You know what that's like: you go to open a bag of chips and accidentally tear the bag apart and chips end up all over the floor. Well, in this case it was lion guts spilling out.

Samson probably had a well-cut body, but his strength went way beyond what normal muscles do. So where did all this superpower come from? "The Spirit of the Lord came upon him in power." Cool! You're probably wondering, "Is all that good stuff gone?" Well, odds are that the Holy Spirit won't make you as strong as Samson, but God knows there will be times when you do need extra bursts of strength.

So, your body comes fully loaded with adrenal glands. In emergencies these little doo-dads dump power juice called adrenaline (ah-dren-ah-lin) into your blood, and for a few seconds or minutes, dude, you have far greater strength than you normally have. It's like the jet engines of Batman's car kicking in. Don't expect to twist steel girders, but in real emergencies the power's there for you. (Ta-daaa! It's Adrenaline Man!)

Talk about wonders of the human body! God thought of everything!

SHOUTING MATCH MISTAKE

But the men of Judah responded even more harshly than the men of Israel ...
So all the men of Israel deserted David.
—2 Samuel 19:43; 20:2

I n this story, enemies had chased King David across the Jordan River, When danger was past, the men of Judah brought David back. Then the Israelites showed up, all steamed because no one had called them to help bring the king across the river. They argued until they got in a shouting match. In the end, the boys from Judah may have won the shouting match, but it got the men of Israel so upset that they rebelled against David's kingdom.

These days, instead of arguing over who gets to have a boat ride with the king, kids fight over whose turn it is to manage the TV clicker or who gets which seat in the car. The arguing gets louder until someone wins the shouting match. Some victory. Then Mom or Dad takes away everyone's TV privileges or cancels the outing and no one rides in the car.

There are smart ways to avoid shouting matches. The men of Judah could've said, "Oh, man! We forgot to invite you? Sorry. Our bad!" It's often ridiculously easy to make peace. You may not want to let someone take his turn first or sit in a certain seat, but think about it—is it really worth it to keep arguing until everyone suffers?

Sure, everyone wants to insist on his or her rights. Everyone wants a fair turn. But it's not worth losing a friend over or getting everyone grounded.

SAVAGE APPROACH TO BIBLE READING

The lions roar for their prey and seek their food from God. The sun rises, and they steal away; they return and lie down in their dens.

—Psalm 104:21–22

If you're a lion, you spend your time tracking down food. And when you spot a delicious four-legged lunch, you sneak up on it, rush it, leap on it, and take it down. Then you bite off chunks and swallow them. When your belly is full, you flop yourself down in some shady, bone-littered cave, belch, blink your eyes the way lions do, and digest.

You can do that with the Bible too. You get hungry to know something about God, so you grab your Bible, flop down on your bed, and go hunting through its pages. It's like moving through the grass. Then when you spot an interesting truth, you leap on it and begin devouring it. You don't just lick it once and walk past; you spend some time eating it. Then you blink and think, "Now, how does that apply to my life today?"

That's the savage approach to Bible reading, and it works for some people. You move when hunger strikes; you get up and go after some truth. Of course, some people like to read devotions at the same time every morning or evening. Fine. Do that. But when you get a sudden hunger for truth, there's nothing like prowling in your Bible.

Have you gone hunting for wisdom and truth today? Have you lain back in some cave and digested what the verses mean? Go for it.

KEEPING A CLEAR CONSCIENCE

"I strive always to keep my conscience clear before God and man."
—Acts 24:16

God has given everybody on earth a conscience. It's part of the package. A conscience is your mind knowing the difference between right and wrong. When you do wrong, your conscience makes you feel bad. When you do what's right, you have peace. The apostle Paul said he tried to keep a clear conscience by doing what was right before God and before people.

If you think that a conscience is a tiny angel fluttering at your right ear telling you to do good, and a tiny devil at your left ear tempting you to lie or take another cookie, you've been watching way too much TV. A conscience is the knowledge that certain things are right and certain things are wrong. For example, your conscience tells you that caring for the weak is right and honoring your parents is right, but stealing is wrong.

When you're tempted do wrong, your conscience reminds you that it's wrong. If you go ahead and do it anyway, your conscience kicks in again, making you feel guilty. If you apologize to the person you wronged, then you have a clear conscience again. And guess what? If you have a clear conscience and obey God's commands, you can be confident that God will answer your prayers. (See 1 John 3:21–22.) That's one of the benefits of having a clear conscience!

Your conscience is a gift from God. Don't ignore it. When it tells you to do something good, obey it. When your conscience tells you not to do something bad, well, duh, don't.

DEVOTION 20

WISE GUYS FOR FRIENDS

He who walks with the wise grows wise, but a companion of fools suffers harm.
—Proverbs 13:20

The computer game you got for your birthday is a blast. After you get the hang of it you start downloading custom scenarios from the internet, and before you know it your machine is slower than waiting for Christmas. Finally when you boot up one day you get the alarming message that your software has found a virus on your system. Some joker who created that custom scenario thought it'd be fun to burn you with his tweaks to the software. And not only is it a pain to have to deal with it, but suddenly you realize it's wiped out all sixteen levels that you've already beaten! But thankfully it's only your computer.

In real life it's a much bigger deal to hang out with people who don't look at life like Christians do. Not that our friends are always wrong. But just because something is legal doesn't mean it's wise. Wisdom goes deeper than being smart. Wisdom means using our brains to make good, godly decisions. A fool is someone who mocks godly wisdom and pigheadedly continues doing unwise things, sometimes dismissing their foolishness by saying, "Hey, it's not illegal."

Now, we may be wise, but if we pick fools for buddies, after a while we may begin acting the way they act. It's not magic. It's called peer pressure. Sometimes just the fact that we're with those guys when they get into trouble puts us at risk of getting in trouble too.

RESISTING PEER PRESSURE

Do not follow the crowd in doing wrong. When you give testimony in a lawsuit, do not pervert justice by siding with the crowd.

— Exodus 23:2

In ancient Israel, when someone hurt someone else or caused an accident, or somebody's property was stolen or damaged, people took the matter before a judge. And back then, like today, people often argued for their friends. If you were a witness, they might pressure you to twist the truth to keep their friend out of trouble. The Bible called that "perverting justice."

Crowds aren't always wrong. Sometimes they're fun, like if you're playing soccer or enjoying yourself at a carnival. But there are times when you need to break away from the herd. If a group of guys starts lying about some kid to get him in trouble, or want him to get all the blame for some fight when it was only partly his fault, don't go along with it—even if they tell you, "He has it coming."

Why go with the crowd just to be accepted? Who needs friends who act like that? Of course, sometimes kids will say that if you don't go along with them that they'll get you in trouble. That's when it takes guts to do the right thing and to refuse to lie. Eventually liars will be found out and when they are, you'll be glad you didn't go along with them.

Don't side with kids if they're setting somebody up. Tell the truth, even if it makes you unpopular. It's a sign you are becoming a mature Christian.

GETTING ALONG

How good and pleasant it is when brothers live together in unity!
—Psalm 133:1

Yeah, good and pleasant, all right. It beats brothers beating each other up. Now, living together in unity doesn't mean we have to think and act exactly like our brother or sister. We're not clones. We're definitely different. But being in unity means that despite the small things we disagree about, we agree on the stuff that really counts.

How does being united on important stuff help make family life good and pleasant? Well, let's say that your family has a rule, "No humming or singing at the dinner table," but though your sister knows how much it bugs you, she keeps doing it. Wouldn't things be good and pleasant if she suddenly thought, "Oops! I'm bugging my brother. Maybe I should be quiet."

But it works both ways. We know how to get under the skin of our family too. Sometimes we do things that bug our brothers or sisters or parents too. And sometimes it's a "good" feeling to know that we have that kind of control over them. But just because it's a good feeling doesn't mean that it's right. The harder work for a man is to figure out how to keep the peace—it's way harder than driving people crazy.

Keeping peace in the family and making our homes a good and pleasant place to live is simple. It's just not easy. And it's impossible without the Holy Spirit's power. We'll take great strides in becoming men when we seek God's help in staying united with others on the important issues like being considerate and learning to overlook the small stuff.

MADE FOR ACTION

"Moses was educated in all the wisdom of the Egyptians and was powerful in speech and action."

—Acts 7:22

One day Pharaoh's daughter went down to the Nile River and found this cute little Israelite kid floating in a basket, so she adopted him and named him Moses. He grew up as a royal prince—and Egyptian princes back then got a top education. So he was smart, but Moses was also strong. He loved action! He got out and did stuff! One of the favorite sports of Egyptian princes was hippopotamus hunting. Can't you just see Moses snatching a spear and jumping into the thick of it? Talk about action—foaming and bloody water, capsized boats, snapped spears, snapped legs ...

Hmmm ... maybe you'd better give hippo hunting a pass. Your local zoo probably has rules against spearing hippos anyway. But there are other cool, active things you can do: white-water rafting (okay, maybe not yet), racing go-carts, wrestling, swimming, bicycling, or playing a game of soccer.

Boys' bodies are packed with energy. God designed you for action, so don't sit around all day playing computer games. Exercising your thumb does not count as a full-body workout. You may not be into sports—maybe you'd rather be watching TV. Fine. Get in your TV and computer time, but you also gotta get out and move it if you don't want to end up looking like a Jabba the Hutt.

Talk about action figures—God made you to be one. You need exercise! Have you had yours today?

DEVOTION 24

FULL-MEAL DEAL

"See how my eyes brightened when I tasted a little of this honey."
—1 Samuel 14:29

One day the Israelites were fighting the Philistines, and King Saul said something dumb like, "Nobody eats until the battle's won!" So here are the Israelites chasing the Phillies through the forest, but they're out of energy 'cause no one's eaten for hours. Suddenly they see honey oozing out of a bee's nest. No one goes for it except Prince Jonathan, and he immediately perks up. Jonathan's attitude was, "We'd do a better job fighting if we weren't famished out of our skulls."

Jonathan said, "See how my eyes brightened!" The moral? When you're beat, a snack can give you an energy boost and keep you going. In fact if you don't eat a good breakfast, your brain won't have the energy to work properly in school. Do that often enough and your grades will sink like the Titanic.

Your intestines break food down into natural sugars, and it's those sugars that drive your engine. That doesn't mean go for candy and chocolate though. Sure, they'll give you an energy jolt ... then leave you flatter than you were before. Your body needs the full-meal deal. Shovel it all in: the potatoes, the beef, the carrots, and the fruit. Your intestines know what to do with that stuff even if you don't.

Want bright eyes and a bright brain? Eat your breakfast. Eat your lunch and dinner.

ANGELS ON UNDERCOVER ASSIGNMENTS

Do not forget to entertain strangers, for by so doing some people have entertained angels without knowing it.
—Hebrews 13:2

The Bible says that angels are powerful spiritual beings who bring messages from heaven. Angels are not humans, and people don't turn into angels when they die, but sometimes angels appear on earth in human form so that they won't stand out in the crowd.

We can only imagine what angels look like. What picture comes to mind when you think of an angel? Maybe you see a blond guy in a long white robe with giant wings sprouting from his shoulder blades. Maybe he even has a glowing Frisbee over his head. Or maybe you think they look pretty much like regular humans.

Although the Bible tells us that angels wore robes in Bible times, that's what everybody else was wearing back then. Who knows what angels are wearing today? And though we usually picture angels with wings, the Bible never actually talks about angels having wings. Spiritual beings like cherubim and seraphim that do go for the feathered look may have as many as six wings! Can you imagine some guy walking down the street with six wings? It would kind of blow his cover, right?

We don't know what angels might look like as they do their work on earth today. Maybe the girl sitting next to you in math class is an angel on an undercover assignment. Since we can't recognize angels and you wouldn't want to offend a messenger of God, it would be wise to be kind to everyone. It can only make the world a better place.

BEEFING UP YOUR BRAIN POWER

To these four young men God gave knowledge and understanding of all kinds of literature and learning.

—Daniel 1:17

King Nebuchadnezzar wanted some new servants, so he told his man Ashpenaz to pick youth who were good at learning and quick to understand. Ashpenaz tapped Daniel and his friends, gave them a crash course in Babylonian, plopped big stacks of literature in front of them, and said, "Here, learn this." Sure, Daniel and pals were smart, but they were overwhelmed. So they prayed, and God helped their brains learn even better than they normally did.

Maybe you're naturally smart: your dad's a rocket scientist and your mom's a nuclear physicist, so of course you were born with a beefed-up brain. But what happens when you need to learn stuff that's way over your head? Sure, you can do some extra studying, but even smart kids burn out. And hey, let's be real: chances are good that your parents aren't rocket scientists or nuclear physicists, and you're about average in the brains department. What then?

Do what you can do: pay attention in class and study hard. Those things are huge. But if you don't want your brain to wear out like an overused eraser, pray for extra ability to understand. Need wisdom and knowledge? James 1:5 says, "If any of you lacks wisdom, he should ask God, who gives generously to all." That's a promise! But you gotta ask.

Remember, God's not limited to helping you with just the stuff you're naturally good at. God helped Daniel and his friends with "all kinds of learning."

DULL AXES, DULL MINDS

If the ax is dull and its edge unsharpened, more strength is needed but skill will bring success.

—Ecclesiastes 10:10

B ack in King Solomon's day, some woodcutters couldn't be bothered to stop chopping long enough to go to the blacksmith to get their axes sharpened. They kept hacking away with a dull blade, and the job kept getting harder ... and harder ... and harder. Finally, they were using all their strength and sweating like pigs just to make a dent in the tree. C'mon, guys! It doesn't take Sherlock Holmes to figure this mystery out.

You think those woodcutters were clueless? What about the kid who gets a complex toy, doesn't bother to read the instructions, and starts trying to assemble the parts? Not exactly brilliant. Sure, with enough glue you can make just about anything stick together, but would you really want that hideous thing in your room? Or what about the kid who won't take time to tighten a loose wheel on his skateboard? Good way to save time? Not really.

Save yourself a headache by reading instructions. Study how things are supposed to fit rather than grunting and groaning and forcing parts together. Things will fit together, work well, and look cool if you take the time to do it right. And you spare yourself a cracked skull by taking the time to tighten loose skateboard wheels and adjust the brakes on your bike.

Don't go through life like a dull woodcutter with a dull ax. Sure, muscles are great and glue is awesome, but using a little skill and wisdom makes things work easier and better.

HOW WE GOT THE BIBLE

"How did you come to write all this? Did Jeremiah dictate it?"

"Yes," Baruch replied, "he dictated all these words to me, and I wrote them in ink on the scroll."

—Jeremiah 36:17 – 18

How did we get the Bible? The words in the Bible were inspired by God. In some cases, God spoke directly to prophets who wrote down his words. And Jeremiah spent forty years repeating God's exact words to his scribe Baruch and the people of Judah. Jeremiah was even put into jail for the difficult news he spoke, but he continued to repeat God's message. And later in ancient Israel, flocks of scribes had the job of making exact copies of the prophets' books. Today, thanks to those scribes, we have a reliable record of God's Word.

Has a teacher ever given you a complicated explanation that you didn't write down? Then when you tried to remember it later, you forgot it completely, remembered only a word or two, or got it totally mixed up. And memory loss even hits with short, simple messages! Think how many times you say to your mom, "Yeah, I'll do it," but a minute later whatever she said is totally wiped out of your mind.

That's why God had his prophets write down what he said right away. God inspired many prophets and writers because he wanted to be sure that people knew what he was telling them. So, people like you, living today, know exactly what he wants you to do.

Thank God for ink and scrolls and paper! Thank God for prophets and scribes who knew how to write! Thank God that these words have been preserved and delivered to us. That's how we got the Bible.

HOWLING KILLER MICE

Ask the animals, and they will teach you, or the birds of the air, and they will tell you; or speak to the earth, and it will teach you, or let the fish of the sea inform you.

—Job 12:7 – 8

The Bible isn't saying to go snorkeling and start quizzing schools of fish. It's not saying you should go to the zoo and ask the elephants to help you with your history assignment. (Their memory isn't that good.) This verse is saying that if you watch animals in action, you can learn a lot about God. Like Proverbs 6:6 says: "Go to the ant ... consider its ways and be wise!"

Nature shows are good for learning about the hand of God on earth. You learn that elephants travel hundreds of miles through jungles to find a single salt lick or that a South American bird goes wild doing a high-speed moonwalk to attract females. And what about the grasshopper mouse that hunts deadly scorpions and howls like a little wolf? Talk about wild! It seems God really cut loose when creating certain critters.

When you tune in to the animals, you learn cool stuff about nature and see the amazing thought that went into creating creatures. You begin to get an idea of how super-intelligent God is. After all, he's the one who designed every creature—from the microscopic to the humongous—with cool features, like built-in navigation systems for birds.

The more you study nature, the more wise you become as you learn to appreciate God's wisdom and design in creation.

PLANNING, PLOTTING, AND PRAYING

Many are the plans in a man's heart, but it is the Lord's purpose that prevails.
—Proverbs 19:21

I f we didn't need brains and didn't need to plan stuff, God could've filled our skulls with a second stomach so we could pack away extra hot dogs without getting a big gut. But God wanted us to think and plan and try to work things out. We just need to remember that God has the best plans and his plans will prevail.

What are your plans? Do you want to get a job to earn cash or make some team or go on an outing? Then plan and work to make it happen. Just remember, you're not in control of all the factors, so although you should do your best, there's no guarantee things will work out the way you planned.

While you're getting excited about dreams and plans, remember that God is the best planner of all, and whatever he wants to happen is what's going to happen. Yes, you need to work hard to try to figure things out, but you also need to pray and ask God to show you his will. Ask him to work with your brain and help you get it right. Even if he doesn't show you, ask him to work things out.

God gave you a brain because he figured you'd need it, so fire the thing up and use it. But being truly smart means letting God help you make the best plans come true.

LEARNING FROM THE MASTER TEACHER

When they saw the courage of Peter and John and realized that they were unschooled, ordinary men, they were astonished and they took note that these men had been with Jesus.

—Acts 4:13

Peter and John were telling the crowds about Jesus when the temple guards snagged them and dragged them before the top religious council. Now, the religious rulers could see that Peter and John were just regular guys. They were rough-and-tumble working-class guys and hadn't received higher education, yet these boys were so sure of the facts and so bold declaring them, it was clear they'd been with the master teacher, Jesus.

Now, like Peter and John, you are probably a regular guy—you try to do your best, and there is something you are really good at. Maybe you aren't pulling an A+ in math, but you love to read. Maybe you're good at designing and creating art. Maybe you are very generous with your friends. Maybe there is something that makes you stand out in a crowd. Most likely, you have your strengths and your weaknesses, and you blend in with average people.

If you know Jesus and you know the Bible, you're not just one more average person. If you know the Man, then you know the truly important things about life, and you can't help but stand out. Get close to Jesus and it will show! Other people can't help but notice something different about you.

It's important to be smart about science and math and other stuff, but it's most important of all to have a relationship with Jesus.

LIGHT YEARS AHEAD

"Though you soar like the eagle and make your nest among the stars, from there I will bring you down."
—Obadiah 4

I n the verse above, God was talking to Israel's enemies, the Edomites, who lived high up in carved-out cliffs like something out of an Indiana Jones movie. The Edomites were about to find out how powerful God was. God was not saying that the people of Edom had built spaceships and started colonies around distant stars. (They hadn't, by the way.) God was saying that even if they had done that, he could still bring them down.

If God can bring down a star colony that's light years away—and we're not even there yet—we'd better not get a big head. Our cutting-edge technology still doesn't cut it. These days we can get so awed by modern gadgets, powerful computers, and DNA engineering that we sometimes wonder if we really need God. Like the ancient Edomites, we've become over-confident. We think we're standing tall and strong without God.

It just isn't so. Our nation—and each of us personally —needs God. We haven't even got a colony on Mars yet—or even the moon! And even when the day comes and we're there, we'll still need him. Hey, if you join the space program and end up being one of the first Mars astronauts, stay humble.

God is way out there—light years ahead of all of us—and he's got a lonnnng reach. So don't think you have things together without him.

GIRLS ARE COOL

"There is neither ... male nor female, for you are all one in Christ Jesus."
— Galatians 3:28

Many ancient peoples—including Israelites—looked down on women. That's the way it was back then. In ancient days, a woman's word really didn't count. She couldn't even be a witness in a court case. When Jesus came along, he put that attitude out on the curb with the trash. Instead of putting women down, Jesus showed the world how important they were. Did you know that the very first people to witness that he had been raised from the dead were women? It's true!

Paul is saying that we can't judge people by whether they're male or female. Now, that doesn't mean that men and women are the same. They're different, to be sure, but men are not better than women. They're equal. Yet even today some boys think they're cooler than girls. They say stuff like, "Boys rule, girls drool." Listen guys: babies drool, Jesus rules, and both boys and girls are cool.

No sweat if you'd rather hang out with guys than girls. Boys are interested in boy stuff, so that's perfectly normal. But the thing is, you've got to treat girls with respect. That doesn't mean you need to like all the things that girls like; no one's asking you to paint your fingernails. Let girls do girl stuff. That's their thing. Just don't look down on them for it.

Girls are different than boys—no one's arguing with that—but Jesus loves both guys and gals the same! That's the bottom line.

COOL WOMEN

God heard Manoah, and the angel of God came again to the woman while she
was out in the field; but her husband Manoah was not with her.

—Judges 13:9

Manoah's wife was cool. One day, out of the clear blue sky, the angel of the Lord appeared to her—to her, not her husband—and told her she'd have a super-hero son named Samson. When she told her husband, Manoah prayed for the angel to return. The angel returned, sure, but he appeared to the Manoah's wife again. When Manoah finally did see the angel of the Lord, he wailed that he was going to die, and his wife had to calm him down.

Some guys have the idea that girls are inferior to boys. Why? Because some girls aren't as tough as boys and often get emotional over stuff that boys don't think twice about. Some guys also think that males are more special because God only spoke to men in the Bible—you know, prophets like Moses and Elijah. Right?

Wrong. Lots of Bible women heard from God. Let's see now: there was Hagar, Rebekah, Miriam, Deborah, Huldah, Manoah's wife, Mary, Joanna, Elizabeth, Anna, Lydia, Tabitha, and Philip's daughters among many others. Sure, some girls wear cutesy jewelry, pretty shoes, and pink dresses with ribbons. There's no denying that they're different. But if God and his angels think that girls are cool, who are you to disagree?

RESPECTING THE ELDERLY

Rise in the presence of the aged, show respect for the elderly and revere your God.
— Leviticus 19:32

This wasn't just an ancient Israelite custom. Once upon a time even in America, if you were sitting when an elderly man or woman entered the room, you stood up to greet him or her. You did it to honor the person. You also offered him or her your chair. An old man named Job was so respected that when he arrived at the meeting place, the other elders rose to their feet (Job 29:7–8). It was like getting a standing ovation.

What about today? If your grandparents are visiting, is your brain riveted to what they might be planning to give you? Or do you respect them even if they don't lead in camels loaded down with presents?

We should respect older people, and there are lots of ways to do this: one of the most important is to show them love and appreciation. Hugs work. Another way to show respect is to listen carefully when they speak and to answer their questions. If you want to show respect, don't pass them in the food line or do your wounded baboon imitation when they're trying to rest.

One of the cool things about honoring and respecting the elderly is that you're also honoring God because you're treating the elderly the way he wants them to be treated.

DEVOTION 36

A FAITHFUL FRIEND

What a man desires is unfailing love ... Many a man claims to have unfailing love, but a faithful man who can find?
— Proverbs 19:22; 20:6

When the Bible says that people want unfailing love, it's not talking about mushy romantic love. What it means is that we want friends we can totally count on. If a friend says he'll help overhaul a car engine, we like it when the guy shows up. We dislike it when the guy doesn't. We aren't happy if someone's our friend one day but not talking to us the next.

Guys have emotions, true, and if your buddy made a joke about you and you were offended instead of finding it ha-ha funny, you really won't feel like keeping your word and helping him do stuff. So what do you do? Find a way to punish him? Deliberately let him down when he needs your help the most? If you don't care about a friend, yeah, it's tempting.

But if you really have "unfailing love" and aren't just saying that you do, then you're not faithful one day and unfaithful the next. Sure, you tell the guy that you think he was a jerk, but you stay friends. You can't just claim you'll stand by him through thick and thin. You have to actually do it, even when he's acting thick and your patience is thin.

If you're someone's best bud and you tell him, "You can count on me," then you have to be faithful and be there when you said you would.

LIFE CHANGES

"After Abraham's death, God blessed his son Isaac, who then lived near Beer Lahai Roi."
—Genesis 25:11

Jacob and Esau were young teens when Grandpa Abraham died. Right afterward, their dad (Isaac) moved his family south from Hebron out into the desert. The well of Lahai Roi was the farthest shepherd's outpost; there was nothing past it but rocks and dust. Isaac and his sons went from a house to a tent, from a bustling town to the last whistle stop before nowhere. See, Isaac had to fulfill his life's mission, and he figured his boys would love the change.

Sometimes your family has to move: your dad gets a job in another city or you uproot from your old neighborhood and move across town to a new house. It's hard when you can't see your old friends anymore. They might as well be living on Mars for all you get to visit them. Sure, there's email and telephones, but it's still rough leaving friends behind.

Changes are exciting, fun, and difficult all at the same time. When you grow up and leave home, you may move again and again. You'll probably change jobs several times until you find one you like. Right now it's your parents' job to make those difficult decisions, and you have to trust that they're doing what's best for your family.

When a move seems hard to make, or it looks like you're moving from a good situation into a tough one, remember Isaac's family. God provided for them even when they were far away from everything they knew and loved.

USELESS INFORMATION

Moses was educated in all the wisdom of the Egyptians and was powerful in speech and action.

—Acts 7:22

Okay, so Moses had the best education Egypt could offer. He learned good stuff like math and hieroglyphics and how to build things. But he also had to memorize boring stuff like the names of every pharaoh who had ever lived, and study myths about pagan gods, and learn hymns to Khepri—the scarab-beetle, their creator-god. (When dung beetles hatched out of dung-balls, Egyptians thought they'd been miraculously created, so they worshipped the dung beetle as their creator.)

A lot of Egypt's wisdom wasn't very useful to Moses, and it may sometimes seem the same to you in school today. You wonder why you need to memorize how many people live in Australia. Or maybe you sit in class and study the elevation of the lowlands in South America or the formula for standard deviation. Sometimes you have to learn things that seem like a waste of good brain cells.

Don't zone out. A lot of subjects you might think are useless turn out to be very helpful after all—like boring math problems and science trivia about how flowers are pollinated. Relax. You have plenty of brain cells to spare.

It pays to pay attention and learn the boring subjects in school, even if they seem useless. You never know when they'll come in handy.

ADMITTING YOU DON'T KNOW

"Do you understand what you are reading?" Philip asked. "How can I," he said, "unless someone explains it to me?"

—Acts 8:30–31

A Christian named Philip was walking down the road when he saw an Ethiopian official riding by in a chariot. The guy was reading Isaiah chapter 53. Now, Philip knew this chapter was a prophecy about Jesus, so he asked the Ethiopian if he understood it. When the man admitted that he didn't, Philip hopped up in the chariot with him and began to teach him about Jesus.

Ever been sitting in class when the teacher's trolling up and down the aisles, looking over everyone's shoulder at their work? The teacher sees you scrunching up your face and asks, "Do you need help?" What do you say? Or, ever been playing a video game and Gazooka the Ogre is stomping you? Then your kid sister skips up and says, "I can tell you how to beat him." What do you do?

Okay, okay, if you want to let Gazooka continue stomping you until all your lives are gone rather than let your kid sister be able to say she saved you, that's one thing. But when you really need help—like with interpreting the words of the Bible, your schoolwork, or some serious problem—that's not the time to play cool and say no. If you need help, ask for it.

Don't be too proud to admit that you don't understand something. Asking questions is how you get answers.

BUILT UP, NOT PUFFED UP

Knowledge puffs up, but love builds up.

—1 Corinthians 8:1b

If you just get knowledge but don't have love, you end up with a big head that is empty of true meaning. You get puffed up. It's like a bullfrog puffing up to try to look bigger. Is he really bigger? Nah. He's just full of hot air. And since he can't hold his breath forever, the ugly green dwarf will soon go back down to his real size.

"Knowledge puffs up." You can fill your head with facts and figures, but if you don't have love, you won't know how to use that information properly. It's just taking up space. You might as well be stuffing your skull full of sawdust. You'll be like the scarecrow in *The Wizard of Oz*, who was so completely clueless that he set off walking down the road to find a brain.

"Love builds up." The most important things in life are to love God and to love your neighbor as yourself. If you love yourself, you'll take care of yourself and build yourself up—like a bodybuilder building up muscles. If you love others, you'll say kind things that will encourage them. Instead of showing off how smart you are or quoting facts to cut others down, build them up.

If you have love, then you build yourself up and you build others up. Avoid the bullfrog syndrome. Live a built-up life, not a puffed-up life.

RUNNING OUT OF BOUNDS

"If anyone competes as an athlete, he does not receive the victor's crown unless he competes according to the rules."
—2 Timothy 2:5

The apostle Paul lived during Roman times, which was a great time to be living if you liked sports. The Romans were big into racing, boxing, wrestling, long jumping, discus throwing, javelin throwing, and chariot racing. Back then if you won an athletic competition, you got a crown of leaves. These days you get a colored ribbon. But even then every event had rules, and you had to compete according to those rules.

If your school has a track and field event, and some kid gets ahead by tripping his competition, think he's going to get a ribbon? Nope. He just disqualified himself. Also, cheating by cutting outside the lines may get you to the finish line first, but about three hundred spectators will be leaping out of their seats and howling, "Cheater!" Bodycheck some kid during a basketball game, and you're parking your sorry butt on the bench for a while.

Rules exist for good reasons, and if you don't obey them, all your skill and speed is of no use. You could be the best player on the team, but if you're sitting out a penalty, you'll only be playing with your shoelaces. It's the same with following God. His rules in the Bible aren't just to keep you from having fun. They exist to keep you and others safe.

You want the prize? Remember the rules and don't go running out of bounds.

CONTENT WITH WINNING

"You have indeed defeated Edom and now you are arrogant. Glory in your victory, but stay at home! Why ask for trouble?"

— 2 Kings 14:10

King Amaziah of Judah had just finished defeating ten thousand Edomites. Way to go! But after that huge victory, he became so proud that he got the idea that he was the original Terminator. That's when he decided to pick a fight with King Jehoash of Israel. Jehoash tried to talk him out of it, but Amaziah wouldn't listen and attacked ... and Jehoash tromped him. For the next ten years, Amaziah cooled his heels in an Israelite prison.

Some kids win an arm-wrestling match and begin to think that nothing can stop them. They swagger around, picking fights. Sometimes they win, sometimes they lose, but more often than not a teacher breaks it up, and they end up in detention or suspended from school. If they keep doing that when they're older, they'll end up in prison—like Amaziah.

If you win a wrestling competition, advance to the next level in karate—or whatever—stick the trophy on a shelf, hang the ribbon on your wall, show it to family and friends, and be content with that. Use your strength for good, and you're a hero. But use your strength to push others around, and you're just an ordinary bully.

Jehoash's advice was smart: "Glory in your victory, but stay at home!" If you're strong—great! Just don't look for trouble by trying to prove how tough you are.

WHAT GRUDGES LEAD TO

Do not hate your brother in your heart ... Do not seek revenge or bear a grudge against one of your people but love your neighbor as yourself.
—Leviticus 19:17 – 18

When God told the Israelites not to hate their brothers, not to bear a grudge against their people and to love their neighbors, he was talking about the same people. "Brother" didn't mean just flesh-and-blood brother. The Israelites considered all their neighbors, all their people, brothers. So to keep it simple: don't hate people; love people.

Revenge is getting back at some person for some wrong he did to you, or that you think he did to you. But before actually doing something to get revenge, you generally plan and scheme how to get even, right? You "seek revenge." And you seek revenge when you have a grudge against some guy. Bear a grudge and in the end you'll want to hurt someone.

That's why the solution is, "love your neighbor as yourself" and "do not seek revenge." After all, you don't plot to take revenge on yourself, do you? Every time you see yourself in the mirror you don't scowl and growl, "You dirty dog! Better watch your back, 'cause I'm gonna get you!" So don't do it to others. Don't trudge around with a grudge.

If someone has offended you, it's great if you can talk about it with that person. But if you can't—or they're simply not sorry—then for your own sake, let go of it.

THE SULKING KING

Ahab went home, sullen and angry ... he lay on his bed sulking and refused to eat.
—1 Kings 21:4

W hen spoiled kids don't get their way, they stomp out off to their bedroom and pout. King Ahab was like that. When he couldn't get his own way, he went home and sulked. Another time, when a prophet rebuked him for disobeying God, "sullen and angry, the king of Israel went to his palace" (1 Kings 20:43). Again he went home for a sullen sulk. (To be sullen means to be stubbornly moody.)

It wasn't very mature for the king of Israel to act that way and it's no example to follow. Yet we're all tempted to get upset, right? Some kids slam doors and bang things around when they don't get their way. Others don't leave the room to sulk. They stay right where they are and plead and wail and argue when their parents make a decision they don't like.

When you have your heart set on something or if it seems like everyone but you gets to do it, it can be hard to accept your parents' "no." It's natural to feel upset or frustrated since God gave us emotions. But the thing is, God also tells us that part of being a mature Christian is to exercise self-control. We can choose to control our emotions and not give in to them.

YOUR NEIGHBOR'S TOYS

You shall not covet ... anything that belongs to your neighbor.
— Exodus 20:17

People have a right to their belongings, so God wrote about this in the Ten Commandments. Rule number eight says not to take anything that doesn't belong to you. Then, for good measure, God added rule number ten that says not to even covet anything that doesn't belong to you. (To "covet" means to be upset that someone else owns something we feel we deserve.)

If we want something in the store and we have the money to buy it, good for us. If we're saving our money to buy what we want, way to go. But the problem comes when we want something that belongs to our neighbor, but he or she isn't selling. When we're drooling over someone else's stuff, two things are happening: one, we're not content with what we have, and two, we might start dreaming up ways to get that person's stuff.

The best way to avoid coveting something that belongs to someone else is to first be thankful for what we have. Chances are we want what the other guy has but really don't need it. The second way to avoid coveting is to thank God that the other guy has what he has. You can be happy for someone else, right?

God put laws in the Bible to protect people's belongings because he wants us to keep our hands off them. He doesn't even want us to give other people's things the greedy eyeball.

GO WHERE YOU MEAN TO GO

Do not conform any longer to the pattern of this world, but be transformed by the renewing of your mind.

—Romans 12:2

If you're a Christian, you're a changed person. Once Jesus has saved you, your old ways of thinking begin to get replaced. God sends his Spirit into your heart and starts changing you by giving your mind a new outlook. He knows you'll be tempted to flip back to acting like those who haven't been changed by Jesus so he warns, "from now on don't conform to your old ways."

Have you ever started to go somewhere in your house, and then been distracted? You hop off your bed, walk down the hall, and ... wander into the kitchen. You look around and wonder, "Huh? Why did I come here?" You weren't even hungry, but you just walked to Grand Snack Central out of habit. You were following the old programming, the old pattern. If you want to go to where you really mean to go, you need to remember you have a new direction—then head there.

When God comes into your life, he begins changing you immediately. You go to do something stupid and you realize, "Whoa! I don't want to do that anymore!" So you stop. Sometimes the changes are big and fast. Other times it takes a while to stop mindlessly repeating old habits. It takes time to replace old habits with new habits.

It can be easy to flip back to your old way of thinking. So make an effort to stop that and to let God's Spirit transform your thought patterns.

WHY GOD GIVES US GIFTS

There are different kinds of gifts, but the same Spirit.... Now to each one the manifestation of the Spirit is given for the common good.

—1 Corinthians 12:4, 7

When the Spirit of God lives in your heart, he gives you power to live the Christian faith. But he also gives you some unique "gifts." These gifts are abilities and spiritual talents, and they're different for each person. But the reason is always the same—to help you and others.

Ever wanted to have special powers—like miraculous powers? Well, we humans can't do miracles. But God can! Sometimes he gives people gifts of insight, knowledge, or ability. If that happens, it's not some power you have. God's Spirit is the one who does it. If you could do it on demand, you'd be tempted to use it for selfish reasons ... like kids in the movies do.

God's Spirit gives Christians all kinds of spiritual gifts. Sometimes he gives believers the gift of knowing what others are going through so they can pray for them or encourage them. Maybe God will give you the gift of wisdom or the gift of knowledge. You'll know something that you had no way of finding out. Or maybe your spiritual gift will be something totally different. It might take time for your gift to show up, but it will show up.

Just remember: God doesn't let you do cool stuff to make you look great. That's not the way God operates. He does it to help you and to help others.

AMAZING WAYS THROUGH THE MAZE

In all your ways acknowledge him, and he will make your paths straight.
—**Proverbs 3:6**

The Bible tells us to acknowledge God in everything we do. What does acknowledge mean? It means making an effort to recognize God, to be aware that he's God, that he's powerful and wise, and that you need his help. Acknowledge God and he'll make your paths straightforward and easier.

When you're trying to figure out the maze on the back of a cereal box, there's nothing straight about it. It goes this way and that way, backward, up and down, and all over the place. Or maybe you've wandered through a corn maze. Sure, it starts out as fun, but when you do a thousand-acre maze, you get good and lost. The whole idea of a maze is to make it hard for you to find the path. Life can be like that. Maybe you feel your whole life is one big maze. What do you do?

Well, if you were lost in a corn maze, you'd holler, right? So holler. Call out to God. Pray. If you pray when you're faced with a choice, God will make your paths straight. You'll still make a few wrong turns from time to time, but overall your way will be easier without twenty dozen false leads and dead ends. God can help get you where you should be.

God has a bird's eye view of things on earth, and if you're talking to him, he can help you find amazing ways through the maze.

MONSTERS IN THE CLOSET

I will lie down and sleep in peace, for you alone, O Lord, make me dwell in safety.
—Psalm 4:8

E ven believers thousands of years ago sometimes got afraid at night—which was why God promised that when they lay down in bed, they wouldn't be afraid and their sleep would be sweet. Sounds great, but how do you make it work for you? You can lock your door, sure, and turn on a nightlight, but a big way to not fear is to remember the promises in the Bible, keep them in your heart, and quote them when you're afraid.

You may sometimes worry that there are monsters in your closet, or under the bed. A shadow on the wall can look scary. It's no fun if you're too scared to sleep, so you huddle under your blankets, sweating. Is your sleep sweet or sweaty? Or maybe you don't have problems with that, but one of your friends does. So what's the solution? How do you drive away fear?

Besides obvious stuff like leaving a nightlight on, you need to trust God and remind yourself of his Word. Here are some promises to quote when you're fearful: "Even though I walk through the valley of the shadow of death, I will fear no evil, for you are with me" (Psalm 23:4). "God is my salvation; I will trust and not be afraid" (Isaiah 12:2).

Quoting God's Word is like turning on a spiritual nightlight. Remember, if you're a Christian, Jesus is with you and he's far more powerful than anything. His angels surround your bed.

THE PLANET OF MISSING SOCKS

"Do not store up for yourselves treasures on earth ... But store up for
yourselves treasures in heaven."
—Matthew 6:19–20

Jesus said not to work hard to pile up treasures on earth.
Why? Well, for one thing, they won't last. Moths might eat
your clothes (except for the buttons), rust can ruin your
toys, and thieves can steal your money. I mean, think about it.
Your socks even get lost inside the washing machine—all the
time. Earth's just a bad place to store treasure. It makes a lot
more sense to stack up treasures in heaven.

Sure, you do need food, clothes, and a place to live. Nobody
is saying that you don't. You need gym shoes and you need a
toothbrush. Yes, you even need toys and fun times. Jesus knows
you need all these things. He didn't forget that. So what does he
mean when he says not to pile up treasure on earth?

It means that although you might wow other kids with how
many toys and collectibles you can fill your bedroom with, things
get old, they get broken or ripped or—like your socks—go
missing. Also, a year from now you may not even be interested
in those kinds of things.

You need some treasures on earth. Just don't pile them up.
Don't let them crowd God out of your life. You need treasures
in heaven even more. Start storing up treasures in heaven with
your service to God. After all, you'll live there forever!

HOW TO TREAT ALIENS

When an alien lives with you in your land, do not mistreat him. The alien living with you must be treated as one of your native-born. Love him as yourself.
— Leviticus 19:33 – 34

So does this mean if a flying saucer crashes in your neighborhood and next thing you know you have aliens living nearby, that you're supposed to love them as you love yourself—even if their license plates are from Mars? That's what I thought at first. But really God was telling the Israelites that they should be as kind to immigrants as they were to fellow Israelites.

Let's say some new kid comes to your school and he looks differently, dresses differently, and eats food that looks like nothing you've ever seen come out of a lunch box. Do you make fun of his customs? Do you call him by a bad nickname when you're talking to other kids? Or do you mock his accent or teach him bad words just to get him in trouble?

Lots of kids do that. But that doesn't make it right. God wants you to respect people no matter what state or country they come from. If you love others just as you love yourself you won't treat a newcomer worse than you'd treat a kid who was born in your neighborhood, and you won't pull jokes on him just because he doesn't know your customs.

So how do you treat someone new to your area? The same way you'd want to be treated yourself.

DEVOTION 52

FIRST ON GOD'S LIST

If you are offering your gift at the altar and there remember that your brother
has something against you... First go and be reconciled to your brother; then
come and offer your gift.

—Matthew 5:24

The Israelites gave "thank offerings" at God's altar to show
their thanks for his blessings. God appreciated the gifts, but
he didn't want them to think that this meant everything was
all right if it wasn't. See, God cares about people, so if you've
hurt or offended someone, that bothers him. Jesus said to be
reconciled (make things right) with that person then give God
your gift.

Often, when we argue with people and tell them what we
think, we can be pretty blunt. That's not counting the harsh
words we say in anger that we don't even mean. Now, if you and
your brother aren't talking, or he's hurt because of something
you did, God's not crazy about listening to you go on and on
thanking him for all his blessings.

God hears you, sure, but the whole time he's thinking about
how your brother's hurting and how you need to make things
right with him. God wants to bless you but he also wants you to
make things right with your brother. If you've offended someone,
whether on purpose or by accident, your top job is to try to make
things right.

Of course, if you apologize but he doesn't want to hear it and
tells you to go away, you've done your part; now all you can do is
love him and pray for him.

MIXING AND MINGLING

I now realize how true it is that God does not show favoritism but accepts men from every nation who fear him and do what is right.
—Acts 10:34–35

The apostle Peter was visiting a Roman named Cornelius, and at first Peter felt pretty uncomfortable going to his home. As Peter told Cornelius, "It is against our law for a Jew to associate with a Gentile or visit him" (Acts 10:28). Actually, it wasn't against God's law. God only said that Jews shouldn't worship idols and shouldn't marry Gentiles (non-Jews) who worshiped idols. It didn't say they should refuse to even visit them.

God showed Peter that God doesn't play favorites with any race. The Jews weren't better than all other people in the world who loved God. Peter realized this two thousand years ago, yet some people today still haven't clued in. They feel it's somehow not "right" for people of different races to mix and mingle. They don't associate with people who aren't just like them. Why? Because it's just, well … it's just not done.

But if someone loves God and is living for the truth, God accepts him and you should too. A person's race is not a qualification for being chosen by God. Sure, that kid may look different, speak differently and eat different food, but don't let those things stop you from accepting him. It's time to realize that some of our customs are not God's idea, but are the prejudices of humans.

God loves everyone, so don't judge someone just because he's different. If he loves and obeys Jesus, he's your brother.

IT'S NOT FAIR!

You never gave me even a young goat so I could celebrate with my friends. But when this son of yours . . . comes home, you kill the fatted calf for him!
—Luke 15:29 – 30

When the Prodigal Son came home after wasting his inheritance, his dad threw a party and cooked the prize beef. The older brother thought this was so unfair. Now, maybe dad hadn't offered him a goat barbeque, but he probably could've had one if he'd only asked. After all, everything the father had left now belonged to the older brother. The entire farm was his. Besides, dad was generous.

It's easy to slip into the older brother's mindset. After all, if things don't look fair, then they probably aren't fair, right? No, not necessarily. Maybe you're just not seeing the big picture. Now, if your parents take your sister on a trip to Disneyland and you stay home scrubbing toilets the whole time, that's not fair. You're not missing the big picture on that one.

But if your brother gets to go to the mall and you don't, don't be quick to accuse your parents of favoritism. You may just be missing some facts. Often if you calmly ask them and let them answer, you'll get an explanation that makes sense. Either that, or they'll say, "Oh," and let you have your turn next time. Maybe you just needed to ask.

Most parents usually try to be fair to their kids—all of their kids. If you feel things aren't fair, ask politely about it.

YOU NEED OTHERS

Though one may be overpowered, two can defend themselves. A cord of three strands is not quickly broken.

—Ecclesiastes 4:12

I n a war, if some enemies found one soldier alone, they could surround him and attack him from behind. But if two soldiers were attacked, they could stand back-to-back and defend themselves better. Also, a single strand of rope can be snapped fairly easily, but a rope of three strands twisted together is a lot tougher to break. In the same way, you need good friends. You're stronger when you stand with others.

Now, maybe you're something of a loner or you don't make friends easily—or maybe you just enjoy playing video games or cruising the Internet by yourself. You need time by yourself, but the problem with always flying solo is that if something bad happens, or you're tempted to do something wrong or to visit bad sites, you'll go down a lot easier.

It's not God's ideal for us to spend day after day alone on the computer instead of out mixing and mingling. Sure, you might have a dog or a goldfish, but we need human buddies looking out for us, riding shotgun on our souls. That way we won't be overpowered by bad stuff. We won't break like skinny ropes. So spend time with family and friends.

Human beings weren't meant to be alone—and Christian kids certainly shouldn't be alone all the time. You need others, and fortunately, God made lots of people.

IN TRAINING

"Everyone who competes in the games goes into strict training."
—1 Corinthians 9:25

The apostle Paul lived in the city of Corinth for two years, and after he left he wrote to the Christians there. Now, a funny thing, often when Paul explained spiritual things to them, he used the language of training for athletic competitions. Why? Because Corinthians were passionate sports fans. Corinthians not only trained for the Olympic Games every four years, they also hosted the Isthmian games every two years. And the Christians there went wild in the stands like everybody else.

You still need to train for competitions today. Whether you're into basketball, hockey, or martial arts, it takes dedication and focus to become good at it. It helps if you absolutely love the sport, because all that repetition can get boring at times. You also have to know the game's rules. Like them or not, that's how the game is played, so your coach makes you learn them by heart and makes sure you follow them.

Today, just as in Paul's day, Christian life is like athletic training. You need to be as wild about Christ as the Corinthians were about their sports events. When you're passionate about something, it's easy to be devoted to it. And when you're devoted to something, you accept the repetitive training and strict rules as part of the package.

Stay passionate, stay focused, and all the rest will follow. That's true both in sports and in being a Christian.

VIGOR MEANS POWER

"Of what use was the strength of their hands to me, since their vigor had gone from them?"

—Job 30:2

Job was a wealthy man who owned seven thousand sheep. He needed shepherds to protect them, otherwise wolves and lions would eat them or raiders would ride in and rustle them. Taking care of sheep was hard work, and shepherds needed to be in shape to fight. Now, Job was always helping the poor, but he didn't give a job to just anybody. Some guys were so weak that Job couldn't even put them to work watching his sheep.

It's the same today. You may need to earn money, but there's no way an adult is going to hire you if your vigor, or power, has gone from you. If you're so out of shape that you can't do the job, you'll miss out on fun activities and chances to earn money. You can't help it if you're smaller than other kids, but you can take care of the body you have.

If you don't want vigor going out of you, you have to do three things: (1) eat good food so you can grow like you should to be at maximum strength; (2) get enough sleep, because you can't be strong if you're exhausted; and (3) exercise daily to stay fit. Follow these guidelines and you'll be in shape when a cash-earning job comes along.

Don't want to miss a fun outing? Stay healthy. Want to earn some extra cash? Stay strong.

GROW LIKE A STATUE?

"And the boy Samuel continued to grow in stature."
—1 Samuel 2:26

Samuel didn't grow like a statue; he grew in stature—which means taller and bigger with strong bones and tough meat wrapped around his bones. When Samuel was just a little guy, his mom dropped him off with the high priest in Shiloh. That's where Samuel grew from a boy into a teen and then a young man.

Like Samuel, all kids grow. When you're about ten, you start going through a stage called puberty, and later you begin growing like crazy! This is called a growth spurt. By the time you hit fourteen or so you're shooting up about four inches a year and starting to get some serious muscles. Now, you may be wondering, how come my transformation hasn't kicked in yet? Don't sweat it. It hits some boys earlier and other boys later.

Of course, your body can't grow tall and muscular all by itself. You have to throw fuel in your engine by eating properly and getting sleep. You've heard that smoking will stunt your growth, right? Well, a steady diet of junk food is also a bad stunt. So avoid guzzling down too much soda pop or wolfing down too many french fries, chips, and candy. Otherwise you'll get fatter and unhealthier when you should be getting taller and stronger.

Want to grow? Go for healthy food—meat, starches, fruit, and veggies. You need all of that stuff even if your taste buds try to lie to you and say that you don't.

LIVE LONG AND STRONG

"Moses was a hundred and twenty years old when he died, yet his eyes were not weak, nor his strength gone."
— Deuteronomy 34:7

Figure that one out! You can understand Moses living to be that old — lots of Bible people lived long lives. In fact, today some people live to be nearly a hundred and twenty. The thing is though, usually by the time people reach even one hundred, they're wearing glasses and hearing aids, the teeth come out at night, and they're shuffling around with a walker.

So what was Moses' secret? Was he in good shape because he was like a toy that had never been taken out of its original packaging? Nah. Moses had been through the rough-and-tumble of life, including eighty years in the desert. In fact, that was part of his secret. A lifetime of fresh air, hard work, and eating natural food kept him healthy and strong.

It's the same with you: the way you live now affects how strong you'll be when you grow up. You don't build strong bones and muscles lying on the couch chewing chocolates. Only superheroes get megamuscles when spiders bite them or radiation zaps them. It won't work for you. If you want to be strong, you've got to eat good food, exercise, and get to bed on time.

God designed your body so that if you take good care of it when you're young, it'll still be strong and healthy when you're older. You may not live to be a hundred and twenty, but hey, it's bound to help.

SMART STRATEGIES, SMART MOVES

Joshua marched up from Gilgal with his entire army ... After an all-night march from Gilgal, Joshua took them by surprise.

—Joshua 10:7, 9

The city of Gibeon was an ally of Israel, so when five armies surrounded Gibeon, Joshua got his one army together and set out to help. If they marched by day, lots of Canaanites would see 'em and run ahead to warn the enemy. So what does Joshua do? He marches his army eighteen miles from Gilgal to Gibeon at night. The next morning as the enemy troops are crawling out of bed, the Israelites attack! God then performed miracles and helped the Israelites win the battle!

It pays to use your brain and not just your muscles. If you're trying to put the chain back on your bike, it doesn't help to try to force it on and get all sweaty and frustrated. You'll just cut your knuckles. Or if you're playing checkers, there's no way you'll win by just moving your men forward as fast as you can. And in computer games—even if your character has lots of lives—you can't just charge in and take hit after hit.

You need to think and plan. In any game or sport, it helps big-time to have speed and strength on your side, but it's often strategy—smart moves—that determines who wins and who loses. Strategy is important in war, in football, in chess, and in computer games. In fact, thinking things out before you make your move is important in all areas of life.

Got a problem? Don't try to solve it with brute strength alone. You aren't King Kong. Use your brain! And pray for God's help. He's smarter and stronger than anyone!

MEMOS AND REMINDERS

You will have these tassels to look at and so you will remember all the commands of the Lord.

— Numbers 15:39

God commanded the Jews to wear tassels — little twisty tails of cloth that dangled on the bottom of their robes. Every time someone walked by, you saw the tassels swinging on the edge of their robes, and they saw the tassels dangling on your robes. And everyone was reminded, "Oh, yeah! We're God's people, and we're supposed to obey God's commandments."

Seem weird? Well, having strange, out-of-the-ordinary reminders helps! People are forgetful, and kids with exciting things on their minds are especially forgetful. Has your mom ever sent you to do something and you got tripped up on the way and never arrived? Ever forget to throw your clothes in the laundry or clean the cat's litter box? We forget little stuff all the time, and it's also easy to forget the big things that God wants us to do — like treating others with kindness.

It's no longer the fashion for boys to wear robes with cutesy-tootsy tassels. These days people wear T-shirts that talk about Jesus or put God posters on their bedroom walls. Some people scribble memos on their hand or even tie strings around their finger to help them remember. Some people's fridges are full of magnets holding messages.

We do lots of things today to remind ourselves of important stuff. Do whatever it takes to remember God's Word.

DO THE MATH

Suppose one of you wants to build a tower. Will he not first sit down and estimate the cost to see if he has enough money to complete it?
—Luke 14:28

One day Jesus was talking about being a disciple. He compared it to building a tower. He explained how important it was to think things through before rushing into action. Otherwise, you'll spend all your money building the basement and then have no cash left to build the tower itself. Bummer. Not only are you out all that cash, but you still don't have a tower. Worse yet, everyone who sees your half-built building will mock you.

You can apply Jesus' advice to any project you're excited about. Think about what it'll cost you before you actually start! Like, if you want a tree fort but you can only afford three boards, don't just run out, buy the boards, and nail 'em up—'cause for the next year kids will stare up at those three pitiful boards and joke, "Niiiice tree fort, Tarzan!"

Sit down and take some time to estimate the cost; then count your cash and find out what you can scrounge. While you're at it, ask your parents for advice. You might be surprised, but grown-ups are good at that kind of stuff. They have to estimate the cost on zillions of things. So run your plans past Mom or Dad. They'll give you a good reality check.

When you get an idea for a project, it's fine to get excited. Still. Pull out a piece of paper, grab a calculator, and do the math. Know what you're getting into.

LOSING STUFF ALL THE TIME

These searched for their family records, but they could not find them and so were excluded from the priesthood.

—Ezra 2:62

I n Israel, only those in the tribe of Levi could be priests. It wasn't enough to say you were a Levite, either—you had to prove it. That's why Levites kept family records to show they were descended from Levi. But three guys—Hobaiah, Hakkoz, and Barzillai—got careless. When it came time to show their records, Hob, Hak, and Barz tore their houses apart to find them—but they couldn't. Too bad, boys. You can't be priests. Got a plan B?

Being disorganized and careless can cost you big-time. If your teacher hands you a permission slip but you forget to give it to your mom, well, she can't sign something she's never seen. You just missed a fun outing. Forget your homework, and it costs you marks. Lose your friend's phone number, and you skip that sleepover. Misplace a rented video game, and you pay so many late charges you could've bought the game four times over.

If you have a habit of forgetting stuff or misplacing important papers, then start new habits today. First, make sure you always put your homework in your school bag. Second, give your mom or dad notices or permission slips as soon as you get home. Third, don't leave video games or other important stuff lying just anywhere. Always put them where you can find them again.

If you don't want to be scrambling around searching and crying like Hob, Hak, and Barz, do yourself a favor and get organized.

GARLIC PEELS, ZITS, AND MESSY HAIR

Anyone who listens to the word but does not do what it says is like a man who looks at his face in a mirror and . . . goes away and immediately forgets what he looks like.

—James 1:23 – 24

People in New Testament times had mirrors too, and before they stepped out of their houses they checked themselves out. If they had a garlic peel on their teeth, they picked it off. If they had a zit, they popped it. If their hair was uncombed, they combed it. But James talked about people who read God's Word and saw what they should do, but mumbled, "Yeah, yeah," and then walked off and forgot about it.

You may not be too concerned about what you look like before you rush out the door. Maybe you just want to dash out the door to play. But it pays to care. Otherwise you'll run out to play baseball with jam on your face, your hair standing straight up, or your T-shirt on backwards. So get in the habit of looking in the mirror and then fixing what needs fixing.

Even more importantly, you should care what you look like on the inside. How do you do that? Read the Bible—especially chapters like 1 Corinthians 13—to see what God wants your heart to look like. Compare your thinking and your actions to how the Bible says a Christian ought to behave. Then do what it says to do.

When you see that you need to fix some areas of your life, fix them. Don't just say, "Yeah, yeah," and forget about it. Read God's Word and obey it.

ON YOUR MARK, GET SET, GO!

The beginning of the gospel about Jesus Christ, the Son of God.
— Mark 1:1

There are four gospels in the Bible — Matthew, Mark, Luke, and John. But here's an interesting point about the gospel of Mark: Bible scholars believe that Marks's gospel was originally written for the Romans. The Romans loved action, so Mark included mostly action in his book and hardly any parables or sermons or prayers.

Your youth leader just told you to read the Bible. Your dad agrees. Your mom says there is lots of good stuff for you to learn about. Ready? Set? But where do you start? It can be pretty overwhelming!

Maybe you think it would be best to just flip it open and read whatever you point to first. So you turn to Leviticus 13:47 and read, "If any clothing is contaminated with mildew — any woolen or linen clothing." You close your Bible and then open it to 1 Chronicles 1:40 and read, "The sons of Shobal: Alvan, Manahath, Ebal, Shepho and Onam. The sons of Zibeon: Aiah and Anah." You close your Bible again, and by now you're probably ready to keep it closed and go watch TV.

Listen guys, start with the gospels. And if you really want a high-energy read, start with the gospel of Mark. When Mark talks about what Jesus did, he uses a lot of fast-paced words like "immediately," "at once," and "quickly." Mark also describes the action in colorful detail. That makes it a great book for boys.

If you've never read any gospel story from beginning to end, start reading Mark today.

BEING BORN AGAIN

Jesus declared, "I tell you the truth, no one can see the kingdom of God unless he is born again."

—John 3:3

E ver wonder where the term "born again" came from? One night an old, white-bearded teacher named Nicodemus came to Jesus. Nick nearly fell over backward when Jesus told him that the only way to enter God's kingdom was to be born again. Nick asked if Jesus meant he had to enter a second time into his mother's womb to be born. Jesus explained, "Flesh gives birth to flesh, but the Spirit gives birth to spirit."

See, you've already been born physically. A physical birth lands you in this world, screaming your lungs out. That's what the cake and candles and presents are all about each year. That's a good start, but it isn't enough. You also need to be born spiritually. You may ask, "But how do I do that? How do I become born again?"

Here's how it happens: When you believe in Jesus, the Holy Spirit enters your heart to give life to your spirit. God's Spirit gives you life—eternal life, in fact—and you've just been born again! You've become one of God's own kids. Sound terrific? Why would God do such a fantastic thing? He does it because he loves you.

Do you want to live forever in God's kingdom? Pray for Jesus to forgive you and ask the Holy Spirit to come into your heart. Then you'll have eternal life. That's what being born again is about.

LOCK IT UP!

"He built up the fortified cities of Judah, since the land was at peace. No one was at war with him during those years."
— 2 Chronicles 14:6

What's King Asa doing? No one's attacking him. Everything's peaceful, and this dude is building fortresses all over Judah. Well, there was trouble everywhere else. "All the inhabitants of the lands were in great turmoil. One nation was being crushed by another" (2 Chronicles 15:5). Asa figured that it was only a matter of time before trouble came his way. Good thing he did get prepared, because when a huge army invaded, Asa was ready. He trusted God and won the battle.

Why do your parents lock the doors of your house if it's never been broken into? Why do they set burglar alarms? Why do they lock the car doors? Come to think of it, why do you have a combination lock on your school locker or a chain on your bicycle wheel?

Okay, okay, so you know that you need a lock on your locker or your stuff will get stolen. And it's a no-brainer that an unlocked bicycle disappears. Well, that's the same reason your parents insist on safety stuff. That's why your dad insists that you lock the doors. It may not seem like a big deal, but you'd be surprised at how much grief those kinds of things can save your family.

Don't get sloppy with those details. Those "dumb details"—together with smart prayer—are what keep your family safe.

MUSCLES AND MORE

"The glory of young men is their strength."
—Proverbs 20:29

God designed young men to be strong. You're not a man yet, but chances are you're already stronger than many girls your age. And the good news is, buddy, more muscles are on their way—lots of them! Usually when you're about twelve and a half, your body starts producing testosterone (tes-toss-ter-own) that causes your bones to become thicker and stronger and your muscles to grow bigger—especially in your upper chest and shoulders.

To glory in the strength God gives you doesn't mean you're a glory hog ... unless you're spending hours flexing your muscles in front of the mirror or putting up posters of yourself around town. We're not talking about that. We're talking about when you're just pumped about being what God made you to be—you're confident. Mom needs furniture moved. Who does she call? The kid with the muscles.

But don't just go for massive muscle mass and miss out on other good stuff. Don't just zero in on sports so that you end up a zero in the brains department. And be cool too—be a jock, but get along with others. Most important of all, be deeper—be real with God. Go for the whole package.

God designed masculine muscles on his drawing board and thought the whole thing was cool. You should too. It's your glory.

BRING ON THE ANTS

"Go to the ant, you sluggard; consider its ways and be wise!... How long will you lie there, you sluggard?"
—Proverbs 6:6, 9

King Solomon wrote Proverbs, so he must've spent time studying ants. And since magnifying glasses hadn't been invented yet, you know he wasn't sitting there making them sizzle. Well, Solomon was on to something. Ants work hard. They may live in a dirt hill, but they keep it neat. Considering how small an ant's brain is, it must not take much thinking to keep things neat.

"How long will you lie there?" That is the question, isn't it? You've got to lie down sometimes; you need to veg. But exactly how long are you going to lie there? 'Cause, um, stuff needs to get done. Are your clothes an inch deep all over the floor like a second rug? Has your school bag disappeared somewhere in your room? Is there food all over your bedroom? Are there cookie crumbs on your sheets?

If you don't go to the ants to learn to clean up, the ants will come to you—guaranteed. They just love cookie crumbs and half-eaten food. Of course, once they come into your room you've got to kill them. And what can you learn from a dead ant, right? Better to study the ants outside where they can be a great example to you.

Think about how hard that little ant works and how neat it keeps its digs. It'll make you wise.

WOUNDED BUDDIES

Strengthen the feeble hands, steady the knees that give way; say to those with fearful hearts, "Be strong, do not fear; your God will come ... he will come to save you."
—Isaiah 35:3 – 4

One of your friends has an accident on his skateboard and he's banged-up and scratched. He can barely get up. You're there for him, right? You help him to his feet, get under his arm, prop him up and help him walk. You get him to a place where he can get some bandages and peroxide. You don't just look at him sprawled on the sidewalk and say, "C'mon! Get up, you pathetic weakling." Not if he's in pain.

Sometimes people get overwhelmed when they feel that some problem is too big for them. Or they become afraid. When some people face really big obstacles, they just want to give up and do nothing, as if they have no strength. God says when people feel that way, we need to encourage them to not fear. When they trust that God will be there for them, their strength will return.

If your friend is sad or discouraged or afraid, he may just need someone to encourage him to be strong again, someone to remind him that God sees and cares for us even in his pain. He may need your help even if you can't see any bruises and no blood is spurting out. A phrase you hear some military men quote is a good phrase for Christians to keep in mind too, "No one gets left behind." Let's carry our wounded buddies off the battlefield of life, and encourage them that God will heal them from all their wounds.

STANDING WITH FELLOW CHRISTIANS

He chose to be mistreated along with the people of God rather than to enjoy the pleasure of sin for a short time.
—Hebrews 11:25

Moses was the cool, privileged Prince of Egypt. He rode around in hot, fast chariots and the horses pulling it had big, fancy ostrich feathers waving on top of their heads. Moses wore the finest clothing and probably had more gold hanging around his neck than a movie star. Yet Moses chose to be mistreated along with the despised, grubby, muddy, brick-making Hebrew slaves. Why? 'Cause they were his people! When he realized his Egyptian family and friends were in the wrong, he stood with the Israelites rather than continuing to hang out in style with those who were doing wrong.

What do we do if some not-so-popular kid is being mocked for his faith? Do we speak up for him and tell his tormentors to leave him alone, or do we turn a blind eye because we move with a cool crowd and don't want to be identified with a nerd? This isn't an easy question and it doesn't have an easy answer, but it does have a right answer.

Not all Christians hang with the cool crowds. Some are interested in such totally uncool stuff that there's no way we'd hang out with them. But if our "cool" friends begin mocking Christians for their faith, they stopped being cool and need to be told so. Tell them you don't like what they're doing. If your friends have any coolness at all, they'll listen to you.

Moses walked out of a plush palace to stand with the muddy brick-makers. If someone is a Christian, no matter what you don't like about him, he's your brother. Stand up for him.

TOO GOOD TO WORK?

The next section was repaired by the men of Tekoa, but their nobles would not put their shoulders to the work under their supervisors.

—Nehemiah 3:5

The Jews were rebuilding the walls around Jerusalem, and the boys from Tekoa were working hard, but their noblemen wouldn't help. They didn't want to get dirty and sweaty carrying bricks and tools. They weren't in the habit of working and they didn't want to start now. And they didn't want some supervisor telling them what to do. They were nobles, after all!

That's the thing about work: you get dirty or greasy or sweaty or wet doing it, and usually someone's telling you to do this and not to do that. But if you sneak off, you'll end up with a reputation like the fat cats of Tekoa. C'mon, when you think of the nobles of Tekoa, what's the first thing that comes to mind? How noble they were? Nah. You think of how they were too lazy and proud to work.

If our entire family's cleaning the yard, why should anyone lay back and play king for the day? If our church's youth group is doing a fundraiser—say, washing cars or holding a garage sale to earn money—we should be there to help out. That way, others aren't carrying the whole load.

THE REUBEN RECORDS

Their relatives by clans, listed according to their genealogical records ...
settled in the area from Aroer to Nebo and Baal Meon.
—1 Chronicles 5:7 – 8

Records are a written story of who was who and who did what, and genealogical records are the history of a family—or several families. In this case, they were the lists of the clans of an Israelite tribe, the "Who's Who" of Reuben. Reubenites had kept family records for generations, and eventually the king's scribe copied their records and they ended up in the Bible. You can bet they were tickled pink about that!

Your family tree won't end up in the Bible—it's a little late for that—but it's still important to have an idea of where you came from. Do you know the history of your family? Have you ever drawn up a family tree? Do you know who your great-grandparents and great, great grandparents were? Or has some history buff written a book of your family history?

These days most people don't keep genealogical records, so if you want to find out where you come from you have to research. But there are ways to learn about your ancestors. Start by asking your parents. Check out the Internet. Find out which family members were Christians. Check out what town they were born in and what they did for a living.

It takes some work, but the search can be very interesting and rewarding. Your family history and where you're from is part of who you are.

SETTLING DISAGREEMENTS

Let's not have any quarreling between you and me ... If you go to the left,
I'll go to the right; if you go to the right, I'll go to the left.
—Genesis 13:8 – 9

You don't always have to have your way. Let others have first
choice sometimes. This scripture comes from a famous
story in the Bible that reminds us of this principle. Abraham
and his nephew Lot both owned tons of sheep and goats, but
the place they were at had little pasture and few watering holes.
Soon Abe and Lot's herdsmen began fighting. So Abraham took
Lot up to the top of a hill, showed him the entire country and
said, "You choose first. I'll take what you don't want."

Lot naturally picked the best pastures and left the drier land
for Abraham. But Abe didn't mind, and afterwards God mightily
blessed him. Now, you may wonder, is this example relevant
when your little brother wants to play with the X-box, leaving you
the old toys? Does it apply when my sister wants my mom to rent
one video and I want her to rent another?

Yes, this principle applies. When you settle disagreements
be fair and generous. Now, this doesn't mean giving everything
away nor always letting others go first forever and ever, all the
time, every time. But it does mean letting them choose first
sometimes.

Being fair means being fair to all people. You'll try your best
to be fair if you care for the other person—and a man of God
should care for others.

MAGIC BOOKS DISAPPEAR!

A number who had practiced sorcery brought their scrolls together and burned them publicly.
—Acts 19:19

T he apostle Paul spent a couple years in Ephesus. This city was a center for witches and sorcerers and magicians. Then lots of these guys became Christians and decided to burn their "spell" books. They torched 50,000 drachmas' worth! Since a drachma is worth about a day's wages, that's a lot of abracadabras going up in smoke! (Poof! Watch me make these magic books disappear!) These guys were serious about cleaning the junk out of their lives.

Today there are tons of spell books and movies around. We're not talking about Merlin or other fantasy stories about magic. We're talking about the old pagan religion of witchcraft itself. People read the witchy books because they're interested in secret wisdom and figure these books have it. Not smart. Or they figure that by mumbling magical rhymes they'll get quick answers to problems. Not. It's just bad poetry.

If you really want wisdom, plug into the one true God—not the false goat-god of witchcraft. Our God has the answers. He also has the power to give genuine answers to prayer. His miracles may take a while to happen, but they're worth waiting for. Best of all, faith in Jesus gives you eternal life in heaven, something witchcraft can never do.

Take a tip from the ancient sorcerers of Ephesus! When they found new life in Jesus, they gladly burned all their old spell books! They didn't care how much it cost them.

ACTUALLY ASKING QUESTIONS

They spoke against God, saying, "Can God spread a table in the desert? When he struck the rock, water gushed out ... But can he also give us food?"
—Psalm 78:19–20

The Israelites had been dying of thirst in the desert, so Moses grabbed his staff, whacked a rock, and voilà—instant water fountain! "Okay," the Israelites said. "So God can do miracles to give us water. Big deal! But can he also give us food?" The answer was plain: of course he could! But the Israelites were showing that they didn't really trust God.

Here's a modern example of an insincere question: "How come all I do is homework, and I never get to do anything fun?" Or this one: "How come I only got to go to the waterslides and I can't go to the movies afterward?" Usually the complainer already knows the answer, but his brain's gone into lockdown and he's just not getting it.

There are good answers to sincere questions, but honestly, how do you expect God or your parents or anybody to respond to a child who simply won't stop complaining or repeating a request? The sad thing about complaints is that they show the person isn't thankful for all the good already received.

It's fine to ask questions, but make sure you're actually asking questions, not just complaining. There's a big difference.

TRUSTING THE TRUSTY

He left in Joseph's care everything he had; with Joseph in charge, he did not concern himself with anything except the food he ate.

—Genesis 39:6

Potiphar was a high-ranking Egyptian official, head of the palace guard. His job was protecting Pharaoh, so he had a lot on his mind and didn't want to think of anything else. So when he discovered that his slave Joseph was a top-notch worker, Potiphar put him in charge of his entire household. He knew that if he gave a job to Joseph or that if Joseph oversaw a job, things would get done and get done right.

Now, Joseph was a slave and worked hard for no pay —ever—day after day. Thankfully, you don't have to work like that. Probably the most you have to do is to be faithful to do your homework, clean your room, drop your clothes in the laundry and do odd jobs around the house.

When you're given a job or a chore, do careful, faithful work. You'd be surprised at the benefits that will come your way if you get known for doing a good job without fooling around. If you're known as a trustworthy worker, you end up at the front of the line for paying jobs. People will think up ways to reward you.

No matter whether you're doing a big job or a little job, or even an odd job, make sure that you do a good job.

OBEYING AUTHORITIES

It is necessary to submit to the authorities, not only because of possible punishment but also because of conscience.
—Romans 13:5

In New Testament days, most Christians lived in the Roman Empire, a super-power that stretched all the way from Britain to Egypt. The Romans were civilized and had many good laws, but they also had some totally harsh rules. Just the same, since God had given rulers their authority, Christians were to respect that authority and submit to (obey) the laws.

You don't want to be punished for breaking the law, right?—not even for littering. You wouldn't go to jail for that, but you could pay a hefty fine. Also, it's a matter of conscience, doing the right thing just because it's right. But hey, if you live in a town that has crazy laws like, "It is forbidden for chickens to walk on Main Street after sundown"—you can always change that law. But until you do, keep the chickens off the street.

When God judges the world, he will judge perfectly. In the meantime, the police aren't perfect. Neither are judges and courts and laws. So some people think, "Okay, Christians had to obey authorities back in Bible times, but we don't still have to today, do we?" Yes, we do. Christians yesterday had to obey yesterday's laws, and we have to obey today's laws.

By the way, "authorities" doesn't just mean police and mayors and people like that. It also means schoolteachers and even moms controlling traffic at crosswalks.

THE A-TO-Z FACTOR

"The race is not to the swift or the battle to the strong . . . but time and chance happen to them all."
—Ecclesiastes 9:11

King Solomon had done his best to be a fair king and rule well. He had appointed judges all over Israel and ordered them to judge fairly. But he couldn't put an end to all injustice. He couldn't control the weather, prevent freak accidents, or eliminate crime. By the time Solomon was old and had ruled for many years, he came to the conclusion that life wasn't always fair. Good guys didn't always come out on top.

If you practice hard, you may become the best, but you won't necessarily win. Even the fastest runners strain muscles. Even the best figure skaters fall on their butts doing a triple Axel—whatever that is. Even the strongest warriors go down in battle. Now, usually the fastest runners do win the race. Usually the best warriors do win the battle . . . but not always. There's always the X factor, the uneXpected.

Sometimes you just have to deal with it when you should've won, but you didn't. Other times you can avoid losing out by praying to God for protection and help. Remember, he's bigger than the X factor. God is the A-to-Z factor, the Alpha and the Omega. So pray ahead of time for his protection from accidents, X-idents, and other X stuff.

In heaven, things will be perfectly fair and just, but right now we're still living in an imperfect world. So just do your best . . . and pray.

DEVOTION 80

SPIRITUAL DEFENSES

"Have you not put a hedge around him and his household and everything he has?"
—Job 1:9

When the devil wanted to attack Job, his big complaint was that he just couldn't get at Job. In the spiritual realm, God had put a hedge around Job and his stuff. Now, in Bible days hedges weren't made of pretty green cedars. Think of a hedge of thorns like the bomas that Africans used to build around a camp at night to keep lions out. Can't you just picture the devil trying to get through a thorn hedge and finally backing out, all scratched up?

You simply can't avoid all accidents, sicknesses, and problems. Yet many Christians tell stories about God protecting them when they prayed for protection. Have you ever taken a major spill on your skateboard or bicycle but walked away with only a few small scratches? Why? Probably someone prayed for you.

Be as strong as you like, but problems can still take you down. That's why you need serious protection. If you stay close to God, he can turn away problems and protect you from trouble. That doesn't mean nothing bad will ever happen, but God can stop a lot of grief before it hits. God's protection is like being surrounded by strong bodyguards—or a thorn hedge.

God put up spiritual defenses to protect Job, and he can do the same thing to protect you today.

STRENGTH FROM INSPIRATION

"Blessed are those whose strength is in you, who have set their hearts on pilgrimage.... They go from strength to strength."
—Psalm 84:5, 7

A pilgrimage is when you go on a journey for spiritual reasons, like when the Pilgrims left England to find religious freedom in America. Or it can mean taking a trip somewhere to worship God. Well, three times a year, the Israelites headed for Jerusalem to worship God at the temple there. Some of them had to walk long distances. Sometimes they had to sneak through enemy lines. The Israelites really had to have their hearts set on the trip to make it through such obstacles.

If you wake up Sunday morning and find that you're snowed in, unless your heart is set on going to church, you probably won't want to help shovel out the driveway. Or if it costs fifty dollars to go to your church's summer camp, unless you're really motivated to go, you won't put out and do chores to earn the cash.

When the Psalm says that you will "go from strength to strength," it doesn't mean that God will miraculously make your muscles bigger. After all, it's up to you to exercise. But God can make you strong in other ways. He gives you the vision for something, you set your heart on it, and you're inspired—so inspired that instead of getting worn out, you're pumped by the time you're done.

Set your heart on serving God, and he'll give you the physical and mental strength to see it through, step by step.

BE CONSIDERATE OF ROSES

"He must wash his clothes and bathe himself with fresh water, and he will be clean."

—Leviticus 15:13

When God gave Moses this law, the Israelites had just spent 430 years in Egypt. Now that they were leaving the pagan Egyptian culture behind, God wanted to make sure they didn't stop the good stuff—like washing. See, the ancient Egyptians were clean freaks. A historian named Herodotus wrote that the Egyptians would rather be clean than good-looking. They were very careful to always wear newly washed linen. The Egyptians bathed in the canals every morning and used soap. They even had mouthwash.

It was hard for the Israelites to stay clean all those years in the dusty desert, but once they reached the rivers of Canaan … "Okay boys, it's time for a scrub! Wash them armpits! Wash them clothes!" These days, unless you're out camping, you don't need to wash your clothes yourself. Your washing machine will do that for you. But one thing you can and must do is bathe yourself.

Don't wait till you're so stinky that you kill roses simply by walking past them. Bathe regularly. And bathing doesn't mean lying in a sudsy tub blowing bubbles and playing with the rubber ducky. Sure, take the goggles in if your parents let you, but just remember this: to get clean you have to use soap, you have to scrub the grime off your body, and you have to shampoo your hair.

Wash up often. Be considerate of other people's noses … and the roses.

TOO MUCH OF A GOOD THING

"If you find honey, eat just enough—too much of it, and you will vomit."
—Proverbs 25:16

T he ancient Israelites weren't big into raising bees, so bees were wild back then. If they wanted some honey, they had to go look for a beehive—out in the forest or among the rocks. Since Israelites didn't eat honey often, no wonder some guys completely pigged out on it when they found a stash. Not smart. Too much of a good thing, and they were vomiting up honey-flavored puke.

These days it's not so hard to find honey. It's usually near the jam in aisle eight. In fact, the shelves have tons of sugary stuff like cereal, soda pop, candy, chewing gum, chocolate bars, syrup, juice, and cakes—not to mention doughnuts smothered with gallons of glaze! We are a sugar society, and most North Americans eat as much as an entire bathtub full of sugar each year. No wonder some kids get hyper. Worse yet, this constant craving for candy causes cavities as colossal as caves.

It's okay to have a sweet tooth once in a while, but the danger is if you like sugary foods so much that you barely want to eat regular food. So take it easy on the sweets. Wolf down the good stuff like meat, veggies, and bread and treat yourself to candies only once in a while. And remember to brush your sugar-covered teeth.

God invented honey, chocolate, and sugarcane so he obviously wants us to enjoy some sweets, right? Just don't overdo it, or you'll be down on your knees puking in the toilet.

BATTLE LOST TO THE BOTTLE

"Ben-Hadad and the 32 kings allied with him were in their tents getting drunk."
—1 Kings 20:16

It's a bad idea to be sitting around anytime getting drunk as skunks, but this was a particularly bad time for Ben-Hadad, king of the Arameans. At this very moment, the army of Israel was marching out to fight Ben-Hadad's army. The Israelites were hugely outnumbered, but at least they were sober. Ben-Hadad's army was ready to fight, but the problem was that Ben and the 32 wino-kings were so smashed they couldn't lead the battle—so their armies lost.

Alcohol still causes huge losses these days. Talk about wasted finances! Some guys spend thousands of dollars a year on booze. Alcoholism can wreck a successful career, make a mess of a marriage, and break up a family. Drunk driving causes many deaths, and—sad to say—quite a few drunk drivers are teens. What are teens doing drinking?

Alcoholism is a huge problem in America today, so don't you be the next casualty. Don't experiment with liquor no matter how much the other kids tease. Just say no to the bottle and mean it. Come to think of it, don't even hang around with kids who abuse alcohol. They'll constantly be pressuring you to start drinking, and who needs that?

You have your whole life ahead of you. Make the most of it. Don't blow the whole thing like Ben-Hadad and his drinking buddies who lost the battle to the bottle.

LAY THAT CLICKER DOWN

If you give the scroll to someone who cannot read, and say, "Read this, please," he will answer, "I don't know how to read."
—Isaiah 29:12

For hundreds of years, goat herders in Egypt kept finding ancient scrolls in the desert sands. Since they couldn't read, they didn't have a clue that these scrolls were worth hundreds of thousands of dollars—even millions of dollars—and the goat herders burned them to heat water for tea. Oh, man! Talk about expensive cups of tea!

You may think that was crazy, but lots of boys today are in similar shape. No, they're not burning ancient scrolls, but they can barely read. It's a good thing jugs of poison have skulls and crossbones on their labels, 'cause some guys can't read poison warnings. Now, it's one thing if a kid has a learning disability—you can sympathize with his having a hard time—but there's no excuse for sheer, plain, flopped-on-the-couch-with-cookies-and-a-clicker laziness.

If you don't read well, what can you do about it? Simple. Read more. Exercise your brain. If you really wanted to get on a swim team and weren't making it, what would you do? You'd start swimming like crazy, right? And you would get better. It's the same with reading. Don't read well? Read more. Don't understand some word? Ask what it means.

Unhook your fingers from the clicker, tumble off the couch, crawl away from the TV, and go find a good book. Better yet, read your Bible.

REALLY LEARNING

... Always learning but never able to acknowledge the truth.
— 2 Timothy 3:7

B ack in Paul's day, some people were like Curious George—constantly interested in new stuff without thinking about the big picture. They gathered knowledge nonstop, but all their scattered education did was fill up their minds with scraps of information. They still didn't acknowledge the truth, meaning they knew all about the truth, but they hadn't let it change their lives. They were like squirrels storing away nuts they never ate.

It's the same today with some kids raised in Christian homes: they know all about the Bible and Jesus dying on the cross, but they've never given their hearts to him. Other kids have taken that step—and that's a terrific start—but then slacked off on living as a Christian. They learn about the Bible, but it seems like just a collection of interesting stories about talking donkeys and battles and Noah building an ark and yada yada.

It's great to learn more about the Bible, but the most important thing is to know Jesus and to live your life so that it really counts! Don't just read the Bible, but accept it and let it change your life. When you actually acknowledge the truth, it hits you between the eyes: the Bible's about a life-changing relationship with God. The interesting stories are just pepperoni on the pizza.

It's cool to learn about all the bits and pieces, but don't miss the big picture. Get an actual knowledge of the truth, and then keep learning!

PERFECT MESSAGE, IMPERFECT DELIVERY

Blessed is the one who reads the words of this prophecy, and blessed are those who hear it and take to heart what is written in it.

— Revelation 1:3

The apostle John was a Jew who spoke great Aramaic (air-ah-may-ik), but his Greek was kind of rough. Some scribes probably helped him write the Gospel of John, so the Greek came out perfectly. But when he wrote the book of Revelation, John was alone. Bible scholars say that John's Greek was so rough in places, it's clear that Greek wasn't his first language. So what? Revelation has a powerful, encouraging message. It has tons of stuff you need to know.

It's the same when your parents are talking to you: listen to the message. When your mom asks why you haven't cleaned your bedroom yet, try to understand what she means. True, maybe you did pick the clothes up off the floor, but she's looking at the unmade bed and the messy desk.

You may feel that she's not quite right. You did clean up ... sort of. But accept your parents' message even if the delivery isn't perfect. Sure, they may mix up some details or forget some stuff, but is what they're saying right or not? And if it is, then take it to heart instead of picking it apart.

You're blessed if you read Revelation and blessed if you take it to heart—even if John's Greek wasn't perfect. You're also blessed if you listen to your parents and take what they say to heart.

WHY WE WORSHIP GOD

To him who loves us and has freed us from our sins by his blood ... to him be glory and power for ever and ever!
—Revelation 1:5 – 6

Why does the Bible tell us to worship God? Does God have an ego problem? Does he need people to constantly repeat how great he is? No. Worship simply means recognizing how awesome God is—and saying it. We worship Jesus because he's God's Son, and he loved us enough to die for us and was powerful enough to return to life. Does Jesus get proud when we praise him? No. He said, "I am gentle and humble in heart" (Matthew 11:29).

Imagine your dad works in the Air Force, and one day he gives you high-level clearance and takes you into the super secret hangar of the newest experimental jet. (You wish!) You walk in and there's this shimmering, monstrous, powerful thing! Your eyes bug out and you shout, "Whoa! Awesome!" Some things are jaw-dropping awesome.

God is far, far more powerful and awesome than that, and his Holy Spirit packs way more power! And what Jesus did by dying to save us and then coming back to life deserves our praise! Is Jesus glorious? Yes. Is Jesus powerful? You bet he is. So when we worship God, we're simply recognizing how fantastic he is.

When you realize how awesome God is and what fantastic things he has done for you, and you're in awe and feeling grateful—that's worship.

HAVE MERCY – FORGIVE OTHERS

If you do not forgive men their sins, your Father will not forgive your sins.
— Matthew 6:15

Once a guy owed a king millions of dollars, so the king ordered that he, his family, and everything he owned be sold to pay the debt. The man begged for mercy, so the king forgave the whole debt. Then that guy found a fellow who owed him a few bucks and demanded he pay. The fellow begged for mercy, but the first guy threw him in prison. The king was furious. He asked, "Shouldn't you have had mercy on your fellow servant just as I had on you?" (Matthew 18:21–35).

If you're like most kids, you've broken quite a few of God's commandments—sometimes day after day. But if you accept that Jesus died on the cross for your sins and ask God to forgive you, you're forgiven. God doesn't hold your sins against you. So then what do you do when your brother accidentally breaks your Lego model? Punch him? Tell him he's never allowed in your room again?

The point of Jesus' parable is this: God has been merciful to us and has forgiven us for many sins, so we need to turn around and be merciful to those who sin against us. If we don't forgive others when they offend or hurt us, God won't forgive us our sins. He may let us suffer the consequences of our mistakes to teach us a lesson.

God prefers to forgive. He'd rather not discipline you. So be merciful to others, just like God has been merciful to you.

DON'T JUST WAIL! PRAY!

They were at their wits' end. Then they cried out to the Lord in their trouble,
and he brought them out of their distress.

—Psalm 107:27 – 28

One day a merchant ship was sailing along when a terrible storm hit. Monster waves lifted the ship high into the sky then hurled it down into the depths. Then up again, then down again. The storm was so wild, the sailors staggered around the deck like drunken men. They were out of their minds with fear. They began praying! Oh yeah, they prayed! And God answered. He stilled the storm to a whisper, and they reached port safe and sound.

Have you ever been at your wits' end? Maybe you're not staggering and sliding all over the deck of a ship, but have you ever been in danger? Have you ever been afraid? What do you do? Do you cry out to God?

God says, "You will seek me and find me when you seek me with all your heart" (Jeremiah 29:13). That's a promise. Only make sure you're actually praying with all your heart and not just lying on your bed moaning and wailing. God said about the ancient Israelites, "They do not cry out to me from their hearts but wail upon their beds" (Hosea 7:14).

When you're at your wits' end, don't just wail. Cry out to God. He'll deliver you. He'll help you when no one else can, but it might not be in the way you expect.

EATING AWAY YOUR PEACE OF MIND

Do not be anxious about anything, but in everything, by prayer and petition, with thanksgiving, present your requests to God.
— Philippians 4:6

When the Bible says don't be anxious, it means don't worry and be fearful. Worried thoughts nibble at the edge of your mind and eat up your peace, so God tells you flat out, "Don't worry about anything!"

You know how your mom saves you a piece of cake for after school, but your little sister keeps going to the fridge and taking a little nibble here, a little nibble there, ... until by the time you get home, your entire piece of cake has been devoured? Worry devours your peace of mind like your sister devours that piece of cake. What kind of things are you worried about? Your family's finances? A big test? Some kid who harasses you? Being late to a friend's house?

If you find yourself worrying or pacing or biting your nails, stop immediately! Drag that worry to God and pray about it— not just the big worries but the little ones too. God isn't going to groan even if you bring a piddly concern to him. After all, the Bible says, "Cast all your anxiety on him because he cares for you" (1 Peter 5:7). God cares about it all. (By the way, when the verse tells you to petition God, this is a one-person petition. You don't need a thousand signatures on your prayer before you present it to God. Just pray.)

Don't let worry eat your peace of mind. God doesn't want you to worry. He cares for you, so hand your anxious thoughts over to him.

DEFEAT YOUR GIANTS

"You yourself heard then that the Anakites were there ... but, the Lord helping me, I will drive them out."

—Joshua 14:12

When the Israelites left Egypt for Canaan, Moses sent twelve spies ahead to check things out. Those guys came back shakin', saying that there were giants in the land—Anakites! No way could they conquer them! Only Caleb and Joshua believed they could. The unbelieving Israelites had to wander in the desert for forty years until a new generation was ready to invade Canaan. The giants were still waiting, but Caleb believed that—with God's help—he could tromp them. And he did.

Are there giants in your life stopping you from entering your promised land? Do huge doubts make you afraid to try out for a sports team? Are you afraid to be downstairs alone? Do you worry that some giant monster is hiding in a closet? Does it seem like way too much work to finish your science project?

Listen. If God wants you to do something, then you can overcome the giants in the way—no matter how big they are. Whether you're staring at a nine-foot-tall Anakite or facing your worst fears, God can help you. You can jerk open that closet door or try out for that team or put together a huge science display—whatever.

God helped Caleb defeat the giants when others didn't have the faith for it. Your problem may be too gigantic for you alone, but it's not too big for you and God together.

WALKING A LEVIATHAN

"Can you make a pet of him like a bird or put him on a leash for your girls?"
—Job 41:5

Job was a good man—rich and powerful until a whole bunch of bad stuff flattened him. Job wondered why God didn't stop all that bad stuff from happening to him. He felt like he didn't deserve it. God let Job know who was in charge. He reminded Job that he was all-powerful. That's why he asked Job if he could pull a leviathan—a fire-breathing swamp dragon—out of the water with a fishhook. "And Job, once you've caught him, can you lead him like a dog on a leash—without him swallowing you whole?" No can do? Well, God can.

Now, guys like to think that they are pretty strong, but they need to get a grip on the fact that they're not Mr. Incredible. Face it, there are times when you've just done something great and you feel that you're hot stuff. Well, you may be hot, but you're not all-powerful. You're not the most awesome being to walk this planet since T. Rex. Next time you flex your muscles in the mirror, remember how powerful God is.

Or you may groan, "Why doesn't God stop evildoers?" Remember, God's still in charge. They won't get away with stuff forever. You can't stop them, but God's got their number. Stand back, give him time, and let him do his stuff.

You have no idea how truly powerful God is. Bear this in mind next time you wonder if God's still around, still strong, and still in charge.

UNDER PRESSURE

"We were under great pressure, far beyond our ability to endure."
— 2 Corinthians 1:8

The apostle Paul had it so tough in the city of Ephesus, he said he was like a gladiator doing hand-to-hand combat with lions in the arena (1 Corinthians 15:32). Paul was under intense pressure! Sometimes he doubted he'd even survive. Did he go down? No. When troubles hit, he prayed and depended on God more than ever, and God helped him make it.

You know how you feel when your homework or a project comes crashing down on top of you like a tidal wave? You're so overwhelmed that you throw up your hands and groan, "It's impossible!" You probably whine too, but we won't go there. Or you know how wide your mouth hangs open when your dad takes you to the garage on a sunny Saturday and tells you that you have till dinner to finish cleaning it? You get that "gladiator against the lions" feeling.

You only have so much strength, and sometimes you'll be in situations that are far bigger than you can handle yourself. Or at least you'll feel that the task is so huge that you can't do it. Well, God wants you to learn to depend on his strength, not just on your limited strength.

When you feel you can't do a job—it's too big or too difficult—know that with God helping you, you can make it.

QUALITY RESEARCH

Since I myself have carefully investigated everything from the beginning,
it seemed good also to me to write an orderly account.
—Luke 1:3

L uke was a physician living in Greece. It had been almost
thirty years since Jesus had been crucified and raised from
the dead, and Luke wanted to write a gospel for Greek
Christians. He didn't want to do a sloppy job, either. He wanted
to see the places where things had happened and interview eyewitnesses. So Luke sailed all the way to Israel to investigate the
facts. He then wrote an orderly account, meaning an organized,
easy-to-understand, and reliable report.

What about you? When your teacher tells you to write a report
on something, do you check things out on the ground, investigate on the Internet, and interview people who know about it?
Do you check your facts carefully, or do you slide by with as little
work as possible—just enough to pass? Or if your mom wants
to know who's responsible for making a mess, do you check the
facts carefully before blaming someone? Do people know they
can trust you as a source of reliable information?

The kind of careful research Luke did stands the test of time.
You can be sure that your faith is built upon the truth because
Luke double-checked and triple-checked his information. So
take care with your research. Make sure it's not only accurate,
but that people can easily understand it. This is true for
schoolwork as well as telling others the facts about Jesus.

When it comes to investigating facts and explaining them
simply, Luke stands out as a top researcher and an example
to follow.

LEARNING THE GUR AND BÙR

Terah took his son Abram ... and together they set out from Ur of the Chaldeans.
—Genesis 11:31

A bram lived around four thousand years ago and herded sheep for a living, but he wasn't uneducated. In Ur where he grew up, boys went to school and learned to read and write and do math. Like, they had to calculate how many gur of grain grew on 4,325 bùr of land. (Hint: One bùr is about 6.3 hectares and produces 30 gur—9,000 liters—of barley.) Got that? No? Well, Abram had to learn it.

Do you find math hard? Might as well get used to it. Kids no longer have to know the gur and bùr of Ur, but there are still lots of multiplication and division and fractions and decimals to learn. You might ask, "Why should I study math? What good will it do me?" That's like asking, "Why do I need to study the Bible? How will it help me?"

You need to understand math so you can calculate how much money to save or how to count your change at the store. You need to know math when measuring boards for a tree fort. You need math for oodles of everyday stuff. It's the same with reading your Bible. Like math, it may sometimes seem theoretical and dry, but learning how God wants you to live and how to treat others is very practical.

Ever since Abram was a boy in ancient Ur, kids have been learning both math and the Bible. We can't live without either one.

IMAGINATION - GOOD AND BAD

The Lord saw ... that every inclination of the thoughts of his heart was only evil all the time.

—Genesis 6:5

Before the flood—a few hundred years before Noah was born—there was an amazing Age of Invention. Unfortunately, it was mostly evil Cain's kids doing the inventing. A guy named Jabal started making tents and herding cattle; Jubal invented all kinds of musical instruments; and Tubal-Cain was the granddaddy of all metalworkers (Genesis 4:20–22). You'd think all this new stuff was great, but they had no use for God, and by Noah's day, men's imaginations were evil all the time.

In modern times, knowledge is increasing so fast that you can't keep up with all the new information. And talk about inventions! In your grandparents' day, TVs had just been invented, and computers were huge clunkers that took up whole rooms. And video games? They didn't even exist when your mom and dad were kids. These days, computer games with powerful graphics and more RAM than a mountain sheep fit in the palm of your hand.

But does all the amazing technology we have solve the world's problems? No. Despite a lot of cool inventions, people are as selfish as ever. Knowledge alone doesn't change people's hearts. Some great Christian inventors and scientists are using their imagination to help make the world a better place. Unfortunately, some scientists dream up some truly ungodly things.

It's cool to have a fantastic imagination—God gave it to you. Just be sure you also seek God and use that imagination to dream up good things.

CONTROLLING YOUR THOUGHTS

We take captive every thought to make it obedient to Christ.
—2 Corinthians 10:5

Jesus said that you should not only worship God with all your heart, but that you should worship him with your whole mind (Matthew 22:37). But how can you do that if your mind's running all over the place? You have to gather your thoughts. You have to capture them and make them obedient to Christ. The Greek word for captive in this verse means "to take prisoner." Picture prisoners marching along in chains and someone's poking them, saying, "Okaaay, boys, keep moving."

Would you say your thoughts are under control? Or is your brain more like a zoo where every single monkey has broken out of its cage and is swinging all over the place, screaming and going bananas? Example: if you're a Christian, you know you're supposed to forgive others. But if someone crosses you, does your mind plan a hundred ways to hang him up by his toes?

No matter how wild an imagination you were born with, you don't need to let it take you on a mental roller-coaster ride. Maybe you're spacey or creative, but that's not a reason to give your mind an all-day pass to the amusement park. You can control your thoughts, but you have to be militant about it. You have to be aggressive.

You don't want to end up brain-dead from all the confusion, so forget the saying "Take no prisoners." Take your thoughts prisoner. Take as many prisoners as you can. Then put those captive thoughts to work for Jesus.

CHOOSE COOL WATER, NOT DUST

"They have forsaken me, the spring of living water, and have dug their own cisterns, broken cisterns that cannot hold water."
—Jeremiah 2:13

Israel was a very dry land. It didn't rain much. So if you had a spring where water gushed out of the ground, you were happy. The Gihon Spring supplied water for all Jerusalem, but other cities had wells. When the well went dry, the people had to drink water from underground tanks called cisterns. It was bad enough that the water tasted stale, but if the cistern had a leak, there was nothing there! God says in this verse that his people have turned away from him, the living water, and have chosen to worship false gods, which is like choosing to drink from a broken cistern.

Now, who in his right mind would trade something great for something broken? It'd be like if you had a brand new X-box—the box, the controls, the game CDs, the works—and some kid came along and talked you into trading that for his old, broken setup. Would that be smart? No. So why would anyone make a trade like that?

They'd do it if they were tricked into it. Like, if the kid stuffed his old game inside a brand-new box and promised that it was new and worked great. When people forsake God and choose false religions or put their trust in things, they think they're getting something new and better, but they're only getting ripped off.

Have you opened up the box of Christian faith and tried out the real deal? If you've experienced the genuine Jesus, you won't trade him for a cheap imitation.

MYSTERIOUS ANGEL BODYGUARDS

The angel of the Lord encamps around those who fear him, and he delivers them.

—Psalm 34:7

One of the jobs God has given angels is to protect humans from physical and spiritual harm. Several times in the Bible, God sent angels to help people. For example, two angels protected Lot and his family by half-leading, half-dragging them out of a doomed city (Genesis 19:10–16).

Many Christians believe that the same angel guards us all the time. Other people say that each believer has two guardian angels. These ideas may or may not be true. We don't actually know for certain since the Bible doesn't say. What it does say is this: "He will command his angels concerning you to guard you in all your ways" (Psalm 91:11).

What's important to know is that angels are powerful. They are armed and dangerous and—thank goodness!—they're on your side! If you want to find out just how awesome angels are and how scared men get when they see them, read Matthew 28:2–4. The Roman soldiers guarding Jesus' tomb shook so badly they collapsed. Usually angels don't appear in all their power and glory. They know how much it rattles humans.

Since angels are so powerful, it's comforting to know that God loves us and has set them around us to guard us.

TROPHIES WAITING IN HEAVEN

Everyone who competes in the games goes into strict training. They do it to get a crown that will not last; but we do it to get a crown that will last forever.
—1 Corinthians 9:25

When ancient Greek athletes won a competition, they didn't get gold medals. They got to wear a crown made of leaves, usually branches of laurel leaves, olive leaves, or pine needles. Obviously, those things didn't last. Pine needles stay green the longest, but after a while even they dry up. Even Christmas trees eventually have to get chucked.

These days when you win a track and field event, you probably get one of those colored ribbons. It shows that you accomplished something, but unless you pin it to your bedroom wall, it can get lost really quickly. Now a shiny metal trophy is different. Usually that's bigger and not so easy to lose—although, with the disasters that some kids' rooms are, they could lose even that.

Paul said that the treasures of this life were like leafy crowns, wilting like yesterday's salad. As Christians, we're out to earn treasures that will last forever. And the good thing is, you can't lose these rewards no matter how messy your room is, because they're not on earth. God holds onto them for you. "He has given us ... an inheritance that can never perish, spoil or fade—kept in heaven for you" (1 Peter 1:3–4).

When you get to heaven, you'll inherit all the treasures and awards God has been keeping for you. Your whole life of serving God will be rewarded.

STANDING UP TO FRIENDS

Rebuke your neighbor frankly so you will not share in his guilt.
—Leviticus 19:17

This is an actual commandment in the Bible: if some kid—your brother or buddy—is into bad stuff, you should not only refuse to go along with him, but you're supposed to "rebuke him frankly," meaning speak out clearly. Let him know that what he's doing is wrong. That way when he gets in trouble, you won't be guilty of not warning him.

What do you do if your brother has a comic that you know your parents wouldn't approve of? Or what if you learn that he's heading to a friend's house to play a violent video game rated for adults? Do you say something about it? Or do you keep quiet and save that juicy little fact for when he makes you mad—then threaten to tell your parents? No. That's blackmailing. That's wrong too.

When a brother or a friend is doing something seriously wrong or is about to, speak up right then and there. Hey, you might even talk him out of it. Then he won't end up guilty, you won't end up guilty, and everyone's happy. Even if you can't talk sense into him, at least when he gets in trouble—and it will happen, sooner or later—you won't share in it.

It can be hard to stand up for what's right, especially if your friend gets mad at you. Doing the right thing has never been easy. But it's still the right thing.

WHEN HUMOR IS BULLYING

Tobiah the Ammonite ... said, "What they are building—if even a fox climbed up on it, he would break down their wall of stones!"
—Nehemiah 4:3

When the Jews were building walls to defend Jerusalem, an enemy named Tobiah joked that their wall was so weak that if even a light-footed fox hopped up on it, the whole thing would come crumbling down. It sounded like a harmless joke, but it wasn't. See, Tobiah was part of a gang that was doing everything they could to stop the Jews from building those walls.

When a group of kids are bent on teasing or tormenting some poor kid, it may seem harmless, but that kind of stuff causes real grief. Sure, they may just sneer and threaten, but sometimes that's enough. And what if you're the one teasing some kid? If you keep on and keep on teasing—even if you never use force—is that bullying?

Yes, it is, especially if it makes the other kid feel bad, and you mean to make him feel bad or afraid. So how do you tell the difference between good-humored jokes where you're just horsing around, and hurtful jokes? With hurtful humor, someone's getting hurt. If you poke fun at the same person all the time or constantly joke about how clumsy he is or how big his ears are—or whatever—that can be bullying.

We all enjoy a good joke, and if the person you're joking about enjoys it, fine. But if he's being hurt by your "humor," stop immediately.

DEVOTION 104

FOUR KEYS OF FRIENDSHIP

Remind the people ... to slander no one, to be peaceable and considerate, and to show true humility toward all men.

—Titus 3:2

Paul's advice to Christians is: (1) slander no one, (in other words, no mean-spirited trash talking); (2) be peaceable, (don't bulldoze others by trying to push for what we want); (3) be considerate, (duh); and (4) be humble (don't think that we're better than others).

These rules were written to help Christians stay out of trouble with the law, but they're also great advice on how to treat and keep friends. Have you ever noticed how obnoxious, angry kids lose friends by treating them badly?

Okay, so it's clear that people don't like to be slandered and bad-mouthed. And it's also obvious that if we don't insist on our way, but compromise and work things out, people enjoy having us around. And of course, being considerate of others is important. But why is humility a big deal? It's important because if we don't have proud attitudes, we won't end up arguing so much, or putting others down.

God wants us to treat others well because he cares for how they feel. It just so happens that acting like a Christian is also a great way to make and keep friends.

OVERLOOKING MISTAKES

He who covers over an offense promotes love, but whoever repeats the matter separates close friends.
— Proverbs 17:9

Okay, this verse doesn't mean you should cover for yourself if your bicycle runs over the neighbor's cat. This means that if someone has offended you, instead of telling everyone how badly he treated you, you choose to cover the offense. You need a lot of love to do that. That's why the Bible says, "Love each other deeply, because love covers over a multitude of sins" (1 Peter 4:8).

Now, if a bully is tormenting you day after day, don't cover that offense. Don't suffer in silence or be afraid to tell an adult. And in serious matters like lawbreaking or other people's safety, you do have a responsibility to be accountable to an adult. But what if your friend borrows your favorite Manga and accidentally rips the cover or leaves it out in the rain? Do you tell everyone what a scumbag he is? If he hears you've gone around bad-mouthing him, it'll be hard to be friends again later.

But if you don't blab about it—or you don't heap blame on him, and instead say, "Accidents happen"—it shows that you value your friend over material things. Want to save a friendship? Don't gossip about a buddy. One of the surest ways to keep a friendship is to overlook mistakes and forgive offences.

CONSIDERING OTHERS

Like one who takes away a garment on a cold day, or like vinegar poured on soda, is one who sings songs to a heavy heart.
—Proverbs 25:20

Try this with an adult to help you—pour baking soda into a container of some kind. Then pour vinegar into it. The result is really cool. I once tried this with a small bottle, and when I attempted to shove a cork into the opening the expanding gas shot the cork out so fast it nearly put out my eye. So don't try that part.

The lesson about vinegar and soda is obvious—the two don't mix. But isn't it odd that the author of this verse compares this chemical reaction to the way it feels when someone is grieving and another person intentionally acts cheerful around him or her? Imagine your friend discovering that your pet had just died, and instead of being sad with you he tried to sing you the newest rock song on the radio.

In the same way, if you're sensitive to what others are going through you'll consider how your behavior might affect them. If your mom's had a tough day, avoid getting uncontrollably foolish or singing schoolyard rhymes.

You may just be having fun, but part of growing up into a man of God is to be sensitive to what others are going through and to learn boundaries.

THE TOE THING

"The land you are entering to take over is not like the land of Egypt, from which you have come."
— Deuteronomy 11:10

When the Israelites headed to Canaan, God told them what they'd be facing. See, back in Egypt they'd lived on rich land along the Nile River. If they wanted a garden, all they had to do was drop seeds in the dirt, poke the irrigation ditch with their toe, let out some water, and presto! But Canaan was a dry land. The Israelites would have to work hard hoeing the ground and trust God to send rain—either that or lug jugs of water from a well.

Maybe your home is like Canaan. Your parents expect you to work. Instead of picking your shirt off the floor with your big toe, they actually expect you to pick up all your clothes! You might even have to feed the dog or vacuum the rug. Is that rough or what?

Maybe other kids do have it easier. Maybe they get away with only doing the toe thing. But by picking up after yourself and helping around the house, you're learning responsibility, self-discipline, and how to be a team player. As you get older and enter the real world, these lessons will put you miles ahead of kids who have it easy now.

Don't grumble if you have to work a little harder than your friends. Good stuff will come from it.

NOT FAIR!

"Why do the wicked live on, growing old and increasing in power?"
—Job 21:7

Probably because they take vitamin supplements and eat lots of yucky-tasting health food. Seriously though, this has always been a big question. It was a question in Job's day 3,500 years ago, and it's still a question today: if God blesses people who live righteous lives and judges those who do wrong, why do we see wicked men living to old age, getting richer, and having lots of toys to play with?

When you have to scrape your allowance together to buy a movie ticket, and you hear about some drug lord who lives in a mansion on some tropical island who has his own private movie theater and jet, it's easy to wonder, where's God? Did he leave the world on autopilot while he's off doing something else? It's even difficult to see a spoiled rich kid in your school who has it all while you don't have much. You wonder, doesn't God care?

God does care, and he's not way off somewhere out of cellular range. He does judge the wicked. He does bring the proud down. And he does reward the righteous. It just takes time. In the meantime, trust that God knows what's going on. Don't take the law into your own hands or try to even the score somehow. Let justice run its course. Give God space to take care of things.

God's on top of things and sees what's happening. Hang in there and he will reward you for doing what's right.

ENDURANCE

"Joshua waged war against all these kings for a long time."
—Joshua 11:18

I f you read the book of Joshua, you get a wide-screen picture of knockout battles, surprise attacks, and huge military victories. But that all happened during the first couple years of the move into Canaan! Joshua waged war for another four years after that, and by then the Canaanites had dug in. They oiled their chariot wheels, opened new sword factories, and added extra bricks to their walls. Then the war bogged down, and the Israelites sat around besieging cities.

It's not all about being lightning quick with a sword. It's not all about courage and strength. Often you need long-term strength. That's called endurance. For example, you're excited when you first start taking martial arts lessons but after a while you're bored with all the repetition. You need stick-to-itiveness. Or maybe you take on snow-shoveling jobs in your neighborhood then after a few weeks think it's just too much work. You need endurance.

Where do you get endurance? You have to make a commitment. Joshua and the Israelites were committed to carving out a homeland in Canaan. (They had to be! They couldn't just mosey on back to Egypt.) If you're involved in a huge, long-term project, make a commitment that you'll finish it. Then tackle it one day at a time. Do what you can do in one day and leave the rest for tomorrow.

Take a tip from Joshua and set your mind to the fact that for some projects you'll have to "wage war a long time."

BEING THERE FOR FAMILY

Please let your servant remain here as my lord's slave in place of the boy,
and let the boy return with his brothers.

—Genesis 44:33

hen the powerful governor of Egypt said he was going to keep Judah's youngest brother, Benjamin, as his slave, Judah offered to take Benjamin's place. (This governor was their brother Joseph, but Judah didn't know this at the time.) Why was Judah willing to make such a sacrifice? Because he loved his brother and he loved his father. He knew it'd break his father's heart if Benjamin didn't return from Egypt. Wow! Talk about love!

Now, chances are that no one will threaten to take your brother as a slave and you'll have to volunteer to take his place, but hey, you still have opportunities to be there for him. Like what if he needs help cleaning up yogurt that he managed to splatter over half the kitchen? What if he needs help finding photos on the Internet for a Science assignment? Is the little guy on his own?

The modern idea that it's up to everyone to look out for himself is wrong. God gave us families and being part of a family is very important. It's supposed to count for something. When you have brothers and sisters, you have a special obligation to look out for them—whether they bug you sometimes or not.

WEREN'T BORN YESTERDAY?

Ask the former generations and find out what their fathers learned,
for we were born only yesterday and know nothing.
— Job 8:8 – 9

E ver had someone tell you something really basic, and you
reply, "Hey, I wasn't born yesterday!"? Well, this dude
Bildad, who said, "We were born only yesterday," was at
least fifty years old — and he and his friends were smart. Yet
Bildad still felt like they'd only been born yesterday compared to
the really wise old people of the previous generations.

By the time you're ten, eleven, or twelve years old, you know
quite a bit. You've spent years studying stuff in school, you've
read books, watched TV, and even learned a couple of things
from talking to other kids. Since you can play complex video
games that your parents are hopeless at, you realize that you
know more than Mom and Dad about some things.

Okay, so you may know video games, but life is a lot bigger
than a fast thumb and robot-zapping reflexes. When it comes to
the serious things of life — what works and what doesn't, hard-
earned experiences, and just overall knowledge — your parents
have a twenty- or thirty-year head start.

Ask the older generation. Find out what your father learned.
You might be surprised at just how much he knows.

FIGHTING AND BITING

The Lord's servant must not quarrel; instead, he must be kind to everyone.
— 2 Timothy 2:24

Who is this servant of the Lord who must not quarrel? Does this verse mean that pastors and missionaries shouldn't argue, but it's okay for everybody else to bite one another's heads off? No. The Bible warns, "If you keep on biting and devouring each other, watch out or you will be destroyed by each other" (Galatians 5:15). God doesn't want us to be spiritual cannibals! We're all God's servants and shouldn't quarrel over silly stuff.

You may think, "Okay, I can stop quarreling, but do I have to be kind to everyone—even to my sister?" Well, if you just stop quarreling without being kind, you'll be right back at it at the drop of a hat (as soon as the adults leave the room). But if you're considerate and kind, then you'll stop arguing and stay stopped. You may say, "Hey, my sister really bugs me." Still.

This thing about being kind to others goes back to what Jesus said about loving everyone, even your enemies. Jesus said to be considerate to others just like you'd want them to be considerate to you. It's hard to bite your tongue when other kids start arguments over dumb things, but the point is, you don't have to get into it. Some things are worth arguing over, but most things aren't. Know the difference.

If you want to follow Jesus and be God's servant instead of a spiritual cannibal, there are a few ground rules. One, be kind to everyone. Two, don't quarrel over piddly stuff.

WORKING OUT THE DETAILS

The ark is to be 450 feet long, 75 feet wide and 45 feet high ... Put a door in the side of the ark and make lower, middle and upper decks.

—Genesis 6:15 – 16

God gave Noah the basic measurements for the ark, and then Noah spent many years building it. Obviously Noah had to figure out quite a few details. He had to think how to reinforce the beams so the ship wouldn't break up in the storm. He had to invent systems to feed the animals and pipe water to them. He had to dream up a way to suck fresh air into the ark so they didn't all suffocate.

It's the same today: you often know what God wants you to do, but you have to figure out the details. For example, you know you're supposed to go to school. But you don't pass the grade by simply sitting at your desk. You have to plug your brain in and figure stuff out. You may wonder, "Can't God just give me the answers to the test?" You wish!

That's where your brain has to kick in. You have to study and really wrap your mind around problems. Sometimes they're so complicated you think you're mud-wrestling alligators. You're trying hard but not getting it. Well, keep at it and you'll succeed. Pray for God to help your brain work well—then use the thing.

God spells out goals and guidelines just as he did for Noah—and he'll even help you with the details—but you have to do your part and think.

TOP CAMEL MAN

Obil the Ishmaelite was in charge of the camels.
—1 Chronicles 27:30

Obil was a camel expert, and King David had camels—lots of them! Go figure. His kingdom stretched from Egypt to the Euphrates River. Want trade caravans? Gotta have camels. So who should David put in charge of every camel in the kingdom? One name shot to the top of the list: Obil the Ishmaelite. He wasn't an Israelite, true—he was an Arab—but Obil knew the most about camels, and the guy who was best at the job got the job.

If you feel different from other kids, don't sweat it. Millions of families have moved to America from other countries to find a better life in—ta da!—the Land of Opportunity, where your talents and abilities matter more than where you came from. Maybe that's you. Or maybe that's some of your friends. It's cool to be different, but sometimes you wonder, Yeah, but will I fit in? Will I succeed? Look at Obil.

Or maybe your parents weren't immigrants. Maybe your great-great-great-great-grandfather was the first, famous, real McCoy to leap off the Mayflower, climb up on Plymouth Rock, and beat his chest. But still, that was him. You're you. Maybe you feel like you're nobody special and wonder if you'll succeed in life when you grow up. The answer to that is easy: study hard, and you can find your unique talent.

Want to succeed in your future career? Take a tip from Obil: know your stuff inside out, and you'll shoot up to the top of the class.

JESUS' POWER OVER DEMONS

When he saw Jesus, he cried out and fell at his feet, shouting at the top of his voice, "What do you want with me, Jesus, Son of the Most High God? I beg you, don't torture me!"

—Luke 8:28

A long time ago in Israel, a demon-possessed madman lived in a graveyard beside the Sea of Galilee. Then Jesus' boat landed. When the Son of God stepped ashore, the guy rushed out from the tombs to meet him. One look at Jesus, and the demons inside this guy went bonkers. The guy fell down and began screaming at the top of his voice to Jesus, "I beg you, don't torture me!" Right away Jesus cast the devils out of him.

Some movies and comic books have things totally backward. They describe demons and evil spirits as mighty, fearsome beings—which some of them are—but the way they have it, it's usually only some bigger demon who can finally beat them. Modern comic and movie scriptwriters have totally forgotten what the Bible says.

When Jesus met demons, the demons trembled with terror, flopped to the ground, and wailed and begged him not to punish them. When the Son of God looked them in the eyes, they screamed and shrieked and went crazy with fear.

So who's the most powerful? Jesus! You don't have to be afraid of the devil or demons because this same powerful Jesus is still protecting us today.

MIRACLES ARE EVIDENCE

Now while he was in Jerusalem ... many people saw the miraculous signs he was doing and believed in his name.

—John 2:23

When you read the story of Jesus' life, one thing that jumps out at you is how many miracles he did. People who saw these things were astonished. This man was clearly no ordinary man, and many people believed that he was the Son of God. In fact, Jesus' enemies complained, "Here is this man performing many miraculous signs. If we let him go on like this, everyone will believe in him." They knew that miracles were strong evidence that Jesus had divine power.

And miracles didn't only happen in Bible days. God still answers prayers when Christians pray to him in Jesus' name. He still does miracles today: big ones that make you go "Wow!" and small everyday ones. Stop and think about some prayer God answered for your family. You've probably even forgotten some of them. Ask your parents or grandparents to remind you.

People pray for lots of little things every day, and time and again God answers! The problem is that by the time God answers the prayer, people have often forgotten that they prayed for it. We don't always recognize when God does something for us. You know how you take it for granted when your mom and dad do things for you? Well, God does lots of stuff for you too. So pay attention and thank him whenever you can.

Jesus did miracles, and those miracles proved his love and power. Although he isn't walking around on earth today, his power to do miracles is still here. He still answers our prayers today.

PUTTING ON THE ARMOR OF LIGHT

The night is nearly over; the day is almost here. So let us put aside the deeds of darkness and put on the armor of light.

—Romans 13:12

O beying the Word of God is like waking up and getting dressed. When this verse says "the night is nearly over," it means that the world's present evil age has almost ended. "The day is almost here" means Jesus is coming soon. It's time to get dressed. But remember, in order to put on the armor of light, you first have to put aside the deeds of darkness. Wake up and stop doing things that displease God.

You've seen those cartoon shows where heroes of the future prepare for battle. All they do is think *Armor on*, and suddenly these plates of shining armor begin whipping out of nowhere and snap in place all over their bodies. Within seconds they're covered. Maybe you wish you could dress like that in the morning, instead of struggling to button your shirt when you're half-asleep—then finding that you buttoned it wrong.

God's armor is the most fantastic kind of battle armor. You pray for his Spirit to cover you with all the pieces of his armor, and he does. But you also need to grab the weapons he gives, like the Sword of the Spirit. You won't be able to see these things with your eyes though. God's armor is armor of light, all right, but spiritual light. (Read all about it in Ephesians 6:10–17.)

You want to be one of God's warriors? Then ditch the deeds of darkness, put on the armor of light, and get serious about being one of his fighters.

HELPING YOUR FAITH GROW

Faith comes from hearing the message, and the message is heard through the word of Christ.

—Romans 10:17

When you read the gospels or hear your pastor talk about Jesus and God's Spirit opens your eyes to all the amazing stuff Jesus said and did, you just know that Jesus was one of a kind. No one else taught the amazing things he taught or did the miracles he did. And certainly no one else died and came back to life! And once you put your faith in Jesus and trust him to save you, you have eternal life.

But even after you believe in Jesus, your faith is still tested. Like maybe you're confused or afraid. Or maybe you're going through a difficult time. Maybe everything seems hopeless and you just need some hope to hang onto so you don't sink in the "quicksand of gloom."

Where do you get your hope? What helps you believe that God is with you and that things will turn out?

You get that hope and inspiration the same way you received it in the first place—by listening to the truth about Jesus and by sitting down and opening up your Bible and reading it. Are you worried about some problem? Are you afraid? Do you wonder where God is when you need him? Do you feel mentally wiped out?

If you want your faith to grow stronger, read God's Word. That's where your spiritual strength comes from. Plug in to God and recharge your batteries today.

HIDING GOD'S WORD DOWN DEEP

I have hidden your word in my heart that I might not sin against you.
—Psalm 119:11

When this verse talks about hiding God's Word in your heart, it doesn't mean stashing it somewhere so little kids can't find it. When it says to "hide" it, the verse means getting the Bible so deep down in your mind that it's almost part of you. And it's not only talking about memorizing Bible verses, but also about tuning in to them. Do that and you're a lot less likely to sin against God.

If you have to make a decision and wonder what to do, it sure makes it a lot easier if a verse from the Bible suddenly comes to mind, telling you exactly what God thinks of your plans, right? Since you don't always have a Bible handy, plant some verses in your mind. Get them deep in your heart. And how do you do that?

Well, just like you have to memorize multiplication tables or lines from a play, you should memorize important verses from the Bible. Some people only have to read a verse a few times and it sticks. Good for them! But most of us, if we want to write it onto our brain's hard drive, have to actually memorize it. Do that. Then the Holy Spirit can remind you of it when you need direction the most.

If you can't remember what God's Word says, it's easy to sin and do wrong things. If you know what the Bible says, it's a whole lot easier to make the right choice.

BITING YOUR TONGUE

He who holds his tongue is wise . . . Even a fool is thought wise if he keeps silent.

—**Proverbs 10:19; 17:28**

There are times—lots of times, in fact—when it's wise to hold your tongue. That doesn't mean grabbing your tongue with your hands—you can hold it just fine with your teeth. Teeth are practically made for the job. That's not hard for a wise person. But for a fool, trying to hang on to his tongue is like trying to stay on a rodeo bull.

Some kids never stop talking. Know anyone like that? It's fine to be a talker. Chatty people are fun to be around, but not if their mouth pours out a non-ending stream of foolish jokes and grossness. Some kids talk about things they shouldn't just to see how many laughs they can get—like if their little brother wet his bed and they tell all his friends.

It's fun to joke around, but you've got to know what to joke about and when to zip your lip. If you know how to do that, you're wise. In fact, considering how fools like to talk, people may even think a fool is wise if he keeps silent. Like, maybe his mouth was full of pizza and he couldn't talk, but at least he missed saying something stupid.

Know when to hold on to your tongue. It doesn't take a lot of brains to keep your mouth shut, but you've got to use the brains you have.

CHILDISH THINKING

Brothers, stop thinking like children.
—1 Corinthians 14:20

The apostle Paul had just finished writing the following words: "When I was a child, I talked like a child, I thought like a child. I reasoned like a child. When I became a man, I put childish ways behind me" (1 Corinthians 13:11). Then he tells all of us to do the same—to "stop thinking like children." It's okay to think like a little kid if you are one. But when you grow up, it's time to move up a few levels in the game.

If you whine over your breakfast cereal, your older brother might say, "C'mon. Act your age!" Or maybe you gross everyone out by mining boogers in public, and some girl groans, "Oooo, sick! Grow up!" (Okay, you had that one coming.) But sometimes, for no reason, some kid insults you by saying that you still enjoy the purple dinosaur show. But Paul wasn't trying to insult anyone. He was just reminding people not to slip back into childish thinking.

You can tell you're growing up when you stop thinking childish thoughts. That doesn't mean you're suddenly super serious and you never look at a toy again. You stop childish thinking when you start considering other people's needs, not just yours. You don't goof off when it's time to work, and you're not easily offended or quick to quarrel. Those are all signs of maturing.

You can still have plenty of fun. Growing up just means your definition of fun changes. Instead of enjoying childish play and purple dinosaurs, you're on the next level.

PETE TAKES THE HEAT

The circumcised believers criticized him ... Peter began and explained everything to them precisely as it had happened.

—Acts 11:2 – 4

Yup, Peter's in trouble ... again. This is the same disciple who rebuked Jesus. This is the guy who hacked off someone's ear with his sword. This is Peter, who denied that he even knew Jesus. Now he's in trouble again. So what's new? Wait! This time Pete's taking heat for doing good. He'd been preaching the gospel to Gentiles (non-Jews), a big no-no to some Jewish Christians. After Pete explained himself, they believed him and everything was cool.

It's easy for us to believe that Peter was right this time around; we're reading the story two thousand years later. But it wasn't clear for folks back then, so at first they jumped all over him. What about you? If some kid's goofed up in the past, are you quick to presume him guilty before he has a chance to open his mouth? Don't. "He who answers before listening—that is his folly and his shame" (Proverbs 18:13).

Sure, you get an idea what to expect from people because of their past track record, but guess what! People can change. And they do change, all the time. So if you don't want to put your foot in your mouth—or theirs—let others explain. Afterward, if you still think they goofed up, at least you'll know you gave them a chance to tell their story.

Don't criticize people before you even hear them out. Peter changed. Others can change too. Give them a chance.

FILLED WITH SKILL

I have filled him with the Spirit of God, with skill, ability and knowledge in all kinds of crafts.

—Exodus 31:3

God gave Moses the exact designs for the ark of the covenant and the Tent of Meeting. (The ark was like a gold-covered treasure chest, and the Tent of Meeting was like a huge, fancy tent.) God also told Moses to build tables and altars. Fine. Now Moses needed craftsmen to actually build these things. Bezalel fit the bill perfectly: he was smart, he knew how to work with gold and silver and bronze, and he was an excellent carpenter.

When God gives you abilities and talents, you're naturally good at something. Maybe you're a champ at sports, or you lead the pack with drawing or inventing complicated stuff out of Lego bricks. And skill? That's when you practice something so much that you become really, really good at it—like playing computer games or tossing a basketball. And of course, knowledge means learning all the ins and outs.

Okay, so God has given you natural abilities, and if you're willing to learn, you can add skill and knowledge to that. But check out that list again. Before God filled Bezalel with skill, ability, and knowledge, he first filled him with the Holy Spirit. This supernatural power connected him to God and gave his life purpose and meaning, and you've got to have that to truly succeed.

It's cool to have skills and abilities, but make sure—before anything else—that you ask God to fill you with his Holy Spirit.

TOTALLY INFINITE UNDERSTANDING

Great is our Lord and mighty in power; his understanding has no limit.
—Psalm 147:5

Not only is God the greatest muscle guy in the universe, but he knows absolutely everything about everything! His understanding has no limit—it is infinite! You think you're smart? Compared to God, you're like an ant with a brain the size of a bread crumb—a small bread crumb.

Sometimes you're muddling through things, trying to solve problems that just won't go away. Or you're trying to understand stuff you just can't understand, and it gets so frustrating that you feel like screaming or pounding the wall. It could be math, or it could be a problem in life. You think and think, but you don't get an answer. You ask others what they think, but they don't know the solution either. So what do you do?

Pray. God can clue you in. Now, if you're praying for him to show you how to build a time machine, well, forget it. But if it's something you truly need to know, then you can expect an answer. Maybe you'll read the answer in the Bible, or maybe God will lead you to someone who knows. Or maybe you'll wake up one morning to find that God took care of it—even though you still don't understand what was happening.

God has the answers to everything. Obviously he must—there is no limit to his understanding. So tune in to him.

JUNK TALK

Do not let any unwholesome talk come out of your mouths, but only what is helpful for building others up according to their needs.

—Ephesians 4:29

The opposite of wholesome, healthy food is unwholesome food, or junk food. Well, the opposite of wholesome talk is junk talk. Want to know what that is? Think of some kid swearing, acting out-of-control foolish, or trash-talking someone else. That's what the Bible means when it says not to let unwholesome talk come out of your mouth.

Some people don't think before they speak. They just blab whatever pops into their mind—potty humor, sick jokes, or whatever. As long as it's good for a laugh, they don't care who they gross out. It doesn't matter if it builds someone up and encourages that person or knocks them down and discourages them. And sure enough, junk talk drags everyone down.

That's why it's smart to think before you speak. Ask yourself, "What does this person need to hear?" Then say those things. That doesn't mean pouring on false compliments. Just be careful what you say. If you don't care for something, look for something descriptive to say that isn't hurtful. Like if your grandmother asks what you think of her new hairdo, don't reply "Weird! It looks like gray cotton candy." Just say, "It has nice curls." Or if your friend asks what you think of his drawing, stop yourself from blurting out, "It reeks." Tell him what parts you like and offer a suggestion if he needs it.

When you think of other people's feelings before you speak, that's wisdom kicking in. Sometimes you can't help it if foolish thoughts pop into your mind. Just don't let them come out of your mouth.

LAST-MINUTE SCRAMBLE

"A sluggard does not plow in season; so at harvest time he looks but finds nothing."
— Proverbs 20:4

The ground in Israel was usually so hard and dry that plows could barely break it up. But every autumn rains softened the soil. That's when farmers were out with their oxen and plows, planting crops. Everyone except for sluggards, that is. Those lazy guys kept putting the job off. By the time they finally got around to it, the ground was getting hard again. They plowed and scattered seeds, sure, but come harvest (surprise, surprise!) no crop—or a very poor crop.

Sound familiar? Instead of doing your homework or school assignment when you're supposed to, do you put it off till the last possible minute or only remember it at bedtime? If it's due the next day, do you do a rushed, sloppy job and get a low grade? This is called procrastination. A procrastinator knows what he's supposed to do but doesn't want to do it, so he drags his feet until it becomes an all-out emergency.

It's easy to avoid that last-minute scramble: do your homework when you're supposed to. Or if you're getting ready for school or church, stay focused on dressing, combing your hair, and finding your shoes. That way you can walk to the car instead of running there half-clothed and barefoot.

Don't be a sluggard. Roll up your sleeves and do your work when it's supposed to be done. Get it done and out of the way. Then go have your fun.

UNMISTAKABLE SMELL

"When Isaac caught the smell of his clothes, he blessed him and said, 'Ah, the smell of my son is like the smell of a field."
—Genesis 27:27

Jacob wanted to have the oldest son blessing, but there was one little problem: Jacob's twin brother, Esau, was the oldest. That meant the blessing belonged to him. Jacob's mom, Rebekah, had a crooked plan. Since Isaac was blind, Jacob could go in, pretending to be Esau. So "Rebekah took the best clothes of Esau her older son, which she had in the house, and put them on her younger son Jacob" (Genesis 27:15).

Jacob walked into Dad's tent, and when Isaac got a whiff of those robes, he recognized Esau's unmistakable smell—and gave Jacob the blessing. See, Esau was a hunter. He crawled in the dirt, sneaking up on animals. No way his mom could get all the sweat stains and antelope poop out in the wash. But these were Esau's best clothes. What was he doing getting these clothes dirty and smelly?

And the big question: do you do the same thing? No, don't answer that. But when your mom says to change out of your good clothes, do it right away before you forget. Fold 'em, hang 'em up, or hurl 'em in the laundry—whatever it takes. If you crawl around in your best clothes, not even detergent will get out the dog poop smell.

Funny thing about Esau: he was seventy-seven years old, and he still hadn't clued in! Hey, but it's still not too late for you to start taking care of your clothing.

BE HAPPY, YOUNG MAN

"Be happy, young man, while you are young, and let your heart give you joy in the days of your youth."
—Ecclesiastes 11:9

Here's a command kids gotta love: Thou shalt have fun! It isn't exactly a commandment, but it's great advice. Now, King Solomon wasn't saying, "Goof off and play all day." Kids played back then, but they also did chores. And he wasn't saying, "Enjoy yourself now, 'cause it's only work when you get older." It's in the attitude. Anybody at any age can enjoy life. Like Solomon said, "However many years a man may live, let him enjoy them all" (verse 8).

Kids are hardwired to want to have fun, and as long as your homework and chores are done, go for it! We all need to unwind after a hard day. But it helps to have a positive attitude about school, homework, and chores too. If you complain about them, it'll seem like it takes forever to get through them. Hey, things really aren't so bad. You're not shoveling chicken dung all day long.

Whatever the chore, plant the thought in your mind, "I have to do this so I might as well have a good attitude." Even if you don't enjoy it, you can whistle while you work. Well, not out loud during a math test, but in other words, have a positive attitude. It beats whining while you work.

Put your heart into your work and try to enjoy it. It'll make things go faster. Then you'll be done sooner and can have some real fun.

PART OF THE PRIDE

Pursue righteousness, faith, love and peace, along with those who call on the Lord out of a pure heart.

—2 Timothy 2:22

To pursue means "to chase or to follow." You know, like a lion pursues a zebra across the savannah. (Run, zebra! Run!) So the Bible tells you to set your sights on good stuff like righteousness, faith, love, and peace—and then to chase those things nonstop. And don't just go after these things alone. Just like lions hunt in teams, it works best when you pursue good stuff with other Christians. (Scratch one zebra.)

There's an old saying: "If you run with wolves, you'll learn to howl like a wolf." Well, if you run with weasels, you'll start squeaking like a weasel. The point is that if you spend time with a bad crowd, they influence you, right? Hang with a smoking, cursing crowd, and the odds are you'll end up smoking and swearing. (At least you'll be breathing second-hand smoke and getting an earful of curses.) Or if your friends watch sick movies, they'll try to suck you into that too.

It's great to have cool friends who do exciting stuff, but remember: you can do cool, fun stuff with Christians. Believers can have lots of fun too! It's okay to have non-Christian friends, but your closest pals should be other Christians—you know, guys "who call on the Lord." The fun stuff you do can include praying with them and studying the Bible together. Instead of getting into all the wrong stuff, these dudes are doing what's right. So run with lions—not with weasels.

HE WHO WORSHIPS GOD, WINS!

Jesus said to him, "Away from me, Satan! For it is written, 'Worship the Lord your God, and serve him only.'"
—Matthew 4:10

One day the devil tried to tempt Jesus. He showed Jesus all the kingdoms of this world and their glittering splendor and fabulous riches. The devil said, "All this I will give you if you will bow down and worship me (Matthew 4:9)." Jesus told Satan to get away, and then he quoted Scripture, saying that we are to worship God instead—and only God.

The devil doesn't usually come out so bold. Usually he's happy if he can just get you to worship your belongings and your toys—anything but God. See, Jesus said that the first and greatest commandment was to love God with all your heart, but a lot of people think the number one rule is to get as many toys as they can just to enjoy life. Their motto is, "He who has the most toys when he dies, wins." Wrong!

The Bible says that greed is just like idol worship (Colossians 3:5). Now, there's nothing wrong with having toys or fancy new gadgets. It's okay to like them and think they're cool and take good care of them. But the problem is if you obsess over your stuff or put material things before God. Then it becomes like idol worship—like you are worshipping a thing instead of God.

Enjoy the toys and things that God has given you. Just remember that God is the one who gives you cool stuff to enjoy—so make God number one in your life.

JESUS' RETURN FROM HEAVEN

"Men will see the Son of Man coming in clouds with great power and glory. And he will send his angels and gather his elect from the four winds."
—Mark 13:26–27

Christians have different ideas about what earth's final days will be like. The book of Revelation is deep and mysterious, so we don't understand it all—yet. But one thing Jesus was very clear about is that he will return one day. When he comes back in the sky, people all around the planet will see him. For two thousand years, Christians have waited for Jesus to return and end all wars and famines and set up the perfect kingdom of God on earth. Christians living today want the same thing. Or maybe you hope Jesus will wait a while. Maybe you want to grow up, graduate high school, and do stuff first. Maybe you don't want this world to end quite yet.

Don't worry. Jesus' kingdom will be a whole lot more fun than life right now. It's not like we're going to leave earth and then float around on clouds forever. Some Christians think that after taking us to heaven for a wonderful time with him and all the Christians who have ever lived, we'll return to earth. Then, instead of selfish, greedy people running the place, there will be love, peace, and harmony on earth.

We don't know all the details of Jesus' return. But we do know that he is coming back one day with power and great glory, and that life will be better than it's ever been.

KNOW BETTER THAN GOD? NOT!

"You acted foolishly," Samuel said. "You have not kept the command the Lord your God gave you."
—1 Samuel 13:13

God had given King Saul very clear instructions. Saul was to gather his army and wait. Seven days later, the prophet Samuel would arrive, sacrifice to God, and then Saul and his army could battle the Philistines. Samuel had spelled out exactly what to do, but when day seven rolled around and Samuel didn't show up immediately, Saul grabbed the nearest knife and made the sacrifice himself. He wasn't supposed to! Seconds after he finished, Samuel showed up.

Saul wasn't the only willful guy in the history of this planet to think that he had a better idea than God. For thousands of centuries since Saul, people have continued making the same kinds of boneheaded mistakes. God says something in his Word, but it seems to make no sense, so people ignore it. Or they say, "Times have changed. God doesn't still expect me to love my enemies." Bwaaaaaap! Wrong answer.

God's Word doesn't always tell us exactly what to do. God gave us brains, and he intended for us to use them. So you'll do well to put on your thinking cap and figure out what to do. The problem comes when God's Word tells you exactly what to do and you still try to "figure things out." That's where you end up with Saul-utions instead of solutions.

Don't pull a Saul and act foolishly. Use your brain and choose to do what God says to do. That's being really smart.

AVOID CAUSING GRIEF

Early the next morning Abraham took some food and a skin of water and gave them to Hagar ... then sent her off with the boy.
—Genesis 21:14

When God told Abraham to send Hagar and Ishmael away, it was hard on Abraham because he really loved Ishmael. But he obeyed God and did it. Unfortunately, Abe didn't think things through and forgot to send a couple of camels loaded down with gold and silver and food and water. He sent them out with only a bit of food and a water jug. They nearly died in the desert!

Ever slipped up like that? You're supposed to feed your younger brother while your mom's out and you forget—and as soon as Mom walks in the door, he tells her that he's starving. Or your mom says to give your hamster away, so you just leave the cage on the curb with a "Free" sign on it.

If your mom tells you to take care of your brothers or sisters, stop playing video games long enough to see that they get lunch. You'll avoid causing others grief. And about hamsters: if you own one, either take care of the pitiful little fuzz ball or find someone who will. If you give it away, include the hamster food. You don't need that stuff, right? The hamster does.

Abraham slipped up, but fortunately God performed a miracle and took care of Hagar and Ishmael. But don't expect God to cover for you: if you're supposed to care for people or pets, think about it and do it.

NOT COOL!

"A drunkard staggers around in his vomit."
—Isaiah 19:14

I n Bible times, beer and wine were plentiful. Like today, some people had no control over their drinking once they started. The first cupful was followed by a second and a third until they got so drunk they were down on all fours barking like a dog. Some were even staggering around and vomiting on themselves and anyone else who happened to be near them.

Sometimes you hear teens say, "You shoulda seen Billy at the party. He was so drunk he was pukin' over the rail. Then he fell off the back porch and rolled around in his vomit." Everyone laughs, and Billy stands there grinning. He imagines the other kids are thinking, "Wow! How cool! What a man!" Hello? Wallowing around in your own foul-smelling whitewash is cool? Some people's definition of a fun time is pretty weird.

Whatever your parents think about alcohol, or whatever your church's doctrine is on wine, you must definitely not touch it. It's against the law for kids to drink alcohol. So what if some so-called friends mock you for saying no. You have nothing to prove to them. In fact, if they pressure you to drink, ditch them. You go your way and let them go their way.

There's nothing grown-up or macho about kids drinking and staggering around in their half-digested dinner barf. So avoid that whole scene.

WANT RESPECT?

"I chose the way for them and sat as their chief; I dwelt as a king among his troops."
—Job 29:25

R ead the whole chapter of Job 29, and you'll see that Job wasn't kidding! He really was like the King of Uz. He had humongous power and influence. Job was like the top general, a Supreme Court judge, and a bank president all rolled up in one. And how did Job use this power? To get everybody in Uz to bow down to him? To invade the neighboring kingdom? Nope. He used his position to feed the hungry and give justice to the oppressed.

As you grow bigger, stronger, and smarter, you find that you can do a lot of things that little kids can't. And it can be real tempting at times to use your extra smarts to trick them out of something you want, or to use your muscles to push them around. It's not only tempting but a lot of guys do exactly that. No surprise there.

What's cool is if you use your intelligence to keep little kids from doing dumb stuff, or use your strength to help them do things they can't do on their own. Think of ways you can use your power and influence to help others. Want a sure sign that you're growing up? Help others. Don't just look out for yourself.

Want your younger brothers and sisters to respect you and follow your lead? Be there for them when they need you, and they'll get used to respecting you and listening to you.

STRONG, SILENT TYPE

"The stone over the mouth of the well was large. When Jacob saw Rachel ...
he went over and rolled the stone away."
—Genesis 29:2, 10

E sau and Jacob were brothers. Esau was Mr. Hairy-chested He-man Hunter while Jacob was Mr. Quiet Guy. In most Bible storybooks Esau is built like the Hulk and Jacob's a skinny guy. Wrong. One time Jacob went to the Haran town well, and along came his cousin Rachel leading a flock of thirsty sheep. A megasize stone lid covered the well, and it was like a two-shepherd job to move it. But our man seized the stone and rolled it away—by himself. See, Jacob was strong too. He was just the strong, silent type.

Some guys today have a reputation for being tough, but it's mostly just tough talk and pushiness. Sure, they have muscles, but they talk about their arm meat so much that it seems they have more ego than strength. A lot of other kids are strong too, but they're not always bragging about it.

It's great to have muscles, and if you've got 'em—or you're getting them—good for you. Just remember that it takes more than boasts and brawn to succeed at important stuff in life. If you want to do great things, physical strength just isn't enough. You also need to walk with God.

You may not be as strong as Esau or Jacob, but you can use your muscles to do good stuff. Oh yeah ... and don't applaud yourself.

FOLLOW THROUGH

" 'Son, go and work today in the vineyard.' He answered, 'I will, sir,' but he did not go."

—Matthew 21:28, 30

Jesus told a story about a farmer who had two sons. The farmer said to Son One, "Son, go and work today in the vineyard." Son One grunted no, so Dad told Son Two to take care of the vines. This guy promised, "I will, sir." But he never went. Well, that was some help! Fortunately, Son One felt so bad about telling dad no that he went and worked.

Lots of kids are like the second son. They promise, "Sure, I'll do it," but only because saying no would cause trouble. Either that, or they say yes, go right on playing, and forget to follow through. So by bedtime the garbage still isn't out on the curb, the Lego bricks are still covering the bedroom floor three inches deep, and the dog's so hungry it eats the hamster. And then the son hears his name being called ...

Here's how to avoid that scene: when your parents tell you to do something, give them your full attention and listen to what they're saying so you know you got it. Then—unless it's simply impossible—do the chore immediately. That way, the garbage gets put out, the Lego bricks get picked up, the dog gets fed, and the hamster lives.

You get a bad rep with your parents and your friends if you don't follow through on your promises. Be a man of your word. If you promise you'll do something, do it.

SIBLING SOLUTIONS

"Men, you are brothers; why do you want to hurt each other?"
—Acts 7:26

Pharaoh's daughter adopted a Hebrew baby, called him
Moses, and raised him as a prince in the palace. But one
day Moses found out that he wasn't Egyptian. "Gulp! You
mean those ... Hebrew slaves are my people?" Now, Moses
knew that the Egyptians were treating the slaves harshly. He
expected, naturally, that this would cause the Hebrews to stick
close together. Surprise, surprise! He saw them pounding on
each other! He didn't get it.

How many times does this happen in your home—you and
your siblings settling arguments by pushing, hitting, and kicking
each other? It's one thing to quarrel and disagree, even to get
upset with each other, but you shouldn't take your disagreements into the gladiator's arena. God doesn't give you strength
so that you can pound on your brothers and sisters.

Lots of cartoons show superheroes pounding bad guys or
guys with giant guns mowing robots down. This can give the
impression that "might makes right." It doesn't. Sure, if alien
robots invade earth some day, it's probably okay for you to blow
them up. But most of the time, men of God don't use force
to settle arguments. They listen to the other guy, talk things
through, and try to work out a solution that makes
everybody happy.

You don't have to be kind to alien robots. But you do have
to love your brothers and sisters. When you have a quarrel with
them, talk things through. Try to work things out.

THE BULLY OF BAHURIM

He pelted David and all the king's officials with stones. . . . As he cursed, Shimei said, "Get out, get out, you man of blood, you scoundrel!"

—2 Samuel 16:6 – 7

Shimei (Shimmy-eye) was a trouble-maker. You can tell, because one day when King David and his officials were fleeing a large army, Shimei came out of his house and began cursing them and throwing rocks at the king himself! That was pretty bold — and dumb — because David had soldiers with him. But nothing happened to Shimei that day. David let it pass.

Bullies are like that too. It's surprising how bold they can get, harassing and teasing other kids and pushing them around practically in front of adults. Or an adult turns his head for just a second and some goon punches you in the shoulder then denies that he did a thing. How do you deal with that, especially if he gets away with it?

The first thing, of course, is to tell a responsible adult. The second thing is to remember that bullies don't get away with things like that forever. They get known for being like that and adults keep an eye on them. So do other kids. If bullies don't grow up and change their ways, they eventually get the punishment they deserve. Shimei did. David never forgot what Shimei had done, and eventually Shimmy paid the price.

If some kid is constantly being a bully and seems to be getting away with it, tell an adult and avoid him if you can.

PLAYING MIND GAMES

As soon as Joseph saw his brothers, he recognized them, but he pretended to be a stranger and spoke harshly to them.

—Genesis 42:7

Joseph's brothers had sold him as a slave, and now Joseph was a top ruler in Egypt. So when his brothers came knocking, asking the ruler for some food, they did not realize it was Joseph who was talking with them. And after what they'd done to him as a kid, can you imagine how Joseph must have felt toward them? Problem was he played some pretty cruel mind-games with them: he threatened them, scared them, locked one of his brothers up in jail, planted evidence on another and said he'd enslave him (Genesis 42–44).

Okay, your family members or friends didn't sell you as a slave, but maybe they got into your Manga comics and ripped them or scribbled on them, or took your money or walked off with a collectible toy. Of course, even after they've apologized, you still want to be sure they've changed before you let them back into your room. But it's how you go about it that matters.

If you speak harshly to them or threaten them or play mind-games on them, you're not really trying to find out where they are at. You're basically just getting revenge. You're showing where you're at ... and it isn't good. Don't do it, even if you think you're justified and, oh boy, they soooo have it coming.

If you can't trust some kid then you can't trust him. But if he apologizes and promises that he's changed, and you give him another chance, skip the mind games.

REMEMBERING TO SAY THANKS

One of them, when he saw he was healed, came back, praising God in a loud voice. He threw himself at his feet and thanked him — and he was a Samaritan.
—Luke 17:15 – 16

L eprosy is a serious skin disease. Back in Bible days, leprosy ate away at a person's flesh until it finally killed him. What's more, it's very contagious. In Jesus' day there was no known cure for it. You think anyone wanted to hang around with the lepers? One time Jesus miraculously healed ten lepers, and nine of them ran off happy and never came back. Only one returned to say thanks — and he was so happy that he threw himself down at Jesus' feet in gratitude. And catch those last words: " ... he was a Samaritan."

First notice what a big deal Jesus' actions were. He didn't avoid the lepers like everyone else did. He talked to them. And most importantly, he healed them. Ah, but only one came back to say "thank you." And he was a Samaritan, one of those with whom Jews did not get along well. In Jesus' day, Jews thought so little of Samaritans that when they'd see one coming the other direction they'd cross the street just so they wouldn't have to walk next to him.

Yet Scripture points out that of all those who were healed of this life-threatening illness, only the one the Jews liked the least was considerate enough to thank Christ for the gift.

This is still a great message for us today — God does not care one little bit about a person's race or from where he comes. His love is available freely to everyone. And in the same way we ought to love all people without regard to their background or race.

WHO YOU GONNA BELIEVE?

The first to present his case seems right, till another comes forward and questions him.

—Proverbs 18:17

This could be a reminder to judges that they need to hear both sides of an argument before they become convinced and make a decision. Of course the first guy to present his case seems right! Often he is only telling facts that help show that he is right. But most quarrels have two sides and a judge learns about the other side when someone steps up and asks, "Yeah, but what about ...?"

Some people really know how to argue. But just because someone can argue convincingly doesn't mean that he's right. Just because he sounds convinced doesn't mean that things are exactly like he's saying. For example, if you listen to only him, he'll have you convinced that Friend B is a jerk and you should never talk to Friend B again.

It's not smart to take sides before you've heard both sides. If two kids are quarreling and one of them dumps on you and tries to get you on his side, hold off. Seek out the other friend and hear his side. Usually you find out that it's wisest not to take sides at all, but just to try to make peace and let both sides calm down and sort out their quarrel.

Don't allow yourself to be totally swayed because some kid tells you very convincingly that something is so. There's probably more to the story that you need to hear.

EYEBALLS UNDER CONTROL

"I made a covenant with my eyes, not to look lustfully at a girl."
—Job 31:1

When Job got sick and lost everything he owned, his friends came to comfort him. Soon they began accusing him: "Surely you must have sinned somehow for God to let all this happen to you." They accused him of this; they accused him of that. None of it stuck. But Job knew what they were thinking—that he must have sinned sexually. Job let them know in no uncertain terms that he had never cheated on his wife. (See Job 31:9–12.) In fact, Job didn't even look lustfully at other women.

God was the one who invented sex. God was the one who designed men to want sex, but he also had a plan: men and women are supposed to enjoy this beautiful experience only within marriage. You may not think girls are so attractive now, but as you get older, your hormones will kick in and start bringing about big changes in your body. Then you'll be seriously interested in girls.

That's why it's important to notify your eyeballs ahead of time that you won't look at girls with lust—not even at girls in magazines. Why? Because Jesus said that if you look at a woman that way, you've already committed the sin in your heart. So don't go there. Put a channel lock on your eyes.

Keep your eyeballs under control like Job did, and it'll be a lot easier to keep the rest of your body in line.

SHARK ... MUST ... EAT

"They are like brute beasts, creatures of instinct . . . and like beasts they too will perish."
—2 Peter 2:12

Sharks are strong, fearsome creatures, but they don't have huge brains driving them. They go by instinct. If they're hungry, they kill and rip and gulp until they've filled their gut. Ever seen nature shows with sharks going wild in feeding frenzies? They're not thinking of the needs of the shark next to them. They're only looking out for themselves. Their thinking goes like this: Shark ... is ... hungry. Shark ... must ... eat. The apostle Peter talked about guys like that. He called them "brute beasts."

Some guys today live their whole lives in a self-feeding frenzy. They push to the front of the line and grab the biggest piece of birthday cake. They rush home from school, shove their sister aside, grab the video game controller from her hands, and shout, "I'm first!" They're looking out only for piggy number one.

When you pause and think of other people's needs—not just your own—you stop being selfish. You've stopped going just by instinct, and you've started caring about others. The Bible says to love your neighbor as yourself. Do that, and suddenly you're wondering if the next guy is hungry or if he has had his turn at a game.

Learning to think of others' needs is part of growing up. It's a sign that you're maturing and becoming less like a shark and more like a man of God.

A SENSE OF TIMING

The wise heart will know the proper time and procedure. For there is a proper time and procedure for every matter.

—Ecclesiastes 8:5 – 6

It's great if you know the solution to a problem. But just having knowledge is not good enough. You also need wisdom on the best way to use your smarts. There's also a good time to bring things up ... and really bad times to do it. If you pack these two facts into your brain, the Bible says you'll be wise.

For example, if you want to tell your friend how to get rid of a wart, you don't shout it out when he's about to give a speech to the class. There's also a procedure. With a lot of things in life, you need to fill out these forms first, pick a number, and then wait to be called. With your friends, you don't need to fill out a Wart Form, but smart "time and procedure" would be to take him aside privately and tell him after his speech.

It's the same with asking your mom if you can go over to a friend's house. Don't just burst through the door after school and blurt it out—especially if she's talking to her long-lost aunt Harriet on the phone, the spaghetti sauce is boiling over, and a bowl just broke. You'll probably get no for an answer just because of your incredibly bad timing.

Want good results? Before you say something, ask yourself, "Is this a good time?" and "Is this the right way to go about it?"

TAKING CARE OF BUSINESS

"Your servant my husband is dead, and you know that he revered the Lord. But now his creditor is coming to take my two boys as his slaves."
—2 Kings 4:1

This lady's husband was a prophet who honored God. Everybody knew that. Even the great prophet Elisha knew about him. But Mr. Prophet had borrowed a lot of money, and when he died his wife and kids were left with debts they couldn't pay. Now the bill collector was coming to grab the prophet's sons ... as slaves! Fortunately, God performed a miracle and paid the debt, but that was a close call.

Now, the main lesson of this story is that God performed a miracle to deliver a faithful servant. Still, there's another lesson here, and that is you need to stop and think about your habits. Like, if you're always borrowing money and don't pay it back, after a while you'll owe so much you can't pay it back. Lose library books, and reading gets expensive. You won't get yourself sold into slavery, but you can cause yourself major pain.

The solution? Take care of details. Don't forget to pay your debts. God shouldn't have to perform a miracle to pay your bills for you—and most of the time he won't. He leaves it up to you to pay them, and if you don't, he lets you suffer the consequences. So change that habit and avoid grief.

Make sure you honor God like Mr. Prophet did. But also be smart and honor others by paying them what you owe them. You'll avoid lots of problems.

TINY DETAILS, BIG SOLUTIONS

The Jebusites said to David, "You will not get in here" ... David said, "Anyone who conquers the Jebusites will have to use the water shaft."
— 2 Samuel 5:6, 8

When David became king of Israel, he wanted the city of Jebus for his capital. It sat on a steep hill, had high walls, and was the perfect fortress. Problem was, the Jebusites were already there. They mocked, "It's impossible for you to conquer us." Well, almost impossible. There was one way. David had grown up near Jebus, and he remembered a secret passage — the water shaft. So he sent his soldiers climbing straight up that slippery tunnel into the city.

Sometimes you face difficult problems, and no matter what you try, nothing works. Maybe you're trying to get a TV remote to work and it won't. Or you've locked yourself out of the house and you can't get in. Or you need to study for a math test, but you left your math book in your school locker.

That's when you have to use creative solutions. You need to turn up the amps in your brain. At this point, remembering tiny but important details can be a real lifesaver. Like realizing that your toy car has the same kind of batteries as the remote, or remembering where your mom hid the spare house key, or getting permission to go study with a friend next door.

When you're facing an almost impossible problem, think outside the box. Ask God to show you any "water-shaft solutions" to the problem.

HAPPY THOUGHTS VS. SICKNESS

A cheerful heart is good medicine, but a crushed spirit dries up the bones.
— Proverbs 17:22

They didn't have a lot of medicines back in the days when Solomon wrote this, and they certainly had no X-rays or antibiotics. But Solomon realized a very important fact: "a crushed spirit dries up the bones." Not literally, of course. You won't turn into a fossil. But when you're seriously discouraged, it's like you have the energy drained right out of you. You don't feel like doing anything.

The thoughts that you think can affect your health. If you constantly worry, or you're bummed out day after day, or you have a negative, angry attitude, it can actually make you ill. You don't need to have some bozo sneeze in your face to get sick. You can make yourself sick simply by thinking downer thoughts all the time. These are called psychosomatic (sy-ko-so-mat-ik) illnesses.

On the other hand, having a cheerful heart is like good medicine. Science has proved this. Hospital patients have sometimes improved their health by watching slapstick comedy shows and laughing their fool heads off. God designed it so that when you laugh, your brain releases healing chemicals into your bloodstream. And hey, trusting God and being happy because God loves you works wonders! Nehemiah 8:10 says, "The joy of the Lord is your strength."

Want to stay healthy and strong? The next time you're tempted to drag yourself around in a grumpy, growling mood, stay focused on positive, happy thoughts instead!

GENEROSITY WITHOUT GRUMBLING

Offer hospitality to one another without grumbling.

—1 Peter 4:9

To offer hospitality does not mean to offer to drive someone to the hospital. It means to be generous toward guests, to make them feel welcome. Back in Bible times, it was important to open your home to guests. But you weren't supposed to just do it, grumbling the whole while. You were supposed to do it with a smile. As Paul said, when you're showing mercy, "do it cheerfully" (Romans 12:8).

If relatives are visiting and you let them have your bedroom for a few days, it doesn't make them feel welcome if you grumble about it the whole time or tape up signs saying, "Don't touch." Or if a new family attends your church and your parents invite them to your home for lunch, it's not cool to run out of the room moaning if their baby dribbles food.

You have to be careful about inviting total strangers into your home, but the idea of hospitality is the same. You need to be compassionate to those who have needs, and when you help them, you need to do so happily. Avoid offending them. (Yes, that also means that if one of your sister's classmate's stays for dinner, that you don't deliberately gross her out by belching at the table.)

Even if you're not super-thrilled about a certain guest and you can't work up a killer grin to greet him or her with, at least avoid grumbling. It really helps.

HOW TO REALLY ARGUE

I waited while you spoke, I listened to your reasoning ... I gave you my full attention.
—Job 32:11–12

Y ou've probably heard the famous story about how God tested Job by letting him get sick and lose all his things. Job's friends showed up and began to criticize him and explain why they thought all this bad stuff had happened. But one friend, Elihu (pronounced: E-lye-who) was a young guy, so he sat there, politely letting the old men speak. For days he didn't say a word. He just listened and thought about what they were saying.

Many people today don't know how to listen. Sometimes when someone is saying what he thinks or telling his side of a story, some kid will interrupt him and not even let him finish. Or if he is quiet when the other kid's talking, he's not really listening to what he's saying—he's only thinking of his own comeback. He's certainly not giving the speaker his full attention.

King Solomon said, "He who answers before listening—that is his folly and his shame" (Proverbs 18:13). If you don't want to end up feeling foolish for misjudging the other guy, then listen to what he's saying. You might find out that your quarrel is just a misunderstanding. But whether you truly disagree with him or just think that you do, give him your full attention.

If you want to really argue wisely and well, listen to the other guy's reasoning and wait until he's done. Then speak up and tell him what you think.

ANAH'S CLAIM TO FAME

This is the Anah who discovered the hot springs in the desert while he was grazing the donkeys of his father Zibeon.
—Genesis 36:24

Like, big deal. Who cares if Anah stumbled across some hot springs while he was in the desert? And do we really need to know that he was watching his dad's donkeys at the time? Well, it may be small news to us today, but it was important to Anah's people, the Edomites. It got mighty cold in the desert at night so for shepherds to have a hot tub to soak in was a huge deal. Anah was the hot springs hero.

Now, you may not know a boy named Anah, and maybe you never met anyone who discovered hot springs in the desert, but you probably meet kids all the time who are excited about something they've done that you consider pretty small. After listening to some kid, you may blurt out, "So what?" Or maybe you snort, "Big deal!"

Well, it may be nothing to you, but if it's important to him, you need to be considerate and don't put him down. Sure, some kid's claim to fame may not make front-page news, but listen when he's talking about something he thinks is cool. Even if it really isn't a big deal, or it bores us, listening to someone shows that you respect him.

PLUNGING INTO THE SEWERS

They think it strange that you do not plunge with them into the same flood of dissipation, and they heap abuse on you.
—1 Peter 4:4

Back in New Testament days, many Greeks and Romans enjoyed wild, drunken parties and sexual immorality. Dissipation means to go whole hog into wild pleasure with no sense of right and wrong. Well, these guys were plunging into a flood of hog-wild pleasure, whooping and laughing as they did. They thought it was great, and if some Christian didn't agree, they'd dump verbal abuse on him.

Some kids today have that attitude. They'll steal and laugh about it, vandalize someone's property and think it's cool, or watch X-rated movies and visit pornographic Internet sites and think that's perfectly normal. To them, someone who's not into that muck is strange. Their problem, right? But what if they pressure us to join them?

If our town flooded and the sewer lines were backed up into Main Street, and some kids were swimming in it, would we dive in with them? No. Well, we shouldn't jump into this flood either. Sure, we may get called a "mama's boy" if we refuse to join them. They may swear at us and call us all kinds of names, but remember: they are the ones who are truly strange.

Do what's right even if some kids mock you for it. It's no fun being called names, but it sure beats plunging into the toilet just to belong.

BRING HONOR TO YOUR PARENTS

A wise son brings joy to his father, but a foolish son grief to his mother.
— Proverbs 10:1

You don't have to be an Einstein to be wise. When the Bible talks about being wise, it's not talking about being clever or being such a brain that you get 100% on every test. Sure, that'll make your parents happy, but wise means a deeper kind of intelligence—it means perceiving God's ways and following them. That will bring your folks real joy.

Now, you can't live your life concerned about people's opinions, but it is important to be concerned about your parents' opinions. You need to be careful that what you do brings them joy and honor instead of grief and disgrace. The Bible says, "Honor your father and mother," so you have to think about how your actions will bring honor to them. How can you do that?

To honor your parents, you must respect their authority and obey them. But if they're not around when you have to make a choice—to go along with something or not to—you honor your parents by doing the right thing and making godly choices. Hey, we all slip up and make bad choices sometimes. But the question is: what kind of choices are you in the habit of making day after day?

If you continually misbehave, you bring dishonor on yourself and on your parents. When you continually behave wisely, you bring honor and joy to yourself and to your parents.

WISDOM AND WRINKLES

Rehoboam rejected the advice the elders gave him and consulted the young men who had grown up with him.
—1 Kings 12:8

Rehoboam was a young guy when he became king. The Israelites said, "Make our lives easier! Lower the taxes!" So Rehoboam checked with his counselors about that. The wise old elders said yes, that was definitely a good thing to do. But Rehoboam dumped their advice and asked his young pals. They said, "Nah! Increase their taxes! Make their lives harder! That'll show 'em who's boss!" Rehoboam listened to his buds and lost most of the kingdom.

It's great when you're old enough to start thinking things through for yourself and making your own decisions. It's a sign that you're growing up. But sometimes boys are so eager to prove they're independent, they deliberately ignore their parents' advice—even when it makes lots of sense. Yet if their friends advise them to ride their skateboard off a killer ramp, hey, they'll listen to that!

The rule of thumb is old people have lived long enough to get old because they didn't do dumb stuff like plunging off fifty-foot ramps. They learned what was smart and wise and made the most sense, and avoided doing some of the truly dumb things their friends told them to go for. Okay, your parents have done dumb stuff too, but they learned from it and it made them wiser.

It doesn't pay to ignore older people's advice. People with wrinkles really do have smarts.

BRINGING UP THE PAST

Then he sent his brothers away, and as they were leaving he said to them, "Don't quarrel on the way!"
— Genesis 45:24

Years earlier, Joseph's brothers had sold him as a slave into Egypt. Reuben had wanted to return Joseph to their father, and was very upset that his brothers had sold Joseph. Now they had met Joseph again and were returning to Canaan. Joseph knew that his brothers would blame each other, so he warned them not to start quarreling. The time had come to leave the past in the past.

An old quarrel is when people got in a fight years ago, or one of you wronged the other one and neither of you have made up or really forgiven each other. So the quarrel's never settled. Then, whenever anything happens that reminds you of the old fight, it comes back up and you're arguing about it again. Nobody's changed his mind. Nobody's saying anything new.

The problem with old quarrels is that they've been argued several times already. You might as well tape-record your quarrel and play it when you get upset. Or, better yet, forgive each other. That's what Joseph told his brothers. He forgave them and said, "Do not be angry with yourselves for selling me here" (Genesis 45:5). Well, if the brothers weren't supposed to be mad at themselves, why should they be mad at each other, right?

Let bygones be bygones. You only hurt yourself and others when you hold onto grudges and refuse to forgive. There comes a time when you have to let go of past hurts.

MOTIVATED TO WORK

"When he sees ... how pleasant is his land, he will bend his shoulder to the burden."
—Genesis 49:14–15

Thousands of years ago a guy named Jacob had twelve sons. When Jacob blessed his sons, he compared his son Issachar (Issa-car) to a donkey. A donkey is a strong beast that—if it is motivated—can work hard and carry heavy saddlebags. Issachar liked to lie around resting as much as the next guy, but when he caught the vision of how good life could be if he worked, he put out.

It's the same today. A newspaper route is hard work. You can't sit at home watching TV if it's time to walk the block delivering papers. So what motivates you to get off the couch, strap on your skates, and pull your cart full of papers down the street? Money, and the good stuff it can buy, makes it worth it.

Hard work is just that—hard work—but it's worth it. Maybe your parents and grandparents give you stuff now, but the older you get the more you have to start earning your own way. And in the world out there, you don't get something for nothing. Maybe you'd rather play on the Xbox than mow the lawn, but unless you find a way to raise cash, you won't be able to buy the new game when you've defeated every level in the old one.

Do you need cash to buy some cool stuff? Then find some paying jobs and "bend your shoulder to the burden."

READY FOR ROUGH TIMES

"You know your father and his men; they are fighters, and as fierce as a wild bear ... your father is an experienced fighter."
—2 Samuel 17:7–8

Young hotshot Prince Absalom had just taken over the kingdom in a surprise attack, and now he wanted to chase King David and finish him off. An old man named Hushai gave Absalom a reality check. He reminded Absalom just how tough his dad and his men were: they were strong and fierce and they had fought dozens of wars. Bottom line: think twice before you mess with these guys. Hard experiences had made them tough.

You may be going through hard times right now. If you are, you're probably not too interested in the fact that it's making you tougher. You just want things to be easier. ("I'll get tough some other way. Yeah, like by eating raw marshmallows.") Well, you often can't choose what comes your way. Usually you have to endure hardships, like it or not.

The upside is that tough times really do make you tougher. Then when you face major problems, you're mentally prepared. You're not fazed if your plane crashes in the Alaskan wilderness and you have to hike out, hopping on one foot. Okay, maybe not that extreme. But being ready to rough it can make all the difference. It means you'll still be standing when the hard times pass.

Sometimes you feel like groaning when you experience tough stuff. Don't overdo the groaning. Like King David, you need enough rough stuff to make you tough.

EYE GARBAGE

"I will set before my eyes no vile thing."
—Psalm 101:3

The vile thing in this verse is not broccoli or spinach. Back in Old Testament days when the Israelites wandered away from God, they often ended up worshiping false gods like Baal or Asherah. The people built on the hilltops huge stone idols of these gods, and for convenience, they bought themselves a Barbie-sized idol made out of clay or wood. Then they set this non-action figure on a shelf in their house so they could see it, kiss it, and pray to it all day long.

These days, setting a vile thing before your eyes could be reading a sick comic book or watching a horror movie that gives you nightmares. It could be playing video games filled with occult images and witchcraft. It could be going on the Internet and seeing stuff that puts strange thoughts in your brain. When you see negative stuff, your mind takes mental photos of it. Then you have those pictures stuck in your head for months or years.

If you want to avoid seeing endless reruns of sick images, avoid looking at them in the first place. Don't even have them in your house. The Bible warns, "Do not bring a detestable thing into your house" (Deuteronomy 7:26). If a vile thing isn't in your house, you won't be tempted to try hiding it under your mattress.

Don't waste time looking at vile eye garbage. Don't bring it home. If you have it already, put it out with the trash where it belongs.

ROLL UP YOUR SLEEVES

"The people of Zebulun risked their very lives; so did Naphtali on the heights of the field."
—Judges 5:18

L ong ago a Canaanite king named Jabin conquered northern Israel, and for twenty years he cruelly oppressed them. Finally, a warrior named Barak sent out an urgent message to all the tribes of Israel to gather an army and defeat the Canaanites. Only problem was, some tribes, like Zebulun and Naphtali, faced the full heat of the battle while others, like Reuben and Dan, didn't even bother to show up.

Afterward, the Israelites had years to sit around, roll up their sleeves to show off their battle wounds, and talk about the heroic fighting that day. But those who didn't show up also had years to ask themselves why they weren't there when they were needed. It's the same today if your youth group is on a major fundraiser and you opt out, or your parents ask everyone to help clean the house, but you skip out and play video games.

There will be times in your life when people will be counting on you to be there. Decide ahead of time that you'll answer the call, roll up your sleeves, and help. Jesus said that if you love others, you'll lay down your life for them. That doesn't only refer to dying on a battlefield. It could simply mean being there and helping out—especially if you promised that you would.

There are opportunities every day for a man to do what a man should do. Let every day be your moment of truth.

TEMPTATION

"Flee the evil desires of youth."

— 2 Timothy 2:22

When the apostle Paul was in prison for being a Christian, he wrote a letter to a young friend named Timothy. Paul warned, "Flee the evil desires of youth." Now, why did he say that? Because a Christian named Demas had just been derailed by evil desires. Paul said, "Demas, because he loved this world, has deserted me" (2 Timothy 4:10). We don't know what exactly Demas was tempted by, but it totally stopped him from following Jesus. Paul didn't want Timothy to go down too.

Things like skateboarding, mountain biking, soccer, and swimming are good. There's nothing evil about desiring to do these things. And movies and video games can be cool. But there are evil movies and video games that you shouldn't desire. And even perfectly normal desires—like a man's desire for sex—can become evil desires if you're not supposed to have them yet.

When it comes to the good stuff you love doing, enjoy it. But wait for things you're supposed to wait for and stay away from evil stuff you're supposed to stay away from. You know what kinds of things tempt you, so be on guard. Your parents know too, so if they warn you that you're getting too close, listen to them. Paul watched out for Timothy; your parents watch out for you.

Don't stand there staring at the temptation while you're trying to resist it. Walk away. In fact, if the temptation is strong, flee!

WISE ABOUT BASIC STUFF

From infancy you have known the holy Scriptures, which are able to make you wise for salvation.

—2 Timothy 3:15

A man in the Bible named Timothy had a Jewish mom and a Greek dad. Down in Israel, Jews wrote Bible verses on their doors or on pieces of paper that they folded and stuffed inside tiny boxes tied to their hands and foreheads. Tim's mom probably didn't make these kinds of decor and fashion statements—her Greek husband wasn't into that—but she did teach Tim the Scriptures.

If you've grown up in a Christian home, then your parents have probably told you Bible stories since you were old enough to hang on to the furniture and walk. As you got older, they quoted Bible verses to let you know how to behave. For example, if you know you're supposed to consider other people's needs, then no kids will go hungry 'cause you oinked down all the pie. Simple stuff, but it helped make you wise.

Best of all, when you listen to the Bible you find out that God loved you so much that he sent Jesus to die on the cross to save you. You might say, "Wise? That's wisdom? That's really basic stuff." Yes, it is. It's wise if you take it to heart, but it's very foolish if you ignore it.

You may not always be thrilled to hear Bible rules, but if you take them in like Timothy did, they'll not only give you faith but teach you how to live.

DEMOLITION DERBY

We demolish arguments and every pretension that sets itself up against the knowledge of God.

—2 Corinthians 10:5

Some smart people have a dumb problem: they don't want to obey God. So they come up with all kinds of pretensions why God doesn't exist. (A pretension is a claim or an argument—in this case, a pretend argument.) Or if they don't want to live a godly life, they claim that the Bible isn't true or that its rules don't apply today. If they can convince themselves that there's no God and that the Bible's outdated, they can live as they please.

As a Christian, you have the power to demolish these anti-God arguments. Picture a big bulldozer with a wide blade demolishing a flimsy house. This doesn't mean you should drive up in an actual bulldozer or use pushy arguments like, "You're dumb if you don't believe the Bible!" It doesn't mean intimidating people by using big words they don't understand, and it doesn't mean arguing angrily.

The things you use to demolish false claims are spiritual weapons like prayer and God's wisdom. Of course, God also expects you to study the questions and come up with intelligent answers. You might hear someone say, "Jesus was a great teacher, but aren't there many ways to God?" You gotta know enough about it to answer, "No, Jesus claimed that he was God's Son, and that he was the only way to God."

You have the power of God and the wisdom of his Word on your side. Now get ready to do some demolition!

SHEERAH THE BUILDER

His daughter was Sheerah, who built Lower and Upper Beth Horon as well as Uzzen Sheerah.

—1 Chronicles 7:24

Long ago, an awesome Israelite lady named Sheerah built three cities in the land of Israel and named one of them after herself. And talk about smarts! Her towns were built in key spots to defend the nation. A super-important road went from the coast into the heart of Israel, so Sheerah built Lower and Upper Beth Horon on two hills guarding that road. (Many years later, King Solomon realized just how important these towns were and mega-fortified them.)

Some guys think that girls are just weak, soft sissies. Sure, tomboys are okay, but the rest of them are all "girly girls" and you don't need to respect them, right? They'd never think of anything awesome that a guy didn't think of first. A girl would never be such a smart military planner that she'd come up with a plan to defend the nation, right? Wrong!

You've got to admit, Sheerah was pretty impressive. But guess what? Girls are impressive in all kinds of other ways too. It's great when they're into the same things as boys are, but you need to be able to relate to girls and respect them even if they're not tomboys. Most girls are interested in very different things than guys, but they're still cool.

Just when you think you have girls all figured out, they'll surprise you. So try not to judge anyone—guys or girls. Everyone deserves respect.

CHOOSING CHRISTLIKE COACHES

Follow my example, as I follow the example of Christ.

—1 Corinthians 11:1

The apostle Paul had been chatting about his personal lifestyle. He had explained how he wasn't seeking his own good, but trying to live unselfishly to help others. Jesus had said to love God and love others and live as a Christian, and though Paul wasn't perfect, he was doing his best to do those things. That's why he could tell others to follow his example.

When you're trying to learn something, it's important to listen to someone who knows what he's talking about and is living what he preaches. If you want to learn to play football better, you listen to your coach, not some kindergartener who doesn't know the first thing about the game, right? So if you want to learn to follow Christ, whose example do you follow—some Hollywood actor whose life is one big train wreck?

If you're trying to follow Jesus, you need to follow role models who are genuinely trying to obey God. Paul was like a coach to the early Christians—and we all need coaches and instructors. Sure, you know you're supposed to love your neighbor, but there's more to Christianity than that. Just like there's more to football than just "grab the ball and run." And who's gonna teach you this stuff? The guys who know it inside out.

Just like you constantly need to improve your game, you need to learn more about the Christian life and walking with God. Choose life-coaches who follow Jesus.

YOUR FAMILY'S WEIRD RULES

We do not drink wine, because our forefather Jonadab ... gave us this command: "Neither you nor your descendants must ever drink wine."
—Jeremiah 35:6

In ancient Israel it was okay for adults to drink wine as long as they didn't drink so much of the stuff that they got drunk. But when the prophet Jeremiah offered wine to Jaazaniah and his brothers, Jaaz said nope, our great-granddaddy said not to. God was so pleased they obeyed their family rules that he promised to bless them forever.

But there is something else very important going on here. When this story happened, the people of Israel were about to be taken captive by another country. They didn't know that for 70 years they were going to be captives in a foreign land. And it was all because they hadn't obeyed God. So when Jaazaniah refused the wine out of obedience to his family's rules, it showed he was clearly a better person than the other Israelites.

Fast forward more than 2,000 years. Do you think times are any different now? You have read God's Word and know what he expects from us. But all around us people live as if God did not exist, or as if he didn't tell us how to act. Sometimes it would be nice to be able to join the crowd without worrying about what we know is wrong. But God clearly tells us that he sees both the right and the wrong we all do, and he desires for us to do right.

Next time you have a choice to make and think that no one will really know or care whether you make the right or wrong one, remember that the kind of people we really are is determined by what we do. And that our obedience to God is determined by what he has said, no matter how long ago he said it.

WARS ON THE EVENING NEWS

"You will hear of wars and rumors of wars, but see to it that you are not alarmed. Such things must happen, but the end is still to come."
—Matthew 24:6

Jesus' disciples had just finished asking, "What will be the sign of your coming, and of the end of the age?" Jesus told them what to look for, but part of his answer was telling them what not to get worried about. "You'll hear about wars. Don't get alarmed. You'll hear that a war might start. Don't freak out. Wars are bad, but they're not necessarily the end of the world."

These days, with newsmen reporting right from war zones and blown-up cars smoking all over your TV screen, it may feel like the war is happening in your living room. You've heard that one day the Battle of Armageddon will mean the end of the world, so maybe you get worried that some new battle you see on TV is going to start it. Or maybe you see some guy carrying signs that read: "Armageddon has begun!"

It's natural to worry, but don't. Don't lose sleep over it. Jesus specifically said not to be alarmed. He wants us to be comforted by the knowledge that no matter what happens, God is in control and we are in his hands. Wars have been happening since the beginning of civilization. Jesus told us that these things must happen. War is serious business, and lots of people suffer in wars. So pray for the people involved.

Jesus knows that people often worry when serious stuff is happening, and that's why he warned us not to worry or get alarmed.

WAR IN THE SPIRITUAL REALM

Then the Lord opened the servant's eyes, and he looked and saw the hills full of horses and chariots of fire all around Elisha.

—2 Kings 6:17

Once the prophet Elisha was in a city, and the king of Aram sent an army to capture him. When Elisha's servant woke up the next morning, he saw hundreds of Aramean soldiers with horses and chariots around the city. (Bet that really woke him up!) "What shall we do?" he wailed. Elisha prayed, "O Lord, open his eyes so he may see." That's when the servant guy saw the hills full of fiery chariots and blazing horses—these angels outnumbered the king's army.

Just because you can't see something, it doesn't mean it's not there. Think about it. Armies usually like to stay hidden and out of sight if they can. That's why Robin Hood's merry men wore green clothes—so they could hide in Sherwood Forest and not be spotted. That's why stealth aircraft use radar-absorbing paint and other technology to make them nearly invisible. Angels already had the stealth stuff perfected 4,000 years ago.

We often imagine one or two guardian angels protecting us, and maybe that's usually the case. But obviously there are times when God sends entire armies of angels to defend his people. That's when there's a huge battle happening in the spiritual realm. Think about that the next time there's trouble in your city or on the news.

God didn't leave us here alone without protection. He has sent his angels to guard us and, when things get serious, he sends out whole armies of angels.

BIG BRAGGING MOABITE MAN

Now Mesha king of Moab raised sheep ... But after Ahab died, the king of Moab rebelled against the king of Israel.

—2 Kings 3:4 – 5

At one time, Israel ruled over ancient Moab. After Israel's king died, Mesha, the king of Moab, rebelled and stopped paying his taxes, which included 100,000 lambs a year! Ever heard of the Moabite Stone? Well, in 1868 a German missionary found a stone tablet east of the Dead Sea. Guess who wrote it? It was none other than Mesha, king of Moab. It was his version of his big rebellion.

This stone tablet confirms what the Bible says—that Israel ruled over Moab, and that Mesha led a rebellion. The writing on the stone details Mesha's successes. He just, um, left out a few details, like the Israelites marching back to re-conquer him—led by the prophet Elisha, no less!

Ever had an older brother or cousin thump on you but when you tell an adult about it, the other kid's version sounds a lot different than yours? But a smart adult can sometimes see through the edited versions. If the kid says, "Yeah, I might have touched him, but he took my Manga book!" See, now the kid just backed up your story, though he probably left out some facts. Same with Mesha.

People constantly find ancient objects and writings that back up what the Bible says. When you've even got Israel's enemies admitting that, well yeah, the Bible told the truth, you can't just sweep the story under the rug.

A WILLING WATER BOY

Then he set out to follow Elijah and became his attendant.

—1 Kings 19:21b

E lijah was a mighty prophet, famous for causing droughts, raising the dead to life, and calling fire down out of the blue sky. Elisha was his attendant, his sidekick, a prophet-in-training, and at first he didn't do any miracles. He listened to the master teach and watched him in action. He was a water boy. All he was famous for was pouring wash-water on Elijah's hands (1 Kings 3:11).

It's not so glamorous being an errand boy. Sure, at first it's exciting to be around a celebrity and to be able to drop names. ("Yeah, as I was saying to Elijah today …") It's cool to even be great man's gopher—"Go fer this. Go fer that." But most of us can't help but feel that we are destined to do more, that God will one day use us in a new way, just as Elisha one day stepped up to the plate and made a name for himself.

The time will come for you to strike out on your own and be your own boss, but you won't be able to do that unless you learn the things you need to learn from the men and women God has put in your life. You have to have humble beginnings if you want to become great. You have to subject yourself to discipline and learn the ropes if you want to prepare for your life's work.

Don't get frustrated if right now you're "just" someone's water boy or gopher. You're learning from guys who know their stuff.

DEVOTION 170

A BAND OF BROTHERS

Jehu greeted him and said, "Are you in accord with me, as I am with you?"
"I am," Jehonadab answered. "If so," said Jehu, "give me your hand."

—2 Kings 10:15

An army officer named Jehu had just done in the evil, idol-worshiping rulers of Israel. Then he set out to wipe idolatry completely out of the land. Jehonadab was the leader of the Rechabites, faithful followers of God, and he got excited about what Jehu was doing. He was in accord (agreed) with Jehu, so he joined forces with him and together they cleaned up the nation.

You know from experiences at school or around your neighborhood that it's sometimes not easy to take a stand for God—like if some guys pressure you to lie or cheat or vandalize things, or to view pornography. It's especially difficult if you're standing up for God but everyone else is going the other direction. Or if they're just staying quiet, putting up with things and not bucking the crowd.

That's why it's important to have good, solid Christian friends. Hang out with guys from your church or youth group, and when times get tough or the peer pressure is turned on full blast and you need to stand up for what's right, you'll have "a band of brothers" there to back you up so the pushers can't push you around.

Don't try to go it alone. Like Jehu and Jehonadab, you need to be part of a group of guys that comes together to stand up for God. God will probably not call you to full scale military battles as he did with these guys, but he will guide you to his purposes for your lives.

THE RETURN-THE-OX RULE

If you see your brother's ox or sheep straying, do not ignore it but be sure
to take it back to him. . . . Do the same if you find your brother's donkey
or his cloak.
—Deuteronomy 22:1, 3

When God says brother, he means fellow man, not just your
kid brother. Now, probably no kid in your town owns an
ox or a sheep, but this principle also applies to another
person's toys, his jacket and his backpack. Whether you found
his stuff laying around or walking off on four legs, you were
supposed to return it to him.

A lot of people seem to think that "Finder's keepers, losers
weepers," is the rule to live by—unless they're the one who
did the losing and are weeping. But that rhyme has it all wrong.
Some years ago, an armored car overturned and money spilled
out onto the highway. A camera caught dozens of people
scooping up cash and running off with it. They felt that it was
theirs for the taking. Was it? No.

Now, if you find a hundred dollar bill blowing along in the
middle of the Mojave Desert, it's okay to claim it. But most of
the time, the Return-the-Ox Rule applies. If you find a towel at
a swimming pool, turn it in. If you find a watch in the school
bathroom, turn it in. If you find a loose boa constrictor in the pet
store . . . run!

You are your brother's keeper, and that also means you're
supposed to help him keep his stuff when you come across it.

HANGING WITH UNCOOL KIDS

Do not be proud but be willing to associate with people of low position.
Do not be conceited.
—Romans 12:16

In the days of the early church, some Christians came from rich and powerful families, while many were poor or even slaves. When the church met to worship God, all different classes came together. Christians were taught to treat rich and poor the same in church. Some rich Christians were willing to do that, but no way they wanted to be seen with workers and slaves throughout the week.

The same thing happens today. Some kids are okay with hanging out with certain kids in church or at family gatherings, but when they get around cool kids they don't want to associate with un-cool kids any more. Paul said people who do that are conceited and proud. They have a high opinion of themselves and think they're too good for others.

You may know some other kid who really needs to hear this, but for now apply it to your life. Do you sometimes let other kids or your own pride tell you who you can be seen with or can't be seen with? In God's eyes, being rich or poor, having a cool rep or being nobody special means nothing. And think about it: most kids believe that everyone is created equal. They know when someone's acting uppity.

Don't be proud or conceited. Hang out with Christians who are different or poorer or richer or cooler or less cool than you.

WHEN DONKEYS FALL DOWN

If you see the donkey of someone who hates you fallen down under its load, do not leave it there; be sure you help him with it.

—Exodus 23:5

The Ten Commandments told the Israelites not to steal from their fellow man, not to lie about him or hurt him or long for his belongings. Some Israelites did all that, but if they saw one of their enemies struggling to get a fallen donkey back on its feet—they'd walk past, snickering, "I'm not hurting ol' Jethro here, but I'm sure not helping him." God said no deal. Even if the guy hates you, help him.

Okay, so most kids who hate you don't own donkeys, so does this verse not apply? Does that mean that if a kid who always bothers you is riding home from school and he spills his backpack on the ground, that you can just walk by laughing and say, "That's his problem"? After all, a backpack isn't a donkey, right?

No, and his bike isn't a donkey either, but it's the principle of the thing. God wants you to help people who need help, not just walk past. So if you see a "nerd" drop his books in school, stop and help him. If some enemy tumbles on his bicycle, help him up. It's called being considerate. Besides, it might turn an enemy into a friend.

FAVORITE FRIENDS AND FAVORITISM

If you really keep the royal law found in Scripture, "Love your neighbor as yourself," you are doing right. But if you show favoritism you sin.

—James 2:8 – 9

L ove your neighbor as yourself," is the foundation for almost half of the Ten Commandments. Love your neighbor as you love yourself and you won't steal from him, hurt him, or lie about him. But the catch is, you should do good to all people, not just close friends, not just those who can do you favors in return. If you treat a friend extra-good but treat another kid like dirt, you're breaking the Royal Law.

We all tend to do stuff for our friends that we wouldn't do for others. Jesus zeroed in on this when he pointed out that even tax collectors were kind to their buddies. Even people who cared less about God had enough manners to greet their pals when they saw them (Matthew 5:46–47). Doing this had nothing to do with having the love of Christ in their lives.

If we care about everyone, not just our buddies, then we'll start treating all people the way God wants us to. Sure, we may hang out with certain guys 'cause we're interested in the same things. It's okay to have close friends we spend most of our time with. It's cool to do things for our buddies. But let's not get a clique mentality and ignore everyone else.

Want to do the right thing? Keep God's Royal Law—love others as much as you love yourself. And don't just love some of them. Love them all.

YOUR FAITHFULNESS RATING

Like a bad tooth or a lame foot is reliance on the unfaithful in times of trouble.
—Proverbs 25:19

If you sprain your ankle and can't put weight on that foot, you just became lame. You can't walk and you certainly can't run. (Sure, you can hop or crawl, but that won't get you anywhere fast.) Same thing if you have a bad tooth. You can't bite with it. It's too painful. That's what relying on an unfaithful person is like when you're in trouble: the job won't get done.

Not naming any names here, but are you ever spacey or do you get tripped-off on your way to do something important then forget what you were doing? Absent-mindedness is not a sin. It's just part of who you are. But ask yourself if you fit into the faithful or the unfaithful camp? Often an unfaithful person remembers what he was asked to do: he just puts it off until it's too late.

When your parents tell you to brush your teeth, is one reminder enough? Do you remember to give school memos to mom always, usually, sometimes, or almost never? If you're asked to do a job, does it get done? When someone is counting on you, are they counting on a faithful or an unfaithful person? If you say you'll do something, do it. Otherwise, you'll get a reputation for being unfaithful, and you'll suffer in the long run.

DEVOTION 176

GOD'S AMAZING UNIVERSE

Can you bind the beautiful Pleiades? Can you loose the cords of Orion? Can you
... lead out the Bear with its cubs? Do you know the laws of the heavens?
—Job 38:31 – 33

These verses may sound like a rodeo roping event or some circus act, but God was actually talking about constellations, or groups of stars. Pleiades is a constellation that is also known as the seven sisters. Orion is also known as the hunter. Today "the Bear with its cubs" is known as Ursa Major (big bear) and Ursa Minor (little bear).

People have been studying stars for thousands of years, but scientists still don't know everything about them. Do you know the laws of the heavens? No, chances are you can't name most of the constellations. Like most people, you don't know how black holes suck in stars like slushies. You don't know why gravity pulls the way it does. (It works, sure, but according to scientists' calculations, it should be a lot stronger.)

Some scientists are beginning to think now that the reason gravity's not stronger is because it exists in another dimension, and only a little bit of it leaks into our physical universe. (Seriously, they really think that!) Obviously, these scientists are making a hypothesis. They are still trying to fully understand stuff like how gravity works. God knows all the laws of the heavens! Well, he should. He invented them.

Since God created all the laws of the universe, imagine how smart he is! That's a good reason to trust what he says in the Bible.

WISDOM VERSUS BOOK LEARNING

How did this man get such learning without having studied?
—John 7:15

Jewish boys went to school in Jesus' day, but their education was mostly memorizing the laws of Moses, discussing the laws' details, and learning to read and write. And that was it. If a young guy wanted more education, he had to find a teacher (rabbi) and study under him. Jesus didn't do that. When he finished school, he went to work full-time as a carpenter. So where did he get his massive wisdom and learning? From God, his Father!

Unless your family's plane crashed on a tropical island and all you learned while growing up was how to wrestle sharks and climb coconut palms, chances are you'll get a decent education. But you'd be surprised at how many highschool graduates don't know important stuff like how to use a credit card wisely, how to take care of a car, how to do their laundry, and how to relate to others. Some are especially clueless when it comes to spiritual stuff.

You can learn about credit cards, cars, and laundry simply by living life. But when it comes to the important spiritual stuff, you need to really love God, spend time with him, and learn from him. You can go to Bible school—that'll help a lot—but it's more important to read your Bible yourself and have a relationship with God.

God can give you wisdom, so pray and ask him to start giving you the kind of deep wisdom you can't learn from just reading textbooks.

THINGS IN COMMON

Do not be yoked together with unbelievers. For what do righteousness and wickedness have in common?

— 2 Corinthians 6:14

Not being "yoked together with unbelievers" doesn't mean standing back while atheists are egged. Rather, it comes from Moses' law to not put a wooden yoke on the neck of an ox and a mule at the same time, to make them pull a plow together (Deuteronomy 22:10). It just doesn't work well. It's like you trying to run a three-legged race tied to a toddler. In the same way, Christians shouldn't be "yoked together" with unbelievers.

Okay, it's a no-brainer that if kids are into wicked weirdness and joking about dark, sick stuff, that you should avoid them. Don't be pals with them. But does this mean that you shouldn't have any non-Christian friends? Does it mean that you should only play baseball with kids from your church or you can't talk to kids of another religion?

No, thank goodness, it doesn't mean that. You can and should be friendly towards all people, no matter how they look, what religion they are, or whether they believe in God or not. But being friendly doesn't mean you super-glue your jackets together. Being "yoked together" is a close relationship, and your closest friends should be fellow Christians. That way when you are in times of need, the advice you get from your closest friends lines up with Christ's teaching.

You may have to play on the same baseball team as a wicked kid, but you need a whole lot more than baseball in common before you make him a close friend.

JOINING A GANG – OR NOT

My son, if sinners entice you do not give in to them ... do not go along with
them, do not set foot on their paths.
—Proverbs 1:10, 15

K ing Solomon talked about a gang who killed and robbed
the innocent. They were recruiting new gang members
and tempted youth by promising them easy money if
they joined. All they had to do was murder and rob travelers
and they'd be rich. Solomon warned that no matter how much
criminals entice you, don't set foot on their evil path.

You don't have to join a criminal organization to be part of
a "gang." It could simply be a group of tough kids pressuring
you to join them. To prove you're with them, you have to steal
something, hurt somebody, or vandalize some property. Or some
drug pusher might offer you easy money if you start peddling
drugs and get other kids hooked on drugs.

If kids tempt you to do evil, don't give in. Don't even set foot
on their paths. Don't even do one thing they say. That'll just give
them something to use against you: "You've already done this,
so what's so bad about doing this other thing?" Some kids really
know how to work you over and put on the pressure, so don't
even listen to them.

Sometimes "belonging" isn't worth it. No matter how cool
gang membership seems at first, there's a very expensive price
to pay, so keep your feet off their destructive path.

FEELING OVERWHELMED

"With him is only the arm of flesh, but with us is the Lord our God to help us and to fight our battles."

—2 Chronicles 32:8

That's King Hezekiah of Judah praying. And he had good reason to be praying! Sennacherib, the king of Assyria, had marched in and conquered all of Judah. The only city left standing was Jerusalem, and now nearly a quarter of a million Assyrians surrounded it. Hezekiah said that "only" the arm of the flesh was with Sennacherib. Most guys would've thought, "That's a lot of arm! That's a lot of flesh!" But Hezekiah trusted God, and that night the Angel of the Lord wiped out 185,000 Assyrians.

Sometimes you face situations like that. Not 185,000 Assyrians, no, but maybe your dad loses his job and your family goes through tough times financially. You hear your parents talking, and they're not sure how they'll pay the bills. You want to help, but what can you do? You could sell your toys, but you wouldn't get much for them. Besides, your mom says no. Times like that are when you learn that some problems are too big for you.

The only thing you can do is what King Hezekiah did when his back was against the wall. Pray. The answer might not come immediately. But when things are serious or it's a life-and-death situation, you can pray like Hezekiah did and expect a miracle like he received.

God is still strong today, and can still do miracles today to help you—if you trust him. When you feel surrounded, ask God for help.

HELMETS AND SHIN GUARDS

"He also went down into a pit on a snowy day and killed a lion."
—2 Samuel 23:20

What is this guy doing? Talk about risk takers! Okay, so Benaiah, one of King David's greatest warriors, needed to kill this lion for some reason, but couldn't he find a rock to drop on its head? Did he really have to jump into the pit and wrestle it? This is definitely one of those don't-try-this-at-home stunts. Benaiah killed the lion, but try something like that, and it'll be you getting killed.

Probably when your dad was a boy, there were no laws stating that kids had to wear helmets when they rode a bicycle or skateboard. Back then when kids went off a bike ramp and came down head first, serious injuries happened. So now we have the helmet rule. Ever feel it's too much trouble to strap on your helmet, elbow-guards, and knee-guards? It's not.

You'll face enough dangers in your life that you can't avoid, so no need to rush into danger you can avoid. Crack your skull by riding without a helmet, and you won't be there when you need to save some kid's life. For what it's worth, Benaiah was probably wearing a helmet when he jumped in the lion pit—an army helmet, that is.

Sometimes you simply have to take risks that can't be avoided. But in the meantime, strap on the helmet and wear protective padding.

READY TO DEFEND

"Fight for your brothers, your sons and your daughters, your wives and your homes."
—Nehemiah 4:14

Nehemiah and the Jews were busy rebuilding the walls around Jerusalem when they heard that their enemies were plotting an attack. Nehemiah immediately posted guards and prayed for God's help. When the threats intensified, Nehemiah put half his men on guard duty. He even had the builders wear swords while they worked. And get a load of this: the men who carried building materials worked with one hand and held a sword in the other. (Careful passing me those bricks, Jeb!)

The good news is, because Nehemiah's men were ready to defend themselves—and because they prayed—they never even had to fight. Their cowardly enemies didn't dare attack. They huffed and they puffed but it was mostly just bluff. Isn't that just like bullies today? They enjoy picking on smaller kids, but when someone their own size stands up to them, they slink away like a walking spring toy going downstairs.

If someone insults you and you let it pass, good for you. Way to go. But when a bully begins pushing around or hurting your little brother or sister, it's time for you to stand up and speak out. Of course, the best thing to do is to tell an adult—and pronto! But if there are no adults around, you've got to protect your loved ones.

Be prepared to defend yourself and your brothers and sisters, but pray that it never actually comes to that. It usually won't.

SPECIAL TRAINING PLAN

What is to be the rule for the boy's life and work?
— Judges 13:12

One day an angel appeared and told a woman she'd have a son — and not just any son! This kid would be Samson, and he'd start delivering his people from the Philistines. This was going to be difficult for Samson's family — a lot was being asked of them — but instead of complaining, they were obedient to God and asked for a detailed plan.

It's cool being good at something, whether it's swimming or drawing or math or killing lions with your bare hands. It's cool if you realize at an early age that God has a special plan for your life. You do something you enjoy, you do it well, and everyone applauds. Your parents want you to succeed, so when they notice you have talents — if they can afford it — they make you take lessons to develop those talents. The fun stuff's still fun, but it just became work too.

You may not be destined to be a lion slayer like Samson or a gold-medal athlete, but whatever your future holds — if you want to become good at it — you need to go at it with a plan. You have to first of all determine to fulfill God's plan, then come up with a training regimen, and then discipline yourself and work that plan — even on days when it's more work than fun and you'd rather lie back on the couch and eat cream puffs and chips.

Be thankful if your talents and abilities show up early. And follow your special training plan — you'll get better at something you enjoy while you train for the future.

LOST: ONE HUNDRED WISE MEN

Where is the wise man? Where is the scholar? Where is the philosopher of this age? Has not God made foolish the wisdom of the world?
—1 Corinthians 1:20

I t's good to be a wise man who figures stuff out and can say exactly the right thing so that a thousand people leap to their feet clapping. It's cool to be a scholar who digs into the Bible and discovers all kinds of ancient facts. It's great if you're a philosopher lost deep in thought, figuring out the mysteries of the universe.

But as smart as all these people are, they can miss out on basic stuff. We're not talking about your dad not being able to figure out how to set the microwave timer or some kid who can win at a high-speed computer game but can't remember where he put his homework. We're talking about brilliant dudes who are clueless about the ABCs of Christian life itself.

A lot of supersmart people can't get their minds around the simple truths of the Bible. Sure, they may know how to map DNA and write computer programs and other complicated stuff, but they're clueless when it comes to understanding that Jesus died for their sins or that it's important to love others. If you don't live the basic Bible stuff, being wise about everything else is just icing without a cake.

So study and learn as much as you can. You should go whole hog for education. Just make sure you understand the simple, important truths of the Bible.

WRONG PLANET? SOOO SORRY!

Let your astrologers come forward, those stargazers who make predictions month by month, let them save you from what is coming ... They cannot even save themselves.

—Isaiah 47:13 – 14

Astrologers believe that distant stars and planets cause things to happen here on earth. They divide the stars into twelve zones, and if you were born when the sun was in the Gemini zone, they say your "sign" is Gemini and the planet Mercury rules you. And if the planet Venus was in the Pisces zone then, well, dude, you're gonna be soooo romantic.

Astrologers make predictions like, "Attention all Libras! July is a great month for summer vacations." Or they make day-by-day predictions: "October 22 is a good day for money and friendship. Start a business while cooking barbecue." Is that what you want to put your faith in? C'mon! How scientific is that? Studying the stars lets you know when to break your piggy bank and run to the corner store? Really?

There are twelve "signs," and each sign needs a planet. But for thousands of years people could see only five planets, so they said that some planets ruled two signs. Then astronomers discovered Pluto in 1930. Oh, boy! Up till then, astrologers claimed that Mars ruled the signs Aries and Scorpio. Pluto had been there all along, but suddenly in 1930 it gets the job. "So sorry, Scorpios! Our bad! You can't stay on Mars! We're shipping you to Pluto!" And now we know that Pluto isn't a planet after all. What a joke.

God's Word warns against putting your trust in things other than God to save you. If you want wisdom on how to live your life, you'll get real smarts by reading your Bible.

LIBRARIES AND LEARNING

A Jew named Apollos, a native of Alexandria, . . . was a learned man, with a thorough knowledge of the Scriptures.

—Acts 18:24

B ack in Roman times, the city of Alexandria, in Egypt, had the largest library on this planet. Like, half a million scrolls and books! It was a major center for learning. Some of the deepest thinkers went there to study and learn—and maybe to get lost in the dusty back aisles a few times. Apollos was one of those learned men. He not only learned math and science and history, but he also knew the Bible back to front and inside out.

Some boys today devour books—especially comic books and manga—but they know practically nothing about the Bible. That's because they read those other books (sometimes over and over again), but when it comes to the Scriptures, they depend on adults to tell them the stories. Or they just get a bit of the action by reading Bible storybooks with big, bright pictures.

How did Apollos get his huge download of knowledge? He read every word in all those books. If you want to learn, you need to read. And while you're reading away, read your Bible, not just comics or storybooks. If you want the really good stuff, you've got to dive into the Good Book itself.

Having someone feed you spiritual food is okay when you're little, but when you get older, you've got to crack open the Bible and feed yourself.

WORTH GETTING ORGANIZED

What you are doing is not good. You and these people ... will only wear yourselves out. The work is too heavy for you.
—Exodus 18:17–18

After Moses led the Israelites out of Egypt, everyone in camp came running to him with their questions and wanted him to settle their quarrels. So he did. Crowds stood around from morning to evening, day after day, while Moses sat there listening and judging. Both Moses and the people were wiped out at the end of each day. Moses' father-in-law gave him some good advice: let other guys handle the easy cases; you just listen to the tough ones.

You can wear yourself out by trying to do the whole job by yourself. Let's say you're building a snow fort and you don't want to let your little brother and sister help you because they'll "mess it up." You'll probably never finish the fort, and you and your brother and sister will be frustrated. What also won't work is if you're doing a school project with friends but you insist on doing the whole thing yourself.

You have to learn to share the job. Give part of the work to other people and let them help you. To do that, you need to trust other people. Sure, you may think they can't do the job as well as you, but you won't do a great job either if you collapse on the floor exhausted.

It paid for Moses to get organized. Learn from him and don't try to do the whole job yourself. Work smarter, not harder.

WE WERE THERE. WE SAW IT HAPPEN!

We did not follow cunningly invented stories when we told you about the power and coming of our Lord Jesus Christ, but we were eyewitnesses of his majesty.

—2 Peter 1:16

Peter left his smelly fishnets to follow Jesus. Peter lived with Jesus for over three years and saw him do astonishing miracles. He was in Jerusalem when Jesus was crucified, and he saw him after he came back to life. So when Peter told people about Jesus' work, if anyone said, "Yeah, sure. Nice story," he insisted, "These aren't cunning, clever, made-up stories! These things happened! I saw them with my own eyes!"

People in Peter's time were used to hearing invented stories about godlike characters. The Greeks and Romans made up myths about Zeus and Hercules and Jupiter to explain the mysteries of the world. Today we hear lots of made-up stories in books and movies, with characters like Superman, Batman, and Spider-Man. They're fun stories, but they are purely fiction. The people that read Peter's book must have wondered if it was also made-up. But Peter makes it clear that he saw these events with his own eyes.

There are so many creative and interesting stories to read today, but it may be difficult to know the difference between fantasy and fact. Just remember, when it comes to the good news about Jesus, there's nothing made-up about it. Witnesses who actually saw these things wrote about them in the gospels.

Jesus was a real man. He lived and breathed and walked this earth and did astonishing miracles. He was and is the Son of God.

LOOKS JUST LIKE HIS DAD

"Anyone who has seen me has seen the Father. How can you say, 'Show us the Father'?"

—John 14:9 – 10

Jesus' disciples knew that he was God's Son, but they wanted Jesus to show them his Father. They wanted to see God. Um ... guys, listen, that's a bit of a problem. God the Father is invisible. You can't see him. But fortunately, Jesus is the "image of the invisible God" (Colossians 1:15). That's why, when God decided to give people a clear idea of what he was like, he sent his son, Jesus, to live on earth as a man.

Maybe you wish you could see God. Actually, even if you could, it's not such a great idea. There's a reason God made himself invisible. God's so powerful that if you look directly at his face, you'll fall over dead. God told Moses, "You cannot see my face, for no one may see me and live" (Exodus 33:20). It'd be like lying down on a launching pad under a rocket so you can get a good, close look at its engines firing up. It's just not a good idea.

You're best looking at Jesus. But you say, "How can I? He's not on earth anymore." Listen, knowing what Jesus is like does not mean seeing how big his nose is, what color his hair is, or if his eyes get crinkle lines when he smiles. That's not the important stuff. In fact, the gospels don't even describe how he looks. What's truly important is who Jesus was and how he lived!

If you want to see God, look at Jesus. And if you want to get a good look at Jesus, read all about his amazing life in the Gospels.

GOD IS STILL IN BUSINESS

"If the Lord is with us, why has all this happened to us? Where are all his wonders that our fathers told us about when they said, 'Did not the Lord bring us up out of Egypt?' "

—Judges 6:13

When Gideon was a kid, his dad and granddad told him all of the Bible stories about God striking Egypt with plagues. They told him about God parting the Red Sea so the Israelites could escape. But in this Bible passage, Gideon was grown up, and raiders had invaded Israel and were stealing everything in sight. The Israelites had fled their homes and hidden out in caves. Gideon needed a miracle in his day.

When things are tough, you may ask the same questions Gideon did. The Bible talks about God doing miracles. So what happened? Why doesn't he still do miracles today? Well, God still does perform miracles. In Gideon's case, God didn't take over and do all the work. He ordered Gideon to fight the raiders. Sure, God did a miracle—the part Gideon couldn't do—but Gideon had to do the part he could do.

God still cares and still performs miracles right now in the twenty-first century. He can heal diseases. He can supply the money you need. God will ask you to do your part—just like he asked Gideon. God expects you to go to the doctor or to do what you can to earn money, but then he does the part you can't do.

Miracles aren't just things of the past. Miracles don't just happen in the pages of Bible storybooks. God is still in the miracle business.

DOING WHAT YOU CAN

If anyone has material possessions and sees his brother in need but has no pity on him, how can the love of God be in him?

—1 John 3:17

I f you're a Christian and you see a person who really needs help, you'll have pity on him or her. And if you can help, God's love will move you to do something. Now, sometimes you can't help with money but you can pray for the person. But if you can help with physical resources and some kid's hungry or cold, it's no help at all to tell him that you hope he gets warm and fed and do nothing else. (See James 2:15–16.)

Of course, when you give you need to give wisely. If you've saved up your money and you're heading out to buy your mother a birthday present, you may see beggars asking for your money. While it is hard to tell if these people really need help, you can make sure you are giving to established organizations like your church or the Salvation Army whose full time jobs are helping those in need. Then when someone asks you for money, you can direct them to one of these places for help.

We can't solve all the world's problems, not even all the problems in our own towns, but often we can find places to help, even if they are only little things. These things can mean a lot. This can mean sharing our lunches with some kid who forgot his, giving away our old toys or clothes to charity, or suggesting that your family sponsor a child in a poor country. There's no end of things we can do.

PHARISEES AND THEIR SEATS

They love the place of honor at banquets and the most important seats in the synagogues.
—Matthew 23:6

The Scribes and Pharisees loved to be honored by others. They felt they were so good that they were worthy of a ton of honor and respect. So they were always trying to snag the best seats at banquets. And when it came time to worship God, they pushed for the most important seats in the synagogue, the front row seats with the best view—and of course, where everyone could get a good view of wonderful them.

Today when you say the word "Pharisee" it's the same as saying "hypocrite," so no kid in his right mind's going to say, "Yup! Look at me! I'm just like a regular little Pharisee!" But if you're always seeking your own honor and trying to grab the best, most comfortable seat, well, you're at least behaving a little bit like a Pharisee.

Remember, life is not a game of Musical Chairs where you fight to get a seat and gloat when the other guy's left standing. Sure, you maybe want the nice seat once in a while. Fair is fair. But if you're constantly combating your brothers and sisters for the best seat in the car, at the table, or on the couch, then it's become too important.

The more you care for others, the less you care about what your chair looks like and whether you get to park your backside on a better, cushier cushion than someone else.

WEAR YOUR CLOAK

"When you come, bring the cloak that I left with Carpus.... Do your best to get here before winter."
— 2 Timothy 4:13, 21

For thirty years, the apostle Paul traveled around preaching the gospel. Then—WHAM!—he was arrested and slammed into the Mamertine prison in Rome. His cell was a damp underground dungeon with rats. Worse yet, winters in Rome can be cold, and with miserable weather moving in, Paul wanted his cloak. (Cloaks were like warm, wooly blankets that men draped over their robes.)

Most guys these days don't wear cloaks, but a sweater or a jacket can keep you warm. Depending on where you live, winters in America can be cold so you've got to dress for it. The problem is that some kids think only sissies wear coats in cold weather. They think that if you're tough, you should wear only a T-shirt in the fall; and if you're cool, you should tromp through snowdrifts without a jacket.

That kind of thinking isn't cool—it's cold! It doesn't prove you're a man if you get chilled and then stumble around clogged up, sneezing, and with your nose dripping snot like a tap that someone forgot to shut off. All it proves is that kids can talk you into doing dumb stuff. Okay, so it's not cool to wear a jacket with cute little mitties safety-pinned to your sleeves, but it is okay to put on a sweater or a coat.

It pays to take care of your body. That way you're not at home sick in bed, missing out on some fun or important stuff.

LIGHTS OUT

"Paul ... kept on talking until midnight.... Paul talked on and on....
After talking until daylight, he left."
—Acts 20:7, 9, 11

S ound like any sleepover you've been to? You stay up real late talking, and man, you're dead on your feet the next day. Well, the apostle Paul had a good reason for talking that long. He had to leave the city the next morning. He thought it was the last time he'd ever see the Christians there, so whatever he had to say, he had to say it then. After talking till the sun came up, Paul headed out on a hike for the next city.

Paul was a tough old crow. He could hack an all night talkathon then get up and head out on a thirty-mile walk. But let's face it, most kids can't. God didn't intend you to. So if your parents give you the green light to stay up later than usual 'cause your cousin is visiting, go for it. But when they say, "Lights out at ten-thirty," don't keep talking after that.

It can be hard to just lie down and go to sleep when you have someone to pillow fight and tell jokes to. But your parents are the ones making the rules and setting the boundaries. You have to honor them. Besides, Mom and Dad were once kids too. They know that you really do need your sleep.

Have your fun, talk your head off, but know when it's time to shut the blab factory down.

TAKE YOUR BENCH TIME

"David went down with his men to fight against the Philistines, and he became exhausted."

—2 Samuel 21:15

hen David was a teen he defeated Goliath. When he became king he battled the Philistines again. When he got old he fought them *again*. Don't these guys ever give up? Well, this last battle went on and on until David was pooped. He couldn't swing that old sword arm anymore. And wouldn't you know it, as soon as he dropped his guard, a giant named Ishbi-Benob came barreling straight toward him. Good thing David's cousin was riding shotgun and took out Big Benob.

It's no sweat if you get tired when you're raking leaves. You sit down for a while and slurp some brain freeze. And if you're wiped from too much homework, you take a break, right? Take some downtime to get a drink of water, relax, and think about what you're doing. After a brief rest, you have more energy to play or work again.

But there are times when you really need to push, or you're jazzed and want to push—like you're in the middle of a game, your team's on a roll, the excitement's high, and you don't want the coach to park you on the bench for a while. If you're excited or afraid, your adrenaline kicks in like emergency fuel and helps you with that last burst of energy ... but when that runs out too, man, you're really spent. Then you start making serious mistakes or you trip and injure yourself. So take your bench time. You can only keep going so long when you're tired.

Don't overdo. If you need a rest, take a rest. When you're good to go, then get back out there!

TURN THE OTHER CHEEK

"If someone strikes you on the right cheek, turn to him the other also."
—Matthew 5:39

Jesus said that if someone strikes you on the cheek, don't start fighting. In fact, offer him your other cheek too. Now, some Christians think this means that if someone starts slugging you, you're supposed to let him keep punching your teeth in. Even if he's beating you to a pulp, you're not supposed to defend yourself. Wrong! When Jesus said strike, he used the Greek word *rhapizein*, which means to slap. You don't usually get hurt from a slap. It's more of an insult than anything.

If you're hotheaded and someone insults you, you probably start screaming insults back. If you lose your temper easily, other kids may have fun provoking you into shouting matches and fights. Don't let them. That bozo with a big mouth isn't taking anything away from you. Don't let him egg you into fights.

If someone's insulting you, it's a reflection of his bad attitude. He may act that way because he has low self-esteem and is trying to feel better about himself at your expense. Letting it pass is a sign of strength. But if someone actually starts slugging you, don't hesitate to defend yourself by telling an adult. Assault (attacking someone) is a crime; it's against the law.

Be patient toward immature kids and show them God's love. That is called "turning the other cheek." But make sure they understand that they can't just walk all over you.

PUSHING PEOPLE AROUND

After Uzziah became powerful, his pride led to his downfall.
—2 Chronicles 26:16

U zziah was the king of Judah, and he was one tough dude. In his early days he hadn't been so strong, but he loved God and prayed, so God made him powerful. Next thing you know Uzziah's strengthening his nation's defenses, leading a well-trained army, winning battles against his enemies, and ... and then he thought he was hot stuff. He became proud, started pushing God's priests around, and fell.

It's bad enough when some kids today are oversized and strong and they throw their weight around and use their muscle to boss other kids and get what they want. But lots of guys aren't really tough; they just think that they are, so they act proud. Worse yet, there are kids that aren't tough and know they aren't tough, but just act macho to impress others.

This kind of thinking is a trap. This no-one-tells-me-what-to-do attitude is opposite of the way Jesus tells us to think. On top of that, it forces you to be mean, and you start boasting to other kids and sassing adults—and get everyone mad at you. Oh sure, it'll get you to the front of the food-line for a while, but as a lifestyle, it stinks big time. And it eventually backfires.

A man of God may he glad that he's strong, but he's not proud of the fact. He uses his strength to defend the weak, not to push them around.

FLAT FLATTERY

Such people are not serving our Lord Christ ... By smooth talk and flattery they deceive the minds of naïve people.
—Romans 16:18

Paul warned Christians in Rome to watch out for those who came teaching a different message than he'd taught them. These Christians had heard the truth, but now false teachers were moving in and dumping weird stuff on them. These false teachers knew how to deceive the naïve (people who are not very wise about the world). How? They used flattery and said stuff like, "Oh, you're so special! That's why I'm telling you this secret, special stuff."

There are smooth-talking deceivers around today too. If someone said to you, "The Bible doesn't say such-and-such is wrong," you might say, "Cool! I've always wanted to do that!" Another false teacher may be in the form of popular books and movies. If some author writes a book telling outrageous lies about Jesus—that he was a magician or that he never died on the cross—the book becomes a bestseller.

The best way to avoid being tricked by smooth talkers is to read your Bible. Know what it says and doesn't say. That way you won't believe every fast-talking trickster who makes a false claim. Of course, sometimes you won't know where in the Bible to find an answer, so ask your parents or your pastor. They've usually spent years studying it. They'll know.

If some smooth talker tries scrambling your brain by telling you weird stuff about the Bible, tell him you're not in the baloney-buying business. Then avoid him.

A "TOUGH TIMES" BROTHER

A friend loves at all times, and a brother is born for adversity.
—Proverbs 17:17

A true friend loves at all times, meaning he doesn't give up on his friends when something happens and they're not much fun to be around any more. He sticks with his friends. And when our brothers are going through adversity (tough times), they should be able to count on us to be there for him. We were literally born for that purpose.

It can be hard on us when someone in our family is going through adversity. Maybe one of them ends up sick for a long time and can't run around and do back flips on the trampoline anymore. Or maybe that person's friends have dumped him or her and now that person wants to hang out with us more than we care for. Or maybe he or she is grounded because the latest report card was not so acceptable. We can be there for those friends, but it'll mean missing other fun stuff.

Being a friend isn't all fun and games; sometimes it means sacrificing what we want to do. But being a friend has always been about more than just playing with someone. Being a friend means you don't pull some amazing vanishing act when your friend is in trouble or gets sick. A friend loves at all times—not just sometimes and not just during fun times.

Be a true brother to your brothers and, yes, to your sisters as well. You'd want them to be there for you if you were going through rough times, right?

TURNING ON THE TAP

Out of the overflow of the heart the mouth speaks. The good man brings good things out of the good stored up in him, and the evil man brings evil things out of the evil stored up in him.

—Matthew 12:34–35

You constantly take in sights and sounds and fill your mind with images. So when your tongue starts wagging, it draws on what's stored in your brain. If eighty percent of your brain cells are taken up by soccer knowledge, chances are high you'll talk about soccer. Sure, you can try to talk only about the knowledge that fills the other twenty percent, but when you're full of a subject, it eventually flows out of your mouth.

Let's say you spend a lot of time playing violent video games and watching TV shows and movies where kids have sick attitudes and bad mouths. Do you really think that stuff will have no effect on the way you think and talk? Some kids argue, "I just like that stuff. I wouldn't actually talk about it or do it." Not at first, maybe, but eventually when your mind is used to it, yes, you will.

The flip side of the coin is that if you focus on good stuff, then good stuff will fill your mind so much that it will overflow and come out your mouth. That doesn't mean you should talk only about Bible verses or watch only Christian videos. There's lots of good stuff out there. Have a good attitude about whatever you think or talk about—from sports to girls.

What you spend your time thinking about and reading and watching really does matter!

THE RIGHT KIND OF WISDOM

I want you to be wise about what is good, and innocent about what is evil.
— Romans 16:19

S ometimes you hear an adult tell his life story and talk about the stuff he was into before he became a Christian. Maybe he talks about drinking, taking drugs, riding with a biker gang, or fighting in prison. You think, "Huh, that sounds exciting." Don't kid yourself. If these guys could do it over, there's no way they'd wallow in the mud again.

A lot of kids today have things mixed up. Instead of being wise about what is good and innocent about what is evil, they know nearly nothing about what is good but are very well informed about evil. Ask them Bible questions, and they draw blanks. But ask them about the newest shoot-'em-dead video game, and they rattle off the names of all the characters and how much power each of their weapons has.

You become "wise about what is good" when you read your Bible and hang around with godly people. You stay "innocent about what is evil" by refusing to watch bad movies, by not playing dark video games, and by steering away from drugs. Now, you may feel sometimes that good stuff is boring—it's more exciting to play games rated for teens than to sit in church. But seeing someone's life changed by a kind act or watching your neighborhood improve by cleaning up a park is pretty exciting.

There's a lot of dark stuff around today, and it takes a deliberate choice to avoid it. You have to keep choosing good, not evil, day after day.

CAFETERIA-STYLE EXPERTS

They want to be teachers of the law, but they do not know what they are talking about or what they so confidently affirm.

—1 Timothy 1:7

I n Paul's day, some guys got odd ideas in their heads ... then read the Scriptures to find verses to prove their theories. Problem was, they hadn't studied the Bible, so they didn't understand what it was really saying. They just went along cafeteria-style, picking this verse and that. They were confidently affirming stuff—meaning they boasted and insisted they were right—but they didn't have a clue what they were talking about.

People do the same thing today. For example, some people think the Bible isn't talking about God and his angels, but about aliens and UFOs. Even though there's nothing in the Bible about this, they read the entire book with that idea stuck in their brain. They read Ezekiel's description of God's throne and say, "Yup! That's a flying saucer if I ever saw one!" They read, "Aliens will shepherd your flocks" (Isaiah 61:5) and scream, "That proves it!"

This is called having selective hearing—choosing information cafeteria-style. For the record, God's throne is God the Father's throne, not some mother ship. The angels are not actually little green men; they're angels. And the aliens that guarded the Israelites' fluffy little sheep were actually foreigners, not E.T.

Before you start spreading alien ideas around, give the Bible an honest reading. Take off the rose-colored glasses—in this case, the little green glasses—and see what it's really saying.

UNREASONABLE DOUBTS

But they did not believe the women, because their words seemed to them like nonsense.
—Luke 24:11

When some women went to Jesus' tomb and found his body was missing, angels informed them Jesus had risen from the dead. The women ran and told the apostles, but the men didn't believe them. Then Jesus appeared and rebuked them for thinking it was nonsense. You can understand the apostles' doubts. People don't rise from the dead every day. So why did Jesus rebuke them? 'Cause hey, guys, he only told you half a dozen times that he'd be crucified and then rise from the dead!

Sometimes doubts are good, like if someone claims they've discovered the Loch Ness monster or the remains of Atlantis. You should be suspicious. You should doubt, because people have lied about that before. In 1922 a scientist found a fossil tooth in Nebraska and announced it was from a missing link. Turned out it was a tooth from a wild pig! Ooops! You learn what to expect from certain people.

Jesus' disciples should have believed because he'd always told the truth in the past. Yet when he rose from the dead, it caught them totally by surprise. In this case, having doubts didn't show how well their brains were working. All it showed was that they hadn't been paying attention when Jesus was talking.

When someone tells you something astonishing, ask questions. Some doubts are reasonable. But remember that we can believe what Jesus tells us about himself!

LETTING GOD DEAL WITH THINGS

Do not take revenge, my friends ... for it is written: "It is mine to avenge;
I will repay," says the Lord.
—**Romans 12:19**

Paul was talking to Christians at Rome who had been persecuted for their faith. Paul knew that these Christians were only human. He knew that they must have felt like getting back at people who were accusing them and hassling them and spitting on them and cursing them. But Paul told them to let God be the one to avenge them. That meant really trusting God.

You probably know the feeling. When your sister kicks you, you probably really want to slug her in return. But if you do, your dad hears the ruckus, walks in, and gives you both a time out. If you can't work it out with your sister, ask for your dad or mom's help. Rather than hitting your sister back, the best solution might be to tell your dad and let him deal with her. Then you're out of the picture. Dad doesn't have to punish you for slugging her, because you didn't.

God is like your dad—only he sees everything, knows exactly what happened, and can deal with things better. God can make sure that people are paid back for the evil they do, so Christians shouldn't take the law into their own hands. Besides, what if God changes that person into a better person instead of punishing him? He often does. So don't get in God's way.

Don't take revenge on those who persecute or hassle you. If God wants to punish people or change them, stand back and let him. In the meantime, pray for your enemies.

HOW THE UNIVERSE WAS FORMED

By faith we understand that the universe was formed at God's command,
so that what is seen was not made out of what was visible.
—Hebrews 11:3

In the time before time, there were no planets, no asteroids,
not even one speck of space dust. There was no light and
no energy—not even enough to recharge one tiny triple-A
battery. There was nothing but God. Then God gave the
command, and the whole universe came into being. And get
this! He created the entire universe out of nothing.

Have you ever looked at the moon through a pair of
binoculars, peeked at Mars through a telescope, or been on
a field trip to a planetarium? Then you probably have a hint of
an idea of how big our galaxy is. Just the small piece of God's
creation that we can observe is amazing, but the universe
includes millions of galaxies like ours.

No humans were around when the universe was formed.
Since we didn't observe its creation ourselves, we have to have
faith to believe what we don't understand. We have God's Word
telling us that the universe was formed at his command. But we
can also observe the amazing complexity of the universe. Just
look around and study science to see that a loving Creator put
tremendous thought into everything, from the greatest galaxy to
the smallest DNA.

Unbelievers think that the earth and everything in the galaxy
formed by accident. It takes faith to believe that God created the
universe, but guys, it takes a whole lot more faith to believe that
everything created itself without God's help.

KEEP THESE FACTS IN MIND

The officer ... said to the man of God, "Look, even if the Lord should open the floodgates of the heavens, could this happen?"
— 2 Kings 7:2

A n army surrounded the city, and with no food coming in, there was a terrible famine. It lasted so long that people gave up hope. Then Elisha the prophet said that the next day they'd have tons of food. An officer snorted and said, "Impossible!" But it happened. You can understand the officer's being skeptical, but he had forgotten two facts: (a) Elisha was a prophet with a track record of fulfilled prophecies, and (b) God had performed five food miracles for Elisha before!

It's easy to get discouraged when you're in a tough situation for a long time and you've prayed and prayed and nothing's changed ... yet. At first you wonder if God was listening. Then you think about it and realize, "Well, he's God! Of course he heard me!" Then you wonder why he doesn't answer, and you're tempted to either give up on prayer or get mad at God.

When you're discouraged, don't overlook important facts that can give you hope. Here are the facts: the Bible is true, God answers in his own way and time, and trusting him has worked before. Often you need to trust even though you don't understand why things are taking so long. But the reason you can trust is because you know that God has delivered in the past.

When you're tempted to doubt that God cares, or think he doesn't have the power to change things, remember his track record and think again!

FAIR AND EQUAL

Our desire is not that others might be relieved while you are hard pressed,
but that there might be equality.
—2 Corinthians 8:13

Paul wrote to the Christians of Corinth about sharing money with the Christians of Judea, because the Judean believers were nearly starving in a famine. But Paul didn't want the Christians of Corinth to give so much that they didn't have any money left to buy food for themselves. He just wanted them to help. This principle applies to many other things as well.

The idea is not for you to give away so much of your stuff or your time or your money that you have none left for yourself. But most of us don't need to worry about that. We're usually pretty good at hanging onto our stuff. I mean look, it doesn't make sense to loan your snowsuit to a friend so that the day of the school outing, you're frozen and begging for clothes. But if you know a friend doesn't have any gloves, it'd be a great thing if you thought of that and brought him your extra pair. The idea is: care for other people and help as much as you can. And remember, this works for other people too: sometimes they need their stuff and just can't loan it to you.

It's wonderful to be generous and to have friends be generous with you. And sometimes we need to be generous now, knowing that later we will need our friends to be generous with us.

HEALTHY AND UNHEALTHY COMPETITION

Do nothing out of selfish ambition or vain conceit ... Each of you should look not only to your own interests, but also to the interests of others.
—Philippians 2:3, 4

There's nothing wrong with ambition. But there's a huge problem with selfish ambition. That's when people have a "me-first" attitude, are only looking out for their own interests and could care less about the other guy. People get like that when they're conceited—worse yet, vainly conceited—and figure they're better than others and deserve more.

Okay, so if you're looking out for the other guy's interests, not just your own, does that mean that you shouldn't be competitive? Should you let him win a video game? (Not likely.) Does it mean you shouldn't do your best in a spelling bee? (No.) Or does it mean that you can be competitive, just don't gloat as the other person loses? (You're getting warm.)

God wants you to really work at things and to do your best, in relationships, in sports, in schoolwork or business. But in doing your best you also need to love others—look out for what's best for them, not just what's best for you. To live this way is to live with the mind of Christ. It is living your life as he lived his life.

The cure for being vainly conceited or having selfish ambition is to care for others. If you're looking out for others too, you'll think of their needs and feelings as well.

STRENGTH WITH MERCY

"Today, though I am the anointed king, I am weak, and these sons of Zeruiah are too strong for me."
—2 Samuel 3:39

The sons of Zeruiah (Zer-roo-eye-ah) were strong, brave warriors who were King David's cousins. So far so good. But there was a problem: these bozos were out of control. David was a strong king, and he wanted to rule with justice and mercy. Not Joab and Abishai, the sons of Zeruiah! When people got in their way—WHAM! Their answer to problems was to run a sword through some guy's guts. One day, Joab killed a righteous man named Abner. David was so sick over it that he felt weak.

What's your reaction when some kid plops down and starts playing with one of your toys? Do you rip it out of his hands and punch him? What do you do if your sister's teasing you and won't stop? Do you kick her or pull her hair? C'mon, guys, you know that's not the solution.

The problem with Zeruiah's sons was that they were convinced that their cause was so right that they were justified in doing whatever they had to do. Not. There are godly ways to deal with problems. Look at King David. He was no pushover, but he knew that strength had to be controlled by mercy and wisdom or it could do more damage than good.

Control your temper and avoid the punch-and-pound solution. Try mercy. You'll be a lot happier and spend less time being lectured.

LAME EXCUSES

"The sluggard says, 'There is a lion in the road, a fierce lion roaming the streets!'"
— Proverbs 26:13

What's this? Lions escaping from the zoo? Well, almost. When flood season hit the Jordan River, rising water often forced the lions living near its banks to find new places to roam. So once in a while a lion might end up near some village. But how come only the lazy guy saw the lion, huh? How come it's the sluggard—the guy who doesn't wanna work—who hears a lion breathing outside? Mighty suspicious.

Lots of kids today make up ridiculous excuses to get out of work. They sound like this: "Put my socks in the laundry? Oh, did you ask me to do that?" Or, "I'm too tired ... by the way, can I stay up late tonight?" Or, "I didn't brush my teeth because there's no toothpaste. Oh, here it is." Or, "Pick up the toys in my room? But I didn't make this mess."

Don't be so lazy that you have to make ridiculous excuses to cover for yourself. Have you noticed how your parents usually don't believe you anyway? You hope they're buying your story, but they're just standing there shaking their heads. The solution is to simply do what you're supposed to do. Even if you're in a lazy mood, use some willpower to get yourself up and going.

Just shrug off laziness and do what you're supposed to do. Avoid lyin' around thinking up lion excuses.

YOUR PERSONAL TRAINER

"Train yourself to be godly. For physical training is of some value, but godliness has value for all things."
—1 Timothy 4:7 – 8

Physical training is of some value, all right! Exercise and self-discipline do good stuff for your body, making you stronger, faster, and better at sports. Whether you have a personal trainer advising you how to zing the badminton birdie low over the net, a guy beside the pool showing you how to swim faster than a piranha, or a martial arts instructor teaching you how to block a punch, it's all good.

When you train, you improve your technique—slide into home base sneakier, slice through the water faster, or kick through a brick wall harder (just kidding). You learn about mistakes you've been making and how to improve—pacing yourself to not wear out quickly and cutting down your time.

The apostle Paul compared sports training to living a Christian life. It takes the same self-discipline and the same focus on the goal—only the results are better than a trophy. If you always try to do the right thing, you become a better person all round. By the way, you have to "train yourself to be godly," but you don't have to do it alone. God is your trainer and he's always with you.

Just as physical training is good for your physical health, spiritual training is good for your spiritual health and your whole life! Do your best—both in sports and in your walk with God.

FORTY-YEAR-OLD JEANS

"During the forty years that I led you through the desert, your clothes did not wear out, nor did the sandals on your feet."

—Deuteronomy 29:5

The Israelites left Egypt to conquer Canaan, but when they learned about the armies and fortresses they'd have to fight there, they chickened out. God punished them by making them wander in the wilderness for forty years. Um, one small detail: they couldn't buy new clothes out in the desert. Normally, after forty years the clothes would be tattered rags on their backs and their sandals would fall apart, but God kept that from happening.

For forty years—exactly 14,610 days—the Israelites didn't need to change their clothes. Boys must have loved this! Now, God can still do miracles like that—make clothes extra durable—but he usually doesn't. These days if you wear the same pair of jeans week after week, you'll tear holes in the knees and wear them completely out. And the smell! Hooweee!

Unless you're an astronaut marooned on the deserts of Mars, you have no excuse for not taking off your dirty clothes. So change 'em before they get so bad they rot right off you. Or if your clothes are still clean after wearing them a day or so, fold them or hang them up so you can find them in the morning. Don't just drop them on the floor.

Take good care of your clothes and they'll stay looking good and last you a long time. Not forty years, no, but at least until you grow out of them.

HAMSTER-CAGE BREATH

"My breath is offensive to my wife; I am loathsome to my own brothers."
—Job 19:17

A long time ago, a guy named Job lived in the land of Uz. We don't know exactly what kind of sickness Job came down with, but painful sores broke out all over his body. Flies laid eggs in his sores and soon maggots began crawling there. The man looked loathsome. (That means disgusting and revolting.) People dodged him when they saw him in the street. Poor Job was so sick that his breath smelled like the bottom of a hamster cage.

Where does bad breath come from? Well, millions of bacteria called plaque (plak) live in your mouth. They like to feast on the food rotting between your unbrushed teeth, and they especially like to live in the roomy condominiums on the back of your tongue. When they're dead and dying, bacteria release a sulfur compound. That's what causes the stink. Take a look in the mirror. Is your tongue a bit white? That's your own personal bacteria graveyard.

To get rid of these filthy creatures, you need to brush your teeth—and that doesn't mean racing 100 miles per hour down the back rows then speeding across the front. It means cruisin' nice and slow. And don't forget to run your toothbrush over your tongue to get rid of the plaque there. Then rinse your mouth with germ-killing mouthwash. This is war, man!

If you don't want your breath to stink like a bacteria compost pile, brush your teeth—and your tongue.

FEARFULLY MADE

"I praise you because I am fearfully and wonderfully made."
—**Psalm 139:14**

When David praised God for the way God had made him, he used the word fearfully as in awesomely or amazingly—not like "Whoa! I look like King Kong!" Another guy named Job asked God, "Did you not ... curdle me like cheese, clothe me with skin and flesh and knit me together with bones and sinews?" (Job 10:10–11) Job was not complaining that he smelled like sour cheese or that God had sewn him together like Frankenstein's monster. Job just had a different way of saying, "Thanks for making me the way you did, God."

Maybe you're one of those guys who look in the mirror and go, "Oh yeah! You are one good-lookin' dude!" Hopefully not. Chances are that you're not Mr. Perfect and you don't like your whole package. Maybe you're too fat or too skinny for your liking, or too short or too tall. Maybe your nose is too big or too small, your teeth are not perfect, and you have a freckle on your eyelid.

Welcome to the real world. None of us is perfect—not even that kid over there, smiling at himself in the mirror. God made you the way you are, and he doesn't make junk. True, he may have had some original ideas. Praise him for the way he made you; you're one of a kind.

Bottom line: accept yourself even if your body is not as perfect or good-looking as you'd like it to be.

LUST OF THE EYES

"Everything in the world — the cravings of sinful man, the lust of his eyes ... comes not from the Father but from the world."
—1 John 2:16

Tons of magazine and TV ads show pretty women selling something while dressed in almost nothing. What's the big idea? Can't they afford clothes? Oh, yeah, they can. Those bikinis are their work clothes. See, automobile companies and other advertisers want to get men's attention, and since they know that guys are interested in sex, the advertisers bring on the beach babes.

This is why there are "men's" magazines on the racks and "adult" channels on TV. All these X-rated images that feed the "cravings of sinful man" and the "lust of the eyes" are called pornography. (Pornography comes from the Greek word *porne*, which means "to sell sex for cash.") Now, it's fine to notice that a girl is beautiful, but the problem with staring at porn is that it gets your mind working overtime, craving sex—and that leads to trouble.

God loves human beings. To make sure humans keep having children, God programmed men to be very attracted to women, and he made sex very enjoyable. But here's the deal: God wants you to enjoy sex within marriage—not before marriage, not outside of marriage. To be sure you got that point, he spelled out some rules in the Bible. Obey them and you'll steer clear of problems.

Make up your mind that you'll honor God by keeping your eyes away from pornography. Stay away from X-rated magazines and videos.

ABSOLUTE PURITY

"Treat ... younger women as sisters, with absolute purity."
—1 Timothy 5:1–2

Paul's advice to young men was straightforward: respect everyone. Respect older men as if they were your dad and older women as if they were your mom. Treat the guys in your church as if they were your brothers and the girls as if they were your sisters. Of course, all these people don't live in your house with you, but they are part of your spiritual family. And this verse focuses on treating girls with respect.

Of course, Paul's advice won't make sense if you punch your sister or tease her. "Yeah," you say, "but my sister teases me. Am I supposed to be kind to her when she bugs me?" Well, if she does that, talk to your parents about it and let them deal with her. In the meantime be patient and kind to your sister. Then turn around and treat all girls the same way.

And don't forget the "with absolute purity" part. Girls are special people created by God. They're not sexual objects to make dumb jokes about. Don't hang around with guys who make sick comments about girls, otherwise you'll end up spewing out their same brain garbage. Tell them to cut it out, and if they don't, then you cut out of there.

If you respect someone, you don't say bad things about him or her. You don't even think bad things about them. That's the attitude God wants you to have toward girls.

PROTECTORS OF THE TRIBE

"Josiah removed all the detestable idols from all the territory belonging to the Israelites."
— 2 Chronicles 34:33

God raises up Josiah, a strong king down in Judah, when there's no ruler in Israel anymore. Josiah looks around, and he's the strongest kid on the block. No one can stand against him. So how does he use his strength? Does he oppress the Israelites? Tax them? No. The first thing he does is smash their disgusting idols and bring them back to serving God.

You have already started doing some serious growing—or you will soon—and you find that you're quite a bit bigger and stronger than younger kids. So how do you use your strength? Do you push your brother or sister around? Do you use your muscles to grab an extra turn on the trampoline? Or do you use your strength to help others?

God gives young men strength for a reason. He meant for men to be the protectors of the tribe. He also meant for men of God to serve him and to help others serve him. So instead of using your mighty superpowers to get your own way, use them to keep younger kids from danger, to stop fights, and to help them to do what's right.

As you grow and become stronger, your mind and your spirit should grow too. When you begin to step up to your responsibility to help others, you're starting to become a man.

LISTENING TO LECTURES

He said to them, "Why do you do such things?" ... His sons, however, did not listen to their father's rebuke.

—1 Samuel 2:23, 25

Eli was high priest of Israel. His two sons were also priests, but did all kinds of disgusting stuff. They offended thousands of Israelites who came to worship God. Eli lectured his sons but they refused to listen. It was a privilege to be priests, so Eli should have taken that privilege away from them. Instead, he let them keep on living out of control. Then God held Eli responsible for not disciplining his sons and punished him and his sons.

Some kids today are like that. They do what they want to do, and when their parents try to tell them that what they're doing is wrong, they answer, "It's not that bad," or "Everyone else does it." Or they accuse their parents of never letting them do anything. Some kids are so self-willed that their parents just give up and let them do what they want.

When a child misbehaves, God holds the parent responsible to talk to him, to lecture him, remove privileges, ground him or find some effective way of disciplining him. It's no fun for a parent and most parents don't enjoy it, so make sure that if mom or dad gives you a serious talk that you listen to them. Thank God for parents who care!

DON'T GET ME STARTED

Starting a quarrel is like breaching a dam; so drop the matter before a dispute breaks out.

—Proverbs 17:14

These days most dams are hydroelectric dams for generating electricity, but in olden days, dams were ponds used to store water during dry seasons. When a farmer wanted to water his garden, he'd open the tap, use as much water as he needed, and then close the pipe again. But if he accidentally breached his dam—knocked a hole in the wall—the water began gushing out, the hole got bigger, and suddenly the whole wall gave way and a flood washed out.

Disagreeing with someone can be like that. If someone offends you or you have a difference of opinion, and you're able to stay calm, that's cool. You can get things off your chest and sort them out. But if you know you'll lose your temper and say hurtful things—or the other person will—then a discussion quickly turns into a dispute (heated argument).

You might mean well, but if things get out of control, fixing the angry mess later can be like trying to stuff toothpaste back in the tube. If you know that's going to happen, drop the matter and don't even go there. If you know that you have a tendency to argue with a certain brother or sister or classmate, avoid getting drawn into a quarrel in the first place.

OKAY, YOU'VE GOT MY ATTENTION!

Then he said to his servants, "Look, Joab's field is next to mine . . . Go and set it on fire."

—2 Samuel 14:30

General Joab was a powerful, feared man, but after Prince Absalom messed up and ran off to another land, Joab talked King David into bringing Absalom back. Now Absalom wanted Joab to do him another favor, but Joab ignored him. To get Joab's attention, Absalom told his servants to torch Joab's barley fields. Oh, yeah! That got Joab's attention, all right. A couple of years later, Joab killed Absalom.

Offending others to get yourself visible on their radar isn't wise. Sure, if you're mad, you feel like "teaching them a lesson." But those kinds of stunts have a way of coming back at you. Like if your mom doesn't let you go out with your friends, you tromp your muddy shoes across the clean floor. Or you take it out on your sister and torment her. Yup, that'll get Mom's attention. It'll also get you grounded.

No matter how upset you feel when your friends don't do what you want them to do, don't lash out in anger at them. There are acceptable ways to let off steam without hurting yourself and others. Like praying, exercising, going for a walk, or pounding your pillow.

Think the consequences through before you do something rash. Sure, you're frustrated, but there are always smart solutions that beat dumb actions any day.

LIVING LIKE PHANTOMS

"Each man's life is but a breath. Man is a mere phantom as he goes to and fro:
He bustles about, but only in vain."
—Psalm 39:5 – 6

When the Bible talks about people being like phantoms, it doesn't mean they fly through walls—unless they do a major wipeout on their skateboard. It means that they're busy and on the go, but they never accomplish anything. They're just a bunch of hot air. Their entire life is like a balloon shooting around the room with air squealing out of it. They live for nothing.

Ever wished you were a ghost so you could walk through walls, fly through the air, and maybe scare people? Okay, scaring people is no fun for them, but the fact is, mankind has always wanted to fly. These days you can get on a plane and do that. For most kids, the closest they come to flying is taking a ride in the Salt & Pepper Shaker at the amusement park.

Flying is fun, but you don't want to live your life like a phantom the way some people do. They bustle about—run around making a lot of noise—but their life never actually makes a difference. They never help others. If you want a real life that counts, love God and others. Not only will it make life better right now, but God will reward you for it in heaven.

If you don't want to live a fleeting, phantom life, then make sure to love God and others. That way, you can live a life that really counts.

CHURCH – BELIEVERS BELONG TOGETHER

Let us not give up meeting together, as some are in the habit of doing, but let us encourage one another.
—Hebrews 10:25

In the early church, believers were sometimes persecuted for being Christians. It could be dangerous to meet. All it took was one spy and you could all get arrested. But often things weren't so serious. A lot of people stopped attending meetings because they simply couldn't be bothered to go. They skipped so many services that they got in the habit of not going to church.

Okay, if there's such a howling blizzard outside your door that the dog teams are freezing solid and even the penguins are falling over dead from frostbite, that's one thing. Or if your family is colonizing Mars, you can't zip back once a week to your hometown church. But hey, if your only reason for not going to church is because you want to sleep in or you just don't feel like going, that really doesn't cut it.

Sure, you can be a Christian all alone, but that's not God's plan. God made people to need other people—to belong to a community. It's important for Christians to go to church. It strengthens you when you spend time with other believers because you encourage each other. Worshiping with others inspires you. And your teachers have prepared important lessons from God's Word to teach you.

You won't always feel like going to church, but meeting with other Christians is a good habit to get into. So dig your dog team out of the snowdrifts, jump in the sled, and go.

DEALING WITH PERSECUTION

Blessed are you when men hate you, when they exclude you and insult you ...
because of the Son of Man. Rejoice in that day and leap for joy, because great
is your reward in heaven.

—Luke 6:22-23

Jesus knew that Christians would be persecuted for believing in him. There would be times when people would mock and insult them. Sometimes their former friends would snub them. So how are Christians supposed to deal with this kind of rejection? Jesus gave a surprising answer. He said that we were supposed to rejoice and be happy about it.

You're probably thinking that no way do you feel happy when kids tease you for believing in Jesus or for going to church. And you're not particularly glad when old pals don't hang around with you anymore because you stand up for what's right. Being cut from the herd can hurt. So how do you deal with it? And what about all this is supposed to make you happy?

First of all, you know you're being rejected or insulted because you're making God happy, and that ought to make you happy. And what should make you even happier is the knowledge that God has promised to bless you for standing up for Jesus. God is going to see to it that you receive a great reward in heaven for your troubles down here.

Leap for joy when other kids insult you? Hey, if you don't wanna leap, at least smile. Your future is very, very bright and blessed.

TAKING THE PLUNGE

"Repent and be baptized ... And you will receive the gift of the Holy Spirit."
—Acts 2:38

Believing in Jesus saves you, so why do you need to get baptized? Surely the water isn't washing away your sins. No. John the Baptist said to Jesus, "I baptize you with water, but he will baptize you with the Holy Spirit" (Mark 1:8). When you get saved, God's Holy Spirit enters your heart and cleanses you. Baptism is an outward symbol of what the Holy Spirit has done and a sign and seal of God's promises.

In the early church, Christians were baptized soon after they believed. Maybe you've believed in Jesus for years but you haven't taken the plunge yet. It's definitely something you should do. Now, different Christian churches have different views on when you should be baptized or exactly how you should be baptized, but the point is, if you're a believer, you should be baptized.

The apostle Paul explained that baptism (going under the water) is kind of like dying and being buried. Then, "just as Christ was raised from the dead ... we too may live a new life" (Romans 6:4). You then rise out of the water to new life. Got that? Just like Jesus died and came back to life, baptism is "death" to your old, selfish life. Bottom line: baptism is a serious, public statement that you've made up your mind to live for Jesus.

Baptism is a huge step. It means turning from your selfish, self-centered ways and going all out for God. If you're a believer, baptism should be next on your list.

HOLDING ONTO CLUES AND KEYS

"If you hold to my teaching, you are really my disciples. Then you will know the truth, and the truth will set you free."

—John 8:31–32

Many things in this world are true. It's true that gravity acts on all objects, and it's true that 3 + 4 = 7. But the most important truths are spiritual truths, such as the fact that Jesus died on the cross to save you. Jesus also taught a lot more truth about loving God and loving others. Hang onto his teachings. You'll know the truth, and it'll free you. How does that work?

It's like a video game where you're trying to find your way through some lost city. You have to remember certain clues to find hidden passageways, and you have to hang onto keys to open doorways. So your little character is running along—pitter-patter, pitter-patter—trying to find the way. And how do you find the passages? By remembering the clues you were given. How do you open the doors? By holding onto the keys you were given.

You have to seriously follow Jesus' teachings—not simply hear them, nod your head, and say, "Yeah, that's true." Do you want to avoid the traps and temptations of this world? Do you want to find your way? Do you want to be free? Then know the truth, remember it, and use it to solve problems. Receive Jesus' teachings and hold onto them.

When you know the truth and obey it, it frees you from doubt and fear and worry and confusion. It sets you free.

SAVE IT FOR MARRIAGE

"It is God's will that you should ... avoid sexual immorality."
— **1 Thessalonians 4:3**

Two thousand years ago when boys grew into teens, their bodies went through huge changes. Their glands released a chemical called testosterone into their bodies that caused them to become very attracted to members of the opposite sex. And the news is testosterone is still doing its thing today. A gorgeous girl walks by and your heart slams around like a basketball, you sweat, and you may even become aroused. Often you can't help those reactions, but you *are* in control of what you do next.

As a Christian, you need to exercise self-control and save sex for marriage. Avoid sexual immorality. (That means stay away from breaking God's moral laws on sex.) Now, some teens say, "As long as you love a girl, it's okay to have sex with her." No, it's not. Besides, if she gets pregnant, the guy usually ditches her and lets her raise the baby alone. Hello? That's love? Moms and dads who protect and care for their kids—that's love.

"Cool" guys brag that they're having sex, but these same guys often get sexual diseases they're not bragging about. That includes penis warts and very painful sores called herpes. And then there's syphilis and AIDS. Sex outside of marriage is simply not Gods' will. Avoiding immorality is God's will.

God knows the problems that sexual immorality causes. That's why he said to avoid it. Just don't do it.

DOG-GODS AND COPYCATS

Solomon's wisdom was greater than ... all the wisdom of Egypt.
—1 Kings 4:30

At times you'll hear people talk about "the wisdom of ancient Egypt." Well, the Egyptians were plenty smart. When it came to planting crops, running cities, doing math, keeping detailed records, and learning the lessons of history, the Egyptians were famous for their wisdom. Some of their wise men wrote practical advice similar to what Solomon wrote in the book of Proverbs. But Solomon was wisest of all.

Sad to say, however, Egyptians worshipped scores of idols, and a lot of their "wisdom" included dirges to dog-headed gods, discussions on how dung beetles created the world, and please-don't-eat-me prayers to crocodiles. So be careful. If someone hands you the Egyptian Book of the Dead and says, "Hey, dude, check out the ancient wisdom of Egypt," tell him you don't dig dead-dog dudes or the mumbling of mummies.

Why try to sift through Egyptian myths when you can read the clear, inspired sayings of Solomon right in the Bible? And while you're at it, get a load of the ancient wisdom in the Psalms. These books tell you how to live and love God and your fellow man. They give you hope! And read the Gospels. You can find life—eternal life—in the Bible, but how can you find life in the Book of the Dead?

FINDING OUT COOL STUFF

I, Daniel, understood from the Scriptures ... that the desolation of Jerusalem would last seventy years.

—Daniel 9:2

Daniel's sitting in Babylon where his people are prisoners. Meanwhile, his hometown of Jerusalem is desolate (in ruins). Daniel's reading the book of Jeremiah and comes to the part that says the Jews will be prisoners seventy years in Babylon (Jeremiah 25:11–12). That catches Daniel's attention! He reads a little further, and his eyes nearly pop out! When the seventy years are up, guess what? The Jews will return to Jerusalem (Jeremiah 29:10). Daniel's thinking, "Good thing I read this! Now I know what's gonna happen!"

Maybe you feel the Bible's so deep that only adults can get stuff out of it, or that it's just full of poetry and history. No, God's Word is packed full of stuff for all ages.

Be glad if your parents require you to read a couple of Bible chapters every day. Sure, some parts won't be exploding with excitement and adventure, but you're bound to run across helpful info and find answers to your questions. There'll also be days where you're reading along and, like Daniel, you'll stumble across some completely mind-boggling facts.

You find out cool stuff when you study the Bible. You might not find it the first day, or even the second. But keep reading, and you'll hit pay dirt.

SAUNA ROOM SCHOOL

He took the disciples with him and had discussions daily in the lecture hall
of Tyrannus. This went on for two years.
—Acts 19:9–10

One time the apostle Paul had no place to teach new Christians, so professor Tyrannus (not Tyrannosaurus Rex) was kind enough to let him use his lecture hall. There was, um, one downside. Tyrannus taught in the cool morning hours. Paul had the schoolroom during the afternoon. The hall was probably free—but hot. This was in ancient Turkey, and the Christians probably felt like they were turkeys baking in an oven. It was like going to school in a sauna.

Unless your class has air-conditioning and an ice-cream break every hour, you can maybe relate to this. When you're sitting in class or Sunday school in the summer heat—and the windows are open but it's not helping—maybe you wish you were somewhere else—like, at the waterslides. The teacher's talking, but your body's approaching meltdown, and your mind is barely there.

What's the solution? Well, if you're gonna get anything out of the class, you have to tune out the heat, turn off the daydreams, and get in the zone mentally. You do that by remembering why you're there. You're in Sunday school to learn about Jesus, the most powerful guy in the universe. You're in school because a good education means a better life.

Just how badly do you want to learn? When school is boring or your classroom is sweltering, remember Paul and the sweating Christians. They stuck it out for two years to learn about God. Stick it out. It's worth it.

OPEN EARS, OPEN MIND

Let the wise listen and add to their learning.

—Proverbs 1:5

When you're really into something, you just devour information about it—whether it's baseball or fishing or dirt biking or video games. Learning comes easy. Your mind's open, your ears are tuned in, and, like a starving piranha, you gulp down new facts because you're interested in more. When you already have lots of learning, and you add to what you know, you're at the top of your game.

One guy in the New Testament was named Philologus, which means "lover of learning." We don't know if Phil lived up to his name, but obviously his mom and dad had high hopes for him. Now, any kid is naturally gonna find some subjects interesting and other subjects boring. But the way life's set up, you can't just focus on video games and skateboarding and let everything else slide. You need to learn the "boring" stuff too.

Even if you're not keen on math, it pays to know how to walk into a store, buy a smoothie, and walk back out again with the correct change. So how do you learn stuff when you're not that interested? By listening. By making yourself focus and refusing to let your mind daydream. By not passing drawings around the class or bouncing spitballs off some kid's head. Whatever you're studying, give it your attention.

Want to learn stuff? Or at least need to learn stuff? Then listen when the teacher's mouth is moving. There'll be time for skateboarding and computer games afterward.

EXTREME RESEARCH

They searched in the archives stored in the treasury at Babylon. A scroll was found in the citadel of Ecbatana in the province of Media.
—Ezra 6:1–2

Way back when the Persians were ruling the land, the Jews began to rebuild their temple. The local Persian official asked, "Um, guys. Do you have permission to do that?" The Jews told him, "Sure we do. Check your records." So the official had the librarians in Babylon search through the documents. They found nothing. Did they give up? Nope. They kept at it and finally tracked the document down in Ecbatana—three hundred miles away!

These days it's a lot easier to find facts. There's Google and a dozen other search engines that blitz through the Internet to supply you with information. But researching can still be work—especially if you don't have the right search words, or you have to jog to the library and check through tons of books. Things are so easy these days that when something's just a bit hard, you can be tempted to throw up your hands and give up.

The key to doing great research—even looking for a pair of socks—is to make up your mind that you're not gonna give up if you don't succeed instantly. Stick to it. Time and time again, victory comes to those who simply refuse to give up.

Keep at it when you have to dig out facts. After all, it's not like someone's making you ride a camel three hundred miles to Ecbatana to hunt down some scroll.

REWARD DAY FOR CHRISTIANS

We must all appear before the judgment seat of Christ, that each one may receive what is due him for the things done while in the body, whether good or bad.
— 2 Corinthians 5:10

When you believe in Jesus, he gives you eternal life, and he prepares a fantastic place in heaven for you. But before you move into your home in paradise, you'll be required to show up at the judgment seat of Christ. Jesus will be your judge, and he'll examine everything you have ever done or said in your entire life.

Maybe you thought that after you left this world, you shot straight into heaven, ran up and down the streets of gold, moved into your new mansion, and maybe took off for a vacation to the moons of Jupiter? After all, all your sins have been forgiven, right? Right, they have. But before you do anything else, you'll have a serious, one-on-one appointment with Jesus Christ.

This is not to judge whether you go to heaven or not. If you love Jesus and have tried to do what he says, your destination's already settled. This session is to gloriously reward you for all the good you've ever done, and to burn away all the garbage you collected in your life. You'll be so happy about all the good you did, but crying about your selfish, bad deeds. Then Jesus will wipe all tears from your eyes.

Knowing that you'll appear before the judgment seat of Christ one day should remind you that what you do in this life really counts.

TAKING A SPIRITUAL SHOWER

Let us draw near to God ... having our hearts sprinkled to cleanse us from
a guilty conscience and having our bodies washed with pure water.
—Hebrews 10:22

Okay, this is not talking about taking a shower before you
pray—though that's not a bad idea if you've just come out
of a mud-wrestling competition. This verse is saying that
when Jesus forgives your sins he cleanses your mind. Then
you no longer have a guilty conscience. You're washed and
showered and you can approach God without worrying that
you stink.

If you're like most kids you probably think you're not "holy"
enough to pray about serious things. Or maybe you think God
won't give the time of day to someone who goofs up like you do.
Sometimes when you go to pray, all you can think about is the
last selfish thing that you did, so you figure God's not going to
answer your prayers. Not true.

If you have asked Jesus to forgive your sins and save you,
then you are clean. You don't need to have a guilty conscience
and keep dragging a big bag of your sins and mistakes in your
mind. If you have sincerely told God you're sorry, then he has
forgiven you. And if you've sinned, then sincerely ask God to
forgive you for that too. He'll wash you clean. Then you can draw
near to him ... no sweat.

Have you asked God to sprinkle your heart today? If not, take
a spiritual shower right now. Let God wash all the dirt out of
your life.

DEVOTION 234

DON'T BE SUPERSTITIOUS

They are full of superstitions from the East; they practice divination like
the Philistines.

—Isaiah 2:6

T he Israelites were often tempted to copycat the superstitious customs of the nations around them—the Philistines to the west and the Arameans to the east. When they needed direction and it seemed that God took too long to answer their prayers, they turned to mediums and sorcerers to divine (figure out) what to do. They also began believing in silly stuff like wearing lucky amulets and medallions to keep evil spirits away.

Many people today are just as superstitious. They carry rabbit feet around with them, figuring that a dead bunny paw will bring them good luck. They flip their lucky penny every time they need a yes or no answer. They're afraid of the number thirteen and freak if a black cat crosses their path.

As Christians, we serve the all-powerful God and our future is in his hands. Our fate isn't in the hands of some non-existent Lady Luck. We don't need rabbit feet to bring good luck and keep bad luck away. God has promised that if we love and trust him, that he will lead us the way we should go, and he will protect us from evil and bless us.

God's answers sometimes take a while to come, but that's because he wants to teach us to trust him and follow the Bible, faithfully. So ditch silly superstitions and listen to God.

IMPERFECT PARENTS

"But Jether did not draw his sword, because he was only a boy and was afraid."
— Judges 8:20

When hoards of Midianites invaded Israel, God told Gideon to gather an army. God then trimmed his army down to a lean, mean strike force of only 300 men. Gideon and his commandos attacked the Midianites and killed thousands of them. It had to be done—it was war—but it wasn't for kids. When they captured two Midianite kings, Gideon had the bright idea to let his son kill those guys. But Jether was only a kid. He couldn't do it.

Some things are for adults only—with good reason—and Jether's dad should've known that this was not a PG–13 activity. War is not for boys. And neither are violent shoot-'em-up video games where you machine gun anything that moves and cyber blood is flying in all directions. And when the label states that a war movie is "rated for mature audiences," that's what it means.

You may wonder why some of your friends' parents let them watch adult movies and play video games designed for older teens. It doesn't matter what standards other parents set for their kids. If your parents have stricter rules, you must honor them—even if they pull a Gideon and allow you to play a certain game or watch a certain video, then later say that it's off limits.

Honor your parents and obey them. They're not perfect, but they're looking out for you.

INTELLIGENT DISCUSSIONS

Don't have anything to do with foolish and stupid arguments, because you know they produce quarrels.
—2 Timothy 2:23

Back in New Testament days, many Christians in the city of Ephesus were puffed up with useless knowledge and weird theories. They thought they were cutting-edge smart, but the reality was they wasted their time arguing about stupid stuff. Now, you can argue intelligently about important stuff, but these turkeys were arguing about foolishness, so it didn't take long for them to end up in childish quarrels and shouting matches.

These quarrels happen when people argue about something dumb like who gets to sit where on the couch or which cartoon superhero is the greatest. No one can prove their point, so soon they don't try to give intelligent reasons. They just shout insults.

Some things are worth arguing about—in a calm, intelligent manner. For example, if someone says that Abraham Lincoln was a famous baseball player, call him on it. If someone says that the math test is a week away but it's happening tomorrow, set her straight. But if they're arguing about whether angels spend their free time hang gliding in the methane storms of Jupiter, forget it! Who knows? Who cares?

A foolish and stupid quarrel is like a light bulb that doesn't work properly. It produces a lot of heat but not very much light.

DIRT ALERT!

"Elisha son of Shaphat is here. He used to pour water on the hands of Elijah."
— 2 Kings 3:11

The Jews have been scrubbing their hands for thousands of years. In Jesus' day, Mark said that they "do not eat unless they wash" (Mark 7:4). That's already great, but there's more: they not only washed their hands before meals, but made sure the water was clean, running water. They didn't have taps, so folks grabbed a jug and poured water on each other's hands. Elisha was the water boy for Elijah.

You'd think with all the running water in North America today, that boys would be cleaner now than they've ever been, right? Well ... the dirt on this situation is that most boys still have to be reminded to bathe. Desperately dirty kids have to be shooed into the shower. And washing hands? Some kids use the toilet and then race out of the bathroom without even noticing that the sink exists. Washing before meals? Yeah, sort of ...

Washing hands means washing hands. The idea is not to get your hands just wet enough so that the dirt smears off on the towel when you wipe 'em. Scrub those fingers! Towels were invented to get wet hands dry. And while you're at it, do the soap thing. Rub your hands till the bubbles fly.

Elisha's not around any more to pour water on your hands, but that's not necessarily a huge problem — most homes have running water, so put it to use after toilet duty and before meals.

NORMAL GROWING UP

"When a man has an emission of semen, he must bathe his whole body."
—Leviticus 15:16

As you grow up and become a man ... Oh, wait! There's a stage between being a boy and being a man, and it's called puberty (pew-ber-tee). That's when changes begin happening in your body. You start getting hair in funny places, your armpits get BO, your voice gets deeper, you often get pimples on your face, and your testicles begin to produce semen.

That's why it's common for boys around thirteen years old to start having "wet dreams." You're dreaming along and then you dream about someone of the opposite sex. The next thing you know you have an emission of sperm and fluid from your penis. (An emission is something that comes out.) Then you've got sticky wet stuff on your pajamas and body.

You can cut down on this by not putting sexual pictures in your brain in the first place, but the fact is, most young men have wet dreams. It just happens. So besides praying for God to give you pure thoughts, you need to take some practical steps. If you wake up and find that you've had a wet dream, put your PJs and underwear in the laundry then take a shower with soap and water.

Stuff like this is a normal part of growing up, so don't freak out. You're not the first boy on the planet it ever happened to. But do remember to wash your mind with God's Word and your body with soap and water.

WHEN FRIENDS ARE DOWN

I could make fine speeches against you and shake my head at you. But my mouth would encourage you; comfort from my lips would bring you relief.
—Job 16:4b – 5

When Job was sick and had lost everything he owned, his friends argued that God must've let bad things happen to him because he'd sinned. His friends meant well, but all their "fine speeches" did was make them feel smart and important. Their criticism didn't help poor Job at all. Job said that if he were in their position, instead of criticizing them, he'd encourage them.

When your brother loses his lawn mowing job, it's easy to remind him about the house he kept missing. Chances are, he's very aware of that house now. Or if some kid gets his pant leg caught in his bicycle spokes and gets cut up, you may be tempted to explain why it happened. Even if you know why, he's probably figured that one out himself now, and it'd just hurt to remind him of how silly it was.

When your brother or buddy is suffering—even if it's because of something dumb he did—chances are he isn't looking for criticism. He needs encouragement, not discouragement. So before you speak, ask yourself whether what you're about to say will cause him even more pain, or whether it will bring him relief. Then choose the Aspirin Approach: be a painkiller.

Save your fine speeches for when you're running for Governor. Right now you have a buddy in pain who needs some encouragement.

DEVOTION 240

EXTRA MILE FRIENDS

When he was in Rome, he searched hard for me until he found me.
— 2 Timothy 1:17

When Paul was arrested and taken to Rome, his friends didn't know where he'd been taken. They searched for a while, and a guy named Onesiphorus (who'd traveled to Rome from Ephesus) refused to stop searching. He asked around, looked hard and finally located Paul. Onesiphorus had always been a big help in the past and he came through once again when it counted.

Ever tried to help a friend find something he lost and desperately needs, but it doesn't turn up? Ever volunteer to help a pal with his homework—only to find out that he's just not getting it and you need to explain and explain? What do you do? If you don't have the time, that's one thing, but what if you just get tired of helping? Do you jump out the window and run away?

There are acquaintances and there are real friends, the kind who go out of their way to help. Sometimes friends need our help but they know they are asking for a big favor, so many won't ask. It is our job to realize they need help and to take care of them as best we can.

If you can help someone with the whole thing he needs help with, congratulations! You're a true friend. If you can't help with the whole thing, hey, do what you can.

WHEN YOU JUDGE OTHERS

Do not judge, or you too will be judged. For in the same way you judge others, you will be judged.
— Matthew 7:1 – 2

In Jesus' day, the Pharisees were trying too hard to be "righteous." Instead of looking at people's hearts and the good they were trying to do, they criticized people and passed judgment on them for every tiny rule they broke. Yet some Pharisees were guilty of more serious sins than they were jumping all over others about. But those who are not merciful will be judged without mercy themselves (James 2:13).

One problem with judging others (even just in your mind) is that sooner or later—usually sooner—your negative opinions come spilling out of your mouth and you start bad-mouthing that person. Also, often when you judge some kid as "bad" you usually start treating him badly too, because you figure a bad kid doesn't deserve to be treated well.

As Christians we realize that we have received mercy from God. Christ died for our sin instead of us having to pay for it. In the same way we must have mercy in judging others. Are they characterized by the wrong things they do? Or is this action an accident, or out of the ordinary for how they typically act? God desires that we be careful in how we evaluate others, choosing wisely between good and bad people and things.

If you must judge a situation—and sometimes you must—make sure that you judge others with love and kindness. Remember, God judges you the way you judge others.

PLUG INTO GOD'S POWER

"They were all trying to frighten us, thinking, 'Their hands will get too weak for the work, and it will not be completed.'"
—Nehemiah 6:9

The city of Jerusalem had been in ruins for years and now the Jews were rebuilding the walls. The work was so tough they complained, "The strength of the laborers is giving out, and there is so much rubble that we cannot rebuild the wall" (Nehemiah 4:10). With their physical strength failing, only willpower was keeping them going. That's why the Jews' enemies tried to make them afraid and discourage them. If they could shake the Jews' willpower, it'd make them weak.

Ever been faced with a situation like that? You're working hard on a science display and you're already frustrated 'cause it's difficult. Then you find you're missing important pieces and you want to just give up. Or some kid says, "Man, that's real sucky-looking!" You feel discouraged and say, "What's the use?" It's like a vacuum cleaner just came along and sucked the strength right out of you.

Fortunately, the Jews had strong faith and believed that God would protect them—and he did! That gave them courage, which in turn gave them the strength to keep working. It'll work for you too! There'll be times in your life when you're pooped, discouraged, and afraid; and faith will be the only thing keeping you going.

Trust in God. When you're feeling weak, plug into the electrical outlet of God's power. Faith in God and a can-do attitude can turn the tide.

PERSONAL BEST

"Do you not know that in a race all the runners run, but only one gets the prize? Run in such a way as to get the prize."

— 1 Corinthians 9:24

In Roman times, there weren't second- and third-place prizes in athletic competitions. There was only one prize, and only the first guy won it. Guess what it was. He got to wear a crown made from laurel leaves. Sometimes the crown was made from celery or parsley. Um ... okaaay. But when he arrived back in his hometown, the good stuff happened: they had a parade in his honor, they built a statue of him, and he could eat free forever at feasts.

In your race for God, you're not going for a head decoration made of salad. You're looking forward to the good stuff. Now, angels won't build statues of you in heaven, but you will be rewarded beyond your wildest dreams—by doing things like feasting with the coolest guys in the Bible.

So how do you get that first-place prize and all the good stuff that goes with it? How you live your life now really does matter. Focus on pleasing God and doing your personal best. Of course, the Christian life is a long race. You can't just do a one-time good deed. You need to choose to follow Jesus every day. If you love God, you'll go to heaven—no question about that.

IMPRESSED HEARTS

These commandments that I give you today are to be upon your hearts.
Impress them on your children.

—Deuteronomy 6:6 – 7

When God gave the Israelites the Ten Commandments (and all the other commands), he didn't just want his people to know about them. He wanted them to really, really know them. They had to have God's commands so deep in their hearts, they practically memorized them and obeyed them quickly and easily. Then they were supposed to impress them on their kids' hearts.

Speaking of impressing, ever take one of those plastic stamp thingies and press it on play dough? It leaves an impression. That's about how God wants his Word to be in your heart. If your parents or Sunday school teachers make you memorize Bible verses, they're helping get God's Word impressed in your heart. As David said, "I have hidden your word in my heart that I might not sin against you" (Psalm 119:11).

It may sometimes seem like a chore and a bore if your mom and dad constantly teach you guidelines and laws, quote Bible verses to you, and write out lists of your duties. But that's what parents are supposed to do, because doing these things helps you in life. That was your most basic education before you even started going to school, and it'll continue to be a part of your learning curve as long as you're growing up.

When you really know God's commands and they're impressed deep on your heart, you're more likely to live by them. And that's the idea.

PUBLIC, UNITED WORSHIP

In the great assembly I will praise the Lord.
—Psalm 26:12

To assemble means to gather people together—so an assembly is a gathering of people. You know, like an assembly in your school gymnasium. So what's David saying? He's saying that it's great for a group of God's people to get together to glorify God. Back in King David's day, God's people assembled in a big old tent called the sanctuary.

Maybe you're one of those kids who wonder why on earth Christians have to all gather in church and praise God together? Why can't you just praise God alone at home while ... um, playing a video game or building something out of Lego bricks? Well, there's a reason. The Bible actually tells believers to get together, focus on him together, and praise him out loud. The only reason not to would be if you were out of breath and basically dead.

And speaking of Legos ... think about putting together a bunch of little pieces. The scattered pieces may not look like much by themselves, but once you assemble them into one big object, then they look cool. That's why a Christian assembly is cool to God. It looks great to him, and it sounds great. And there is another thing: worshiping God inspires and strengthens Christians.

You may not understand why united worship is important now, but at least respect God and others by not zoning out or talking. When you're in church, do your best to focus on God.

LOTS OF PEOPLE SINGING

Sing to the Lord a new song, his praise in the assembly of the saints.
—Psalm 149:1

K ing David loved worshiping God with music. David was a musician and wrote lots of new hymns called psalms. People started singing his songs in the "assembly of the saints," the gatherings of believers. David even played instruments to praise God! (No, he did not play the electric guitar.) Clearly, David loved music.

Now, some kids today like singing; others don't. Maybe you like listening to music on your iPod or singing retro tunes. But when everybody's in church singing together from the hymnbook or the words projected on the overhead screen, you might wonder, "Why are we doing this? Does God actually like hearing all of us sing?"

Yes, he does. That's why the Bible says for believers to sing together. It can be a powerful experience. Think about the theme song from your favorite TV show. What if the creator of the show came to town, and you and a hundred other kids were all belting out that song? That'd be fun, huh? Well, the Creator of the universe is in church, so sing wholeheartedly for him too.

Whether your church is singing an old hymn like "Amazing Grace" or a new song someone just wrote, join in. You may not always feel like singing, but God is always worthy of praise.

AVOIDING THE DARK SIDE

The sacrifices of pagans are offered to demons, not to God, and I do not want you to be participants with demons.

—1 Corinthians 10:20

Back in Roman days, pagans (idol worshipers) sacrificed animals to the idols of their gods and then ate the meat of the sacrifice. It was part of their pagan worship. Most people couldn't afford meat often, so this was a special reward for worshiping Hercules or the other gods. Often they made the event into a feast and invited their friends—including Christian friends. Paul warned Christian believers not to eat that meat. It was like taking part in idol worship.

This principle applies today too. Not that you're going to be tempted to eat a Hercules steak or food dedicated to demons. Think of other stuff that might tempt you. For example, a non-Christian friend may invite you to his house after school to play an adults-only video game. Now, that game may be exciting to play, but it's so evil that it will seriously mess up your mind. Don't participate in it.

The same principle applies to music, videos, comic books, or whatever. There are good videos, good music, and good comic books, but if something is dark and demonic—or if it glorifies violence—then steer clear of it. It will influence you in the wrong direction. Besides, it'll end up giving you nightmares.

There are enough clean books, games, and movies available that it should be pretty easy to find good, fun stuff to do. So stay away from the dark side.

GOD - ALWAYS MERCIFUL AND LOVING

Who is a God like you, who pardons sin and forgives the transgression....
You do not stay angry forever but delight to show mercy.

—Micah 7:18

Micah was a prophet of God, and he lived back when the tough Law of Moses was the law of the land. This was long before Jesus was born. Yet when Micah described God, he didn't talk about an angry God who loved to judge people when they goofed up. Micah said that God would rather forgive sin; he said God loved to show mercy.

Sometimes you might wonder, "Why was God mean and angry in the olden days, yet so loving and kind and forgiving after Jesus came?" Or maybe you've heard unbelievers ask, "Why did God destroy cities and judge nations in the past, yet when Jesus came along he hugged little children and told us to love our enemies?" Why the change?

No change. God hasn't changed. God judged nations in the past because they rebelled against him, persecuted God's people, and did other bad things. And the news is: God still judges nations today. But God is not only into judgment and justice, he's also big on love. Even back in the olden days, he delighted in forgiveness.

God was forgiving and loving and merciful in the past, and he still is today. God said, "I the Lord do not change" (Malachi 3:6). God has always wanted to forgive.

FEAR CAN BE A GOOD THING

The fear of the Lord is pure, enduring forever.
—Psalm 19:9

T he Bible often tells us to fear God. You may ask, "If God is love, why should I fear him? Isn't he on my side?" Yes, he is. But fear is sometimes a good thing. True, a lot of fear is just worry and fretting—like being afraid of the dentist or fearing that World War III will start. But some fear is worthwhile. Since the fear of the Lord is pure, you know it's a good thing.

You should be afraid of some things. For example, if you're afraid to climb up on top of some steel tower during a thunderstorm and get deliberately struck by a billion volts of lightning, that's a good fear. It shows that you're thinking. It shows that you're aware of the power of a lightning bolt and how badly it can fry your molecules. You respect it. That's what the "fear of the Lord" is about: being in awe of God's power.

"Yeah," you say, "but God is love. Lightning is not love." True, but who invented lightning? God. In his Narnia books, C. S. Lewis tells readers that the lion Aslan "is not a tame lion." Aslan can be gentle, but he's also powerful and dangerous. God is like that. You don't mess around with him. He's not a jolly, roly-poly Santa Claus. He's God.

The fear of the Lord is not a bad thing. It's a positive thing. It's pure. When you begin to fear God, it shows you've started to understand who God is and how powerful he is.

TRUTH VERSUS MYTH

They will gather around them a great number of teachers to say what their itching ears want to hear. They will turn their ears away from the truth and turn aside to myths.

— 2 Timothy 4:3 – 4

In Paul's day, some intellectual people liked the idea of a wise teacher named Jesus, but they freaked when Paul said that Jesus saved us by dying for our sins and then coming back to life. To them, that was too easy. They rejected the gospel and began inventing all kinds of complicated myths about Jesus.

Today too, many people are "itchy" for something different. When their ears start itching like crazy, they figure the best way to scratch them is to stuff them full of interesting, bizarre theories. So they gather busloads of teachers and go gaga over old false books like the Gospel of Judas. (According to that so-called gospel, Judas was a hero for betraying Jesus!)

If you think those teachers with their myths are out to lunch, you've got that one right! The simple truth beats mixed-up myths any day. So how do you avoid swallowing interesting lies? By knowing what the Bible actually says about Jesus and by living for the truth. That way, when strange Bible teachers come along, your ears won't be itchy for their lies.

These days, lots of people turn their ears away from the truth because they don't want to hear it. Don't you do that. Read your Bible and listen to godly teachers.

DEAD FRED AND MADAME MAMBA

When men tell you to consult mediums and spiritists, who whisper and mutter, should not a people inquire of their God? Why consult the dead on behalf of the living?
—Isaiah 8:19

A medium is a person who claims she can give you supernatural wisdom because the departed spirit of your dead uncle Fred just entered her and possessed her and is talking through her mouth. Spooky, huh? A spiritist is anyone who claims to have the power to talk to spirits of the dead. The Bible warns against this weirdness.

You may have heard of people who phone mediums with names like the Mysterious Madame Mamba. Why do they do it? Well, they have so little faith in God that they're not content to pray to him and trust him with their future. So they hope old Uncle Fred's spirit is floating around with nothing better to do than advise them on who to fall in love with, how to spend their money, etc.

Don't do it. Madame Mambas are faking it. Yup, they're lying. Uncle Fred is either in heaven or the other place. He's not popping into the brain of some medium. Even if Uncle Fred were around, he wouldn't have any inside scoop.

Why talk to the dead? What do the dead know? You're a lot smarter and a lot better off praying and asking God and reading the Bible to find answers.

PRACTICE MAKES PERFECT

"Among all these soldiers there were seven hundred chosen men . . .
each of whom could sling a stone at a hair and not miss."
—Judges 20:15

When the seven hundred slingers from the tribe of Benjamin trotted out to battle, the guys coming at 'em had swords, spears, and bows. It really wasn't a fair fight. Bows had a pitiful range of only three hundred feet, but a slinger could drop you dead with a man-made meteorite from six hundred feet away. And Benjamite slingers? Ho! These guys were so good, they could nail a single hair! Imagine if that hair was on your head.

It takes years of slinging to get that kind of range and accuracy. These guys had natural ability, sure, but without practice, they'd never have been that good. Benjy's boys whipped rocks over and over again until they hit a hair every time. It's the same today, whether you're kicking a soccer ball or playing Ping-Pong and trying to ping faster than the other guy can pong. You've got to do it over and over until it becomes second nature.

You can apply this to your walk with God too. Get in the habit of doing the right thing so that when a temptation comes along, you automatically do what's right. When some little devil ambushes your mind and tries to get you to do the wrong thing, your defenses go up lightning quick and you block his attack.

Practice makes perfect. Well, maybe not perfect, but real good. (We don't need to split hairs over this.) So keep at it. Practice.

WOMEN ON THE FRONTLINES

"Greet Priscilla and Aquila, my fellow workers in Christ Jesus. They risked their lives for me."

—Romans 16:3 – 4

Priscilla and Aquila were Paul's pals, and this husband-wife team worked hard to help him preach the gospel. In fact, they did dangerous, secret-agent-type stuff and risked their lives to help him. Now, have you noticed that in the Old Testament the guys all have names, but often their wives' names aren't mentioned? Yet every time Priscilla and hubby Aquila are mentioned, she's not just named, but named first. Why? No one really knows why. All we know is that Priscilla was one famous, hard-working, gutsy gal.

If you read through the New Testament, you see how many outstanding women there were. Several women even traveled with Jesus and his disciples around Israel. And take a look around next time you're in church. Notice how many women and girls there are? And lots of women are pastors, Sunday school teachers, and missionaries. Etc... Whoa! Women are on the frontlines, doing a lot for God's Kingdom!

God looks at people's hearts. He's interested in whether you love him and are willing to serve him. You're sitting in church enjoying the ride, but a whole lot of somebodies are working hard behind the scenes to keep things happening. A lot of those somebodies are women.

Women are very important to God. If you still have the idea that girls aren't as cool as guys, it's time to kick that thought out of your head.

HORSE-SIZED JOBS

"If you have raced with men on foot and they have worn you out, how can you compete with horses?"
—Jeremiah 12:5

That is the question, isn't it? If you think track-and-field's tough this year, wait till next year when it's all field and you're up against horses. Seriously though … the prophet Jeremiah was complaining that it wasn't fair that he had it so tough while bad men had lives of ease. God basically told Jeremiah to get ready, "You think it's tough now? Wait till warhorses come. The bad guys you think have it so good will be trampled and good guys like you will be on the run."

Maybe you have to drag the trash cans out to the curb every Thursday. Maybe your mom makes you clean all the Lego bricks off your floor with a snow shovel once a week. Just wait until you have to work eight hours a day at a job you're not crazy about. You think you have a lot of homework now? Wait till you're in college and you have hours of homework every night.

Come to think of it, you have things pretty easy right now. The horse-sized jobs and studies haven't even showed up yet, so don't let the small stuff wear you out. Besides, if you have a can-do attitude now, that same can-do attitude will be there to help you when you're older and things are tougher.

If you think things are too tough, don't just horse around. Instead, remember Philippians 4:13: "I can do everything through him who gives me strength."

WHEN FRIENDS DESERT YOU

You know that everyone in the province of Asia has deserted me, including Phygelus and Hermogenes.
—2 Timothy 1:15

The apostle Paul was arrested for being a leader of the Christians and soon he sat in a small, cold prison in Rome. That was bad enough. But what really hurt was when he learned that the Christians in the Roman province of Asia had turned against him. Paul had led these people to the Lord and he'd taught and trained them for years, but now they had turned against him. Talk about rejection!

It's hard when friends desert you—especially if you've been friends for a long time, you've done lots of fun stuff together, and you have good memories of them. Then suddenly they find "cooler" friends and ditch you. Or maybe someone starts a rumor about you, or tells a story about something dumb or embarrassing that you did, and suddenly your friends are gone.

It hurts when that happens. Paul doesn't get into detail about how he felt, but you know he was suffering. Jesus himself was rejected and told us that there'd be times when that would happen to us too. Times like that show you who your true friends are—the kind who stand by you no matter what—and God is your truest friend of all. He says, "Never will I leave you. Never will I forsake you" (Hebrews 13:5).

Paul had lost a lot of friends in Asia, but true friends like Timothy stayed close to him, and most important of all, God never abandoned him.

WHEN OTHERS ARE DOWN

You should not look down on your brother in the day of his misfortune.
—Obadiah 12

The Edomites were related to the people of Judah, so when the Babylonians attacked Judah, burned their cities and stole all their belongings, the Edomites should've had compassion. But they stood aloof and did nothing. God noticed the Edomites' attitude and what he saw made him decide to punish them.

When some kid suffers misfortune (something bad happens, he loses something, is hurt or is being punished) it can be soooo tempting to stand back and say smugly, "Serves him right. Let him stew in his own juice." It's a natural reaction. Maybe you feel some kid is a real jerk and deserves it. Maybe you even feel like rejoicing that he "got what he had coming."

The thing is that even when something bad is happening to someone else, God is also watching you to see what you do. Will you show love and mercy or will you kick him when he's down? Remember the Good Samaritan? The Samaritans were enemies of the Jews, but when a Samaritan saw a beat-up, wounded Jew lying beside the road, he did whatever he could to help.

Don't stand back and smirk when misfortune hits some kid that you don't like. Reach out and help if you can.

FIGHTING BEASTS OR BEASTLY FEASTS

If I fought wild beasts in Ephesus for merely human reasons, what have I gained? If the dead are not raised, "Let us eat and drink, for tomorrow we die."
—1 Corinthians 15:32

In Roman days, criminals were thrown to the lions in the arena. Sometimes the guys were given weapons to give them a fighting chance. Paul talked about the danger he had faced for the sake of the Gospel, saying it was like he had fought wild beasts. The Bible doesn't say Paul got into an arena to fight actual lions with a sword and a net. This verse is symbolic.

Paul didn't want to do that major fighting for no reason. He was doing it because he understood resurrection through Christ. If there is nothing for us after death—no reward for doing good, no punishment for doing bad—then why try to do good? What's the point in fighting temptation and bad habits? You might as well sit around eating pizza and drinking soda pop all day. If there is no purpose to life, why not live like a slob, never clean your room, and never lift a finger to help? A lot of people think that way.

They're wrong. The Bible puts us on notice that every human being who has ever lived on this planet will be raised from the dead one day and rewarded or punished for how they lived. If you love God and believe in Jesus, you'll be raised to everlasting life. That's true, but guess what? You'll also be rewarded in heaven for how well you obeyed God.

It's worth it to battle wild beasts—temptations and problems—to overcome beastly bad habits. So get up and help others. God will reward you for it!

PUTTING THE BEST THINGS FIRST

I consider everything a loss compared to the surpassing greatness of knowing Christ Jesus my Lord. . . . I consider them rubbish.

—Philippians 3:8

As a kid, the apostle Paul received a top education in a Greek school. He studied poets and philosophers. As a young man, he studied under the top religious teachers in Israel. Paul tried to be the best he could be by obeying every tiny religious rule. But after Jesus saved him, he realized that compared to knowing Jesus, all his accomplishments weren't worth much. He considered them rubbish.

When you are focused on a goal, such as a race or a homework assignment, you don't carry a big old black plastic bag of rubbish with you, do you? No. You drop the garbage off at the curb. And even if other good, cool stuff in your life isn't garbage, it can distract you from getting important stuff done. There is a time for computer games, TV, and hanging out with friends. They are all good and fun activities, but you can't do them while you're trying to play soccer or study for a test. Then they're dead weight, like garbage.

Enjoy life. Enjoy the fun and games. But remember, the main purpose of a Christian is to know God and his Son, Jesus. Don't let anything get in the way of that.

LION ON THE LOOSE

Be self-controlled and alert. Your enemy the devil prowls around like a roaring lion, looking for someone to devour. Resist him, standing firm in the faith.
—1 Peter 5:8–9

The Bible warns, "Be alert!" In other words, watch out, because the devil is as fierce and as dangerous as a man-eating lion on the loose. He's looking for his next lunch. Don't let him ambush you. So what do you do when he attacks? Run? No. Even though he roars to scare you, stand firm. "Resist the devil, and he will flee from you" (James 4:7).

One of the devil's favorite tricks is to ambush you with temptation. But you can control yourself. It helps to decide ahead of time that you won't give in to temptation. Then you won't be caught off guard. Now, Jesus will protect you if you stay close to him. He will help you be strong so you can stand with your decisions.

Stand firm in your faith, resist temptation, resist the devil, and he will flee from you. And remember, it's not like you're so strong that you can resist the devil on your own. No, when you resist the devil's temptations, it is because he is fleeing from Jesus, who is inside you. It's Jesus who makes the devil afraid. Having Jesus close to you is like having a powerful security guard watching out for you. The devil may still be growling as he flees, but he will flee.

Keep on guard for the devil's attacks. If he does attack, stand firm and resist him. You have the authority of Jesus to resist the devil. Do it, and he'll turn tail and run!

DEVOTION 260

WHY GOD GAVE PROPHECIES

These things happened so that the scripture would be fulfilled: "Not one of his bones will be broken," and, as another scripture says, "They will look on the one they have pierced"
—John 19:36–37

Hundreds of years before Jesus was born, God gave his prophets many prophecies about Jesus—and those things came to pass. For example, you know that Jesus was crucified, right? Now, when the Romans wanted a crucified man to die quickly, they broke his legs. But since Jesus was already dead, they didn't break his bones. Instead, they pierced his side with a spear. Two prophecies fulfilled at once!

So what does this mean to you? Well, it shows that God was thinking of you when he wrote the Bible. He knew you'd have questions like, "What proof is there that God exists? Is Jesus really who he said he was?" So right when the Bible was being written—centuries before Jesus was even born—God included some prophecies to help convince curious kids like you.

There's more: King David wrote Psalm 22 a thousand years before Jesus' birth—back before people even practiced crucifixion—yet that prophetic psalm perfectly describes what happened to Jesus when he was on the cross, with his arms being pulled out of joint. (See Matthew 27:32–50.) And if you really want your brain boggled, read Isaiah chapter 53. It was written six hundred years before Jesus, yet explains that he would die to forgive our sins.

Fulfilled Bible prophecies are proof that God exists and that Jesus is the Savior of the world. And there are lots of these fulfilled prophecies in the Bible!

FANTASTIC OUTER SPACE

When I consider your heavens ... the moon and the stars, which you have set in place, what is man that you are mindful of him, the son of man that you care for him?

—Psalm 8:3 – 4

King David, who wrote this psalm, must've loved to climb up on his flat palace roof at night and look up at the moon and the zillion stars stretched out over Jerusalem. Maybe he took his kids up with him, lay on his back, and pointed out the planets and constellations. David was in awe. When he thought about how vast the universe was, he was amazed that God cared so much for people here on earth.

Think about it: David didn't even know a hundredth of what we know today! Back then people only had their eyeballs. Today we have telescopes staring into distant galaxies. We have satellites shooting past the moons of Jupiter taking snapshots of their ice canyons. We can study photos of dust storms ripping across the deserts of Mars and download color photos of stars exploding.

The miracle is that even with all the endless galaxies stuffed with mysterious stars stretching out to infinity, God cares for us! What is it about people that God's mind is full of us? Why can't he just stop thinking about us? Well, he loves us, that's why! And why? People are his special creation.

It's awesome to stare out into space at the universe that God created, but it's even more awesome to realize how much he cares for you.

DEVOTION 262

UNDERSTANDING AND TRUSTING

Trust in the Lord with all your heart and lean not on your own understanding.
— Proverbs 3:5

Does God think that understanding stuff is important? Oh, yeah! The Bible says that no matter how much it costs, get knowledge and get understanding. Getting knowledge is what God made a busy brain for. God also wants you to use that knowledge. But here the Bible says to "lean not on your own understanding," but lean on God and trust him instead. Huh?

Some people misunderstand this verse and think it means they should just drift through life without thinking things through or preparing or asking important questions:

"Have you studied for tomorrow's science test?"

"No, I don't wanna lean on my own understanding."

"Do you understand how to fix your bike?"

"No, God must not want me to ride it."

So what does this verse mean? When God has already given you clear instructions—like don't steal—then you gotta trust him. Don't say, "No, God's way won't work in this situation." Or when God promises, "Call to me and I will answer you" (Jeremiah 33:3), then trust that he'll do that. Don't try to solve an unsolvable mess alone. But yes, use your brain. Yes, think. Yes, plan. But most of all, trust God with your whole heart.

IN IT FOR THE LONG HAUL

"Let us throw off everything that hinders and the sin that so easily entangles, and let us run with perseverance the race marked out for us."
—Hebrews 12:1

This verse compares Christian life to running a race—a long race that is. In fact, it's such a long race that it'll take your whole life to run it. It's not like a hundred-meter sprint to glory. It's more like the Boston Marathon. You wouldn't expect to win that race if you carried a TV on your back, right? So throw off every weight that hinders you.

Paul also said, "I do not run like a man running aimlessly" (1 Corinthians 9:26). It's not like you're going wild, scrambling through a corn maze, and trying to figure out where the path is. In this race the path is marked out for us. The Bible marks the boundary lines clearly—real clearly. But the race is long, so you need to persevere (per-se-veer). That means to keep at something, stick to it, and not give up.

How do you persevere? By keeping your eyes focused on Jesus. Jesus is standing at the finish line, waiting to give you the prize. Also remember that Jesus ran this race already and didn't let anything stop him. Now he's sending his Spirit to help you—so don't give up!

Keep your eyes focused on Jesus—keep your eyes on the prize—and that'll give you the perseverance you need to run the race.

YOU KNOW YOU'RE GOOD

"As long as he sought the Lord, God gave him success. But after Uzziah became powerful, his pride led to his downfall."

—2 Chronicles 26:5, 16

King Uzziah was a terrific warrior! He defeated the Philistines and the Arabs, and even the Egyptians sat up and paid attention. Uzziah's army was a powerful force. He fortified cities and had engineers invent new weapons. He figured he was so great that he could break God's law. WHAM! Next thing you know this warrior king had leprosy, and all he ruled was the one house he lived in.

If you're really good at some sport and you know you're good, fine. If kids come up to you and tell you how good you are, fine. But you're in trouble when you start to lap it all up, 'cause pride does weird stuff to people's heads. Pride makes you think that the rules that apply to other humans don't apply to you—after all, you're special.

Being powerful is not the problem. Getting proud about being powerful is the problem, so steer clear of thinking you're bigger than life. Uzziah was such a fantastic king, that it was pretty sad to watch him go down. It didn't have to happen. He could've stayed powerful if only he'd stayed humble. Want to stay on your feet? Don't get a big head.

BRAND-NAME BLUES

"Why do you worry about clothes? For the pagans run after all these things, and your heavenly Father knows that you need them."
— Matthew 6:28, 32

Back in Jesus' day—just like today—a lot of guys were worried about how they looked. You wouldn't think so, considering that they walked around in robes or wore togas that basically looked like short skirts. But hey, they had their styles and we have ours. They went for togas and sandals; we go for blue jeans and T-shirts.

But seriously, "worry about clothes"? Most boys have to be told to be more concerned. They don't give a rip how they look—and as a result, it's their clothes that get ripped. But ever complain that you don't have brand-name runners? Hey dude, you're gettin' into clothes. If you can get the brand name you want, go for it. But if you can't get them and can't bear to face your friends, you're worrying about clothes ... and running after runners.

Also, as you get older and become interested in girls, you'll find that girls care a lot about how guys look. That makes guys image-conscious reeaaal quick. Just don't get into it so much that you spend all your clothing allowance following fads.

The bottom line is: don't get anxious about how you look. What's in your heart is more important than what's wrapped around your outside.

KIDLOCK!

"Jerusalem will be called the city of truth . . . the city streets will be filled with boys and girls playing there."

—Zechariah 8:3, 5

Jerusalem was in ruins. The Babylonians had battered the walls and burned the buildings. They took the Jews away and enslaved them for seventy years. Finally the Jews were set free and sent back home, but "home" was a wreck. Jerusalem was so full of rubble and heaps of stones that no one could live there. But God said that people would live there once again. And get this! One of the biggest signs of God's blessing was that the city streets would be full of boys and girls playing.

Back then, like now, kids played lots of group sports—kicking balls, playing tag, racing, etc. Since they didn't have any parks or soccer fields, they played in the streets. They literally filled the streets! A traffic jam is called gridlock, but this was kidlock! These days there are public swimming pools, skating rinks, baseball fields, and other safe places to play. Some kids still play street hockey out on the pavement—on the side streets, that is.

It's fine to play alone, but God knew that it's a whole lot more fun when you play group sports. You'll make more friends and get a lot more exercise. Playing group games means getting out and moving your bod, not just sitting around playing computer games, taking cartoon characters through the levels.

Want to make your city come alive? Want to be living proof that God is blessing the place? Get out and play!

PUTTING YOUR HEART INTO IT

Serve wholeheartedly, as if you were serving the Lord, not men, because you know that the Lord will reward everyone for whatever good he does, whether he is slave or free.

—Ephesians 6:7 – 8

In Roman times, millions of people were slaves, and many of them became Christians. Paul advised them that if they could be set free to go for it, but if they couldn't, that God would still reward them for whatever good they did. It was great if their employers noticed and rewarded them, but even if not, God would reward them.

Have your parents ever asked you to do a chore like (gag) cleaning the cat's litter box, or helping clean the garage or the whole house, and you just didn't feel like doing it? Or ever just felt just plain lazy and did as little as you could to get by?

If you have that attitude you'll miss out on huge rewards—not necessarily from your parents, but from God. Your parents may not be able to reward you for each thing you do, but God sees everything. Now don't misread this and think that God will give you wealth or success because of your good deeds. The Bible says that good and bad things come to both saints and sinners. You cannot earn God's love or blessings. But he does promise to reward those who believe in him when they get to Heaven.

No matter who you're working for, put your whole heart into the job as if you were doing it for God himself, not just some person.

REPORTING WRONGDOING

What you are doing is not right.... Give back to them immediately their fields, vineyards, olive groves and houses.

—Nehemiah 5:9, 11

There was a famine in Judea, so the poor people's land didn't produce enough food. But they still had to pay taxes. When they borrowed money for taxes and food, some rich people took advantage of them. They lent them money, sure, but charged interest—which they weren't supposed to do. When the poor couldn't pay them back, the rich took their lands and their houses. The poor told the governor, Nehemiah, and he dealt with the situation.

Often, if a bully forces you to give him money, takes your lunch or copies your homework, he'll also warn you not to tell an adult. Or he'll say that if you tell on him, that you're a sissy or a tattletale. He only says those things because he knows that he's in the wrong and he's afraid of getting caught—because then he'll get in trouble. So what do you do?

Do like the poor people did when the rich ones were oppressing them: since they couldn't get the rich to stop taking their belongings, they reported them to the governor. When kids are making your life miserable, don't put up with it. Tell a parent, a teacher, or whichever adult is in charge.

There are lots of situations in life that you can't change, but you do have rights, and when your things are being taken away, tell an authority who can make things right.

WHEN ADVICE ISN'T APPRECIATED

Do not throw your pearls to pigs. If you do, they may trample them under their feet, and then turn and tear you to pieces.

—Matthew 7:6

Jesus taught his disciples to speak the truth and proclaim the message boldly, but he also advised them to use wisdom and not to waste their words—which he compared to precious pearls—on unreceptive or ignorant people. Some people simply don't want to hear the gospel, don't want to be told that they should change, and just get mad at those who tell them the truth.

Sometimes you see some kid doing bad stuff and know you should say something—so you do. But what if he threatens to pound you if you don't stop giving him advice? Should you keep on talking, or do you turn off the tap? That's not easy if you're hot under the collar and really want to give the guy a piece of your mind. And you don't always have a message from God, right? Sometimes the kid's just doing something that bugs you.

Don't waste your words on the ignorant. Not only will they resent what you say, but they might actually get physical about it. So if you're giving unwanted advice or telling someone off, pick up on the signals when your advice isn't wanted, know when to stop, and avoid getting your nose punched.

You have to tell people the truth. But you also need to have common sense and stop talking when it's clear that people really, really don't want to listen.

DEVOTION 270

GIVING GENEROUSLY TO GOD

Each man should give what he has decided in his heart to give, not reluctantly or under compulsion, for God loves a cheerful giver.
— 2 Corinthians 9:7

Giving is an important part of being a Christian. Jesus taught that his followers should give money to help the poor. The early disciples knew that they should give to help other Christians who were in need. Also, Christians should support pastors and missionaries. "The Lord has commanded that those who preach the Gospel should receive their living from the Gospel" (1 Corinthians 9:14).

In most churches, the offering basket is passed down the aisle every Sunday. Maybe it has sailed past you week after week and you haven't paid much attention to it. (Ho-hum. Just a basket full of holy money.) But think about it: There are lots of needs in your church, and taking care of these needs costs money. Who pays for them? That's where you come in.

When you give to your church, you're helping the poor and helping your pastor and missionaries preach the gospel. Decide in your heart what you think you can afford to give and what you feel God wants you to give. Really think and pray about it. Don't give "under compulsion," meaning don't just give because you feel forced to. Instead, be generous and happy about giving.

Think about what you should give, decide on an amount, and then stick to your decision. Remember, God loves it when you give cheerfully! Your cheerfulness is part of the gift you give.

BUMPED OFF THE PATH

You were running a good race. Who cut in on you and kept you from obeying the truth?

—Galatians 5:7

Two thousand years ago, Paul traveled to the Roman province of Galatia and preached to the Galatians that faith in Jesus—faith and nothing else—saved them. The Galatians believed this, but later some teachers persuaded them that faith wasn't enough; they also had to keep all the complicated laws of Moses. Paul was upset. The Galatians had been running a good race. Now they were stumbling off track.

Ever been running and have someone cut in front of you, forcing you to slow down and lose your stride? Next thing you know you're falling behind. Or ever been riding downtown with your mom and some driver cuts in front of her without signaling? She hits the brakes, lays about twenty feet of rubber, and you make a nose-dent in the seat in front of you. Someone just cut in on you.

Living the Christian life is like running a race. But often when you're flying along, making good time, the devil sends one of his messengers to cut in on you. He wants to bump you so you'll run off the path. He sends along a temptation to distract you or some weird teaching to trip you up and slow you down. Watch out. Don't get ambushed.

Keep running the good race. Obey God's truth and don't let anyone cut in on you. Don't even listen to weird stuff that'll get you off track from the truth.

SERVING GOD FOR REAL

"If God will be with me and will watch over me on this journey I am taking and will give me food to eat and clothes to wear ... then the Lord will be my God."
—Genesis 28:20 – 21

Jacob had lived at home long after he had become an adult, eating his parents' food, wearing the clothes they provided, and coasting along on his dad's faith. Jacob knew about God, sure, but he'd never really depended on God—never given his heart to him. Now he was on his own and in trouble, so he began praying. He realized he needed a relationship with God.

A lot of kids raised in Christian homes are like that. They know all about God and they've heard the Bible stories, but until they face life's tests, they never really devote themselves to God. Then they get in a situation that's bigger than they are. They have to handle things without mom or dad coming to the rescue, and they start taking God seriously.

After a while Jacob realized that God really was looking out for him. Then he began praying to God more and asking for help with his problems. And God came through every time! See, God loves it when we pray to him, whether we're in desperate situations or not. He wants you to realize that he really is God and that he has the power to take care of you.

God wants to look out for you, so start a relationship with him. Don't wait till you're in a tough situation to start praying. Pray today.

HAVING A MEAL WITH JESUS

I stand at the door and knock. If anyone hears my voice and opens the door, I will come in and eat with him, and he with me.

—Revelation 3:20

When people talk about sharing a meal, in Bible times as well as today, it has a deep meaning. It means being good friends, spending time with people, and talking with them.

It's important to pick good friends. You don't just invite anyone over to your house, right? And you certainly don't let just anyone in your room—just your best friends. And Jesus wants to be your best friend. Actually, more like a big brother. Not the kind who pounds on you, but the kind who always looks out for you.

By the way, Jesus isn't really standing knocking at your bedroom door. This verse is talking about the door to your heart—your whole life. And he's not just coming for a visit. He wants to come in and live with you from now on. The apostle Paul said, "I pray that ... Christ may dwell in your hearts through faith" (Ephesians 3:16–17). But you need to invite him into your life.

Jesus wants to always be part of your life, be close to you, and help you and give you peace. So listen to his knocking and let him in.

GOD IS YOUR DAD

Because you are sons, God sent the Spirit of his Son into our hearts, the Spirit who calls out, "Abba, Father"

—Galatians 4:6

Jesus is God's Son. We are not God's sons and daughters by birth. But when you believe in Jesus and ask him to come into your life, God adopts you and makes you his child. He sends the Spirit of his Son, Jesus, to live in your heart. Now, maybe it doesn't come naturally to you to think of God as your dad, but it's perfectly natural for Jesus, so his Spirit in you calls out, "Abba, Father!"

When you talk to your dad, do you normally call him "Father"? Probably not. Chances are you call him dad. Well, that's what Abba means. Abba isn't an English word, as you probably guessed. It's an ancient Aramaic word that means "Dad." The whole idea is that you can have a close, warm relationship with God, just like with a dad.

Jesus talked about this once. He told a bunch of dads one day: "Which of you, if his son asks for bread, will give him a stone? If you ... know how to give good gifts to your children, how much more will your Father in heaven give good gifts to those who ask him!" (Matthew 7:9–11). God is your dad. He loves you and wants the best for you.

Do you want a close relationship with God? Do you want him to adopt you as one of his own kids? Then believe in Jesus, and you'll be one of God's adopted children too!

MAKING SOME PRIVATE SPACE

Jesus did not want anyone to know where they were, because he was teaching his disciples.
—Mark 9:30–31

Jesus loved people, but sometimes crowds practically mobbed him. Talk about no privacy! One time Jesus and his disciples were in a house trying to have a meal, but such a large crowd pushed in around them that they weren't able to eat (Mark 3:20). Imagine being so squeezed you can't get your fork to your mouth! You can't live like that. So when Jesus wanted to teach his followers, they had to slip off to some quiet place.

Now, you probably don't have to escape into the Mojave Desert to read your Bible or pray. Hopefully a sign on your bedroom door will give you the space you need. But the point is you do need quiet space. And you can be "mobbed" by outside noise even in your bedroom if music is playing or if some virtual pet is beeping to be fed.

The word disciple means "someone who follows the Master's teaching." Hopefully, you're trying to do that. And the news is Jesus still teaches his followers today. How does he do that? As you read God's Word, he teaches you and shows you amazing stuff. And when you pray, the Holy Spirit reminds you of what you've read and leads you in the right direction.

Take a break! Get away from all the cartoons and noise and distractions. Let Jesus teach you. Jesus said, "Learn from me … and you will find rest for your souls" (Matthew 11:29).

BE STRONG AND TAKE HEART

"My strength fails because of my affliction."
— Psalm 31:10

David was the best king Israel ever had. He was strong, handsome, and crazy about God. He had a huge kingdom and a palace with tons of gold in the basement. David's enemies bowed down and brought him gifts. Then David made some classic mistakes. His friends turned on him, and his enemies began plotting against him. Dave was emotionally drained. On top of all this, he began having health problems.

Ever been so sick with fever or stomach flu that you were physically wasted? Or even if you still had strength, you couldn't use it 'cause every time you exerted yourself you felt like vomiting? That's how David felt. And having friends badmouth him made him even weaker. David didn't even want to get out of bed. Maybe you've felt that way when a friend turned on you. It's like you're actually sick.

You can't control how friends act, but you can put a lid on germs by keeping clean in the first place. And if you're sick, work on getting better. That means if your mom comes along with a huge tablespoon of foul-tasting medicine and says, "Open up," open up. Another thing, stay focused on the good stuff that's happening, not the bad stuff. You'll feel better mentally and physically.

By the end of this same Psalm, Dave figured out the solution. As discouraged and sick as he was, he said, "Be strong and take heart, all you who hope in the Lord" (Psalm 31:24).

DON'T FALL TWICE

"When he was sound asleep, he fell to the ground from the third story and was picked up dead."
—Acts 20:9

The apostle Paul was in an upper room speaking, and this kid named Eutychus (You-tea-kus) got the bright idea of sitting on the open windowsill—three stories up. He probably figured that if he breathed some cool, fresh air it'd keep him awake. Nice try. Euty was an accident looking for a place to happen. He nodded off. Down he fell and—WHAM!—he was dead. (The fortunate news: Paul prayed for him and he came back to life.)

Lots of accidents happen when you're careless. Here are some scenarios: you don't tie your shoelaces and they get tangled in your bicycle spokes; you're racing through the house to get away from your sister and you slam into your grandma; you step on the marbles you left on the floor and down you go. Even adults get careless and cause accidents.

You can avoid most accidents by obeying commonsense rules—tie your shoes, don't run in the house, and pick up your toys. Sometimes accidents are not serious—you bump your elbow but you're okay. But some accidents leave you in pain and badly injured. So while you're having your fun, remember the rules. Play it safe.

CUTTING CORNERS

"He is like a man building a house, who dug down deep and laid the foundation on rock."
—Luke 6:48

Jesus talked about two men building houses. The first man dug down deep till he struck rock then laid bricks on that. His house had a solid foundation. Guy Two cut corners. Maybe he was in a hurry to go out and play, or maybe he was just lazy, but—bottom line—doing a good job wasn't a high priority. He plopped his bricks right down on the sand. How smart was that? The rains and floods showed up and had fun kicking in his little sand castle.

Do you cut corners? Like, when your dad asks you to dig the dandelions out of the lawn, do you go after the roots or do you leave 'em in so that they pop up again next year? When you put your plate in the dishwasher, do you wipe the spaghetti off first? When you clean out the bird's cage, do you really clean it or just throw new newspaper on top of the soggy ones?

It takes time to do a good job on your homework or chores, and you'll probably be reeaaal tempted to do a quick job so you can run out and play. Nuh-uh. Put in that little bit of extra time to do the job right. That way you don't end up redoing the job later.

Don't be a sandman and cut corners. Whatever you do, do it carefully and well. Be like the guy who put in a solid foundation.

HELPING JESUS

I tell you the truth, whatever you did for one of the least of these brothers of mine, you did for me.

—Matthew 25:40

When Jesus returns he will reward those who have done good, praising them for feeding him when he was hungry, for giving him clothing when he needed it, for caring for him when he was sick and for visiting him when he was in jail. People will ask, "When did I do those things for you?" Jesus will reply that whatever we did for anyone who believes in him we did for him.

Now, if you could travel back in time to Israel and you were sitting down eating lunch and you saw Jesus walking by, and he was hungry, would you share your lunch with him? Sure you would! Or if you came by his camp by night when Jesus and his disciples were sleeping under the olive trees, and Jesus was cold, would you loan him your sleeping bag?

Sure, you'd do these things for Jesus. You'd jump at the opportunity. Well, you do have the opportunity. No, Jesus isn't sleeping under the trees anymore, but when you donate your unused clothes to charity or give food to a soup kitchen or visit a sick friend in the hospital, it's the same as doing it for Jesus himself.

If Jesus loves some kid enough to send his Holy Spirit to live in his heart, then he surely wants you to be kind to him, even if he's the un-coolest kid you know.

DON'T FORSAKE FRIENDS

The king asked, "Is there no one still left in the house of Saul to whom I can show God's kindness?"

—2 Samuel 9:3

Some years after King David had gained the throne of Israel, he was reflecting on his predecessor Saul and Saul's son—and David's best friend—Jonathan. David was wondering if there was anyone left of Saul's family that he could show kindness to as a way of honoring his friend's memory. David would probably have given anything to be able to see his old friend, Jonathan, again.

Sometimes you and your friends grow apart because your interests change. Or maybe you don't hang out with some kid anymore because, well, his family moved to Alaska. (That'll do it every time.) But it's just not right to dump an old friend because you think he's no longer good enough and you want a cooler, newer pal—or if an old friend needs a favor, and you can help, but you give him the cold shoulder.

Good friends are a treasure and old friendships are worth hanging onto. Sure, you may no longer be interested in the same things, but appreciate people for what they've done in the past. Remember the good times. Be loyal to friends and to friends of your family. That means being there for them if they show up totally out of the blue, needing your help.

Being there for family is important. Being there for old friends is important too. You'd want an old friend to be there for you, wouldn't you?

PAINFUL FAVORS

Wounds from a friend can be trusted, but an enemy multiplies kisses.
—Proverbs 27:6

I n Bible times, if you met someone you greatly respected, you bowed down in the dirt to him. Sometimes you kissed his hand. (Yeah, things were different back then.) But hey, if it was a family member or a friend, you just kissed him on his cheek. So this verse is saying: better to trust someone who "wounds" you by telling you the truth you need to hear than some guy who's faking affection.

Some kids just pretend to be your friends. They'll slap you on the back — "Hey there, dude!" — and do a dozen fancy handshakes and high fives to make you feel all buddy-buddy. And maybe they're fun to be around. But if you can't trust them, you can't trust them. They'll tell you what a good pal they are but they're not looking out for you. They won't tell you the truth when you're getting off track.

A true friend may not be quite as much fun at times. But you can trust him to tell you the truth, even when it hurts. He'll talk to you and warn you when you're getting into stuff you shouldn't be getting into. A true friend will point out the ketchup on your cheek, not to make fun of you, but to help you. He'll tell you when you were rude and advise you to stop.

If you're going to make it through life, it helps to have a few close, good friends who are truly looking out for you.

WOW! REVELATIONS FROM THE BIBLE

Open my eyes that I may see wonderful things in your law.
—Psalm 119:18

We don't know who wrote this prayer. King David didn't sign his name to this psalm so it probably wasn't him. But whoever it was, he considered God's Word his greatest treasure. To him, the Scriptures were like a gold mine. He was constantly digging in them. Sure, he'd read them many times, but he prayed for God to open his eyes so he could see wonderful stuff there that he'd never seen before.

Ever been looking for an eraser or a pencil sharpener and you just can't find it? Then your mom walks in the room and points it out to you, like, in five seconds? It was there all along, but you just didn't see it. Well, God's Spirit is like a supermom who can show you stuff in the Bible. God can reveal stuff even to you. You just need to let him open your eyes.

Jesus promised, "The Holy Spirit ... will teach you all things" (John 14:26). Of course, the Holy Spirit usually uses the Bible to teach you. Let's say you've read John chapter 15 a dozen times already, but then God lifts your eyelids and suddenly it's like you're reading it for the first time. A verse you've read before jumps out at you and suddenly makes sense. Then you say, "Wow! I never saw that before!" You just saw wonderful things in God's Word.

Don't just read your Bible half-asleep because it's something you must do. Ask God to open your eyes and make the read worthwhile.

BECOMING MORE LIKE JESUS

When Moses came down from Mount Sinai ... he was not aware that his face was radiant because he had spoken with the Lord.

— Exodus 34:29

Moses climbed up to the top of Mount Sinai and spent forty days and forty nights there, talking to God. After the Lord gave Moses the Ten Commandments, he sent Moses back down the mountain to the Israelites. Moses showed up and suddenly everyone was backing away, afraid to come near. He didn't realize that his face was glowing with God's glory.

If you spend time praying and reading your Bible, God begins to change you, and you become radiant too. You won't start glowing as bright as Moses did, but you will change. You may be saying, "Hold on! This is talking about holy people like missionaries and people who pray all day—not kids like me! God doesn't give skateboarders and computer gamers a touch of glory, does he? Does he?"

Oh yeah, he does. You may not think you radiate much of God's presence, but if you're a Christian, his Holy Spirit lives in you. And God's Spirit is constantly changing you, making you more like Jesus all the time. Instead of walking around full of anger or hate or fear, you'll have God's peace and joy in your face. Even if you can't see it, others will.

Spend time with God and read your Bible and meditate on it. God's Spirit inside you will become more evident in your life. You will change. Guaranteed.

GOD GUIDING YOUR MIND

Then David gave his son Solomon ... the plans of all that the Spirit had put in his mind for the courts of the temple.

—1 Chronicles 28:11 – 12

When David found out that God wanted his son Solomon to build a temple, David drew up the designs for the building. Then all Solomon had to do was follow directions. David probably had zero experience in designing temples, so where'd he get his ideas? God's Spirit gave him the plans. Sure, David knew what Phoenician temples looked like—and Bible scholars say he borrowed ideas from them—but for the most part he did the design with God's help.

God gave you a mind—and he's hoping you'll use it—but he doesn't leave you on your own. God's like a tutor, a special one-on-one teacher. When you have a tutor, you still have to think hard and work to figure things out, but the tutor's looking over your shoulder, explaining and helping each step of the way. God was like that with David. God kept David's thoughts moving in the right direction.

If you're a Christian and have God in your life, then his Spirit can guide you each step of the way. He will give you cool counsel and teach you. John 14:26 says, "The Counselor, the Holy Spirit ... will teach you all things and will remind you of everything I have said to you."

Want to succeed? Think things through and plan well, but also pray for spiritual downloads. Ask God to put his plans in your mind.

PARENTS' BRAINPOWER

Listen, my son, to your father's instruction and do not forsake your mother's teaching. They will be ... a chain to adorn your neck.
—Proverbs 1:8 – 9

Proverbs is full of wise sayings. This wise saying sounds a lot like the fifth commandment, which says, "Honor your father and your mother" (Exodus 20:12). God wants you to respect your parents ... even if you don't think they're so smart. Just do it. Going into a little more detail than the commandment, this Proverb tells you to listen to your dad because he's lived life, knows a thing or two, and is worth listening to.

The Proverb goes on to tell you not to "forsake your mother's teaching." When you were young, Mom was probably the one who taught you stuff, reminded you of rules, and talked to you when you messed up. Now that you're older and not a small kid anymore, you might think you don't need to listen to Mom any longer. Maybe you want to impress your friends by sassing her or ignoring her.

Do yourself a favor—don't do it. Your mom and dad knew what they were talking about all those years, so don't ditch their teachings now. It's all still good. Stuff like being responsible and tidy, having manners, etc., is still important. Besides the fact that your parents are smart, they're looking out for you. They want what's best for you.

Ever see some superathlete with a glittering gold chain around his neck? That's how your spirit will be decked out if you listen to your parents.

GETTING A GLORIOUS BODY

Our citizenship is in heaven. And we eagerly await a Savior from there, the Lord Jesus Christ, who ... will transform our lowly bodies so that they will be like his glorious body.

—Philippians 3:20–21

E agerly await, all right! Our Savior will come from heaven one day, and you are going to get a body that can power up and shine like the sun, step through solid walls, and never die. Jesus will change our ordinary bodies so that they're glorious like his body. (Want to know what Jesus' body is like now? Read Revelation 1:13–16.)

You've seen Transformer toys that start with an action figure, and you zippo-chango-rearrange the parts and turn it into a car or a beast, right? Or maybe you get tired of the way your Lego models look, so you find a Website that tells you how to totally rearrange the pieces, and you redesign your bricks into a super-cool model.

Right now our bodies are like the original models, but they'll go through an astonishing change and become super bodies! "We will all be changed—in a flash, in the twinkling of an eye.... The dead will be raised imperishable" (1 Corinthians 15:51–52). Being raised imperishable means we'll never perish. We'll live forever with God. And not just live forever, dude, but forever with power!

It's already fantastic that Jesus is returning in all his glory, but when he has transformed us, we'll have awesome bodies with all new features and powers. We'll be able to do stuff we've never done before. That's also worth eagerly waiting for.

THE HEAVENLY CITY

The city does not need the sun or the moon to shine on it, for the glory of God gives it light, and the Lamb is its lamp.

— **Revelation 21:23**

The Bible describes heaven as a magnificent city with streets of gold, walls made of twelve different kinds of gems, a river of life with Trees of Life growing by it. And fabulous places to live! Now, how much of this is literal and how much is symbolic we don't know, but one thing we do know: our eternal home will be more wonderful than anything we can possibly imagine.

Maybe you've been to Disneyland and thought that was great! Or maybe you've never been to Disneyland, but you've heard it's the place to go, and you'd like to check it out before going to heaven. Hey, if you miss Mickey, don't sweat it! Heaven will be so much better!

And where will you live? Jesus said, "In my Father's house are many rooms.... I am going there to prepare a place for you" (John 14:2). You'll be living with God! That's the best part: God himself will be there. There'll be no more pain or death or sorrow or crying—just happiness forever.

Heaven isn't a fairy tale or just some fluffy-puffy cloudland. Heaven is a very real, exciting place, and we'll be living there one day.

TEMPORARY TROUBLE, HUGE REWARDS

Our light and momentary troubles are achieving for us an eternal glory that far outweighs them all.

—2 Corinthians 4:17

Back in Paul's day, Christians were often persecuted for their faith. People hated them, told lies about them, spat on them, and gave them grief. Sometimes Christians lost their jobs just because of their faith, and they didn't know where they'd get money. Paul knew these troubles were real. After all, he'd suffered a lot himself. But he reminded Christians that these troubles were light because their heavenly rewards would far outweigh the trouble.

It's no fun going through difficult times. Maybe you've lost a good friend or you've been injured. Or maybe your parents are having a hard time financially and you can't afford things that other kids enjoy. Or maybe kids who were once your friends tease you because you believe in Jesus. It may not seem like your troubles are light. They may seem sandbag-heavy.

But God promises that when you suffer here on earth in his name, he will repay you with heavenly rewards, with "an eternal glory that far outweighs them all." Those eternal rewards won't just outweigh your troubles, they'll far outweigh them. It would be like if you missed out on a lollipop now, but got a dirt bike in three months. It's worth the wait.

Sometimes when you're going through troubles, it's not easy to keep your eyes on the ultimate goal—heaven. It's not easy to tell yourself that it will be worth it all. But just the same, it will be worth it all.

EXCELLENT THINKING

Whatever is true, whatever is noble, whatever is right, whatever is pure, whatever is lovely, whatever is admirable — if anything is excellent or praiseworthy — think about such things.

— Philippians 4:8

Back in Paul's day, just like today, there was lots of sick stuff in society, and Paul knew that Christians couldn't help but see and hear some of it. Then it would get stuck in their heads and bum them out. That's probably one reason he told them to think about things that were inspiring and encouraging. Then the good thoughts would bump the garbage thoughts out.

Ever had some song play on and on in your head like some radio you can't shut off? That's tiring enough if it's just plain dumb, but what if it's bad? There's a lot of garbage in the world today too, and even if you try to avoid the worst stuff by not watching certain TV shows or hanging with certain kids, some junk will still bombard your brain. So what do you do about it?

Deliberately focus on things that are true and good and pure. That doesn't mean you have to sit around thinking about the Bible all day long or humming hymns. But thinking about admirable stuff can mean thinking about your football team. Thinking of excellent stuff can be remembering how you got serious airtime while out dirt biking. All this is cool, excellent stuff.

Are your thoughts pure and inspiring and uplifting? The choice is yours. Enjoy good, wholesome fun and fill your mind with pure, excellent thoughts.

A TIME FOR HUMOR

There is a time for everything, and a season for every activity under heaven
... a time to plant and a time to uproot ... a time to weep and a time to laugh.
—Ecclesiastes 3:1, 4

In ancient Israel, farmers knew that at the beginning of summer they harvested their wheat fields. At the end of summer they harvested dates and figs. In fall they harvested olives. There was a specific time for every activity and if they did stuff at the wrong time—like, oh, cutting down the wheat two months before it was ripe—it was a disaster.

Laughing and joking is perfectly acceptable at a party or when you're horsing around with other kids. It's totally all right to laugh out loud when you're watching a funny video. But there are also times when jokes aren't acceptable. You wouldn't tell knock-knock jokes if your friend's dog just died. If he's grieving, it's time to be quiet and respect his sorrow. Not every moment is party time or time to laugh.

Most kids are pretty carefree compared to their parents, and that's pretty much the way it should be. But be aware of what's happening with others around you—with your family, with your friends. You may be ready to laugh your head off but others may be facing sorrow. If your mom is sad or your dad just lost his job, don't get into wild jokes.

There are times to have fun and laugh, so enjoy those times. Just be aware that there are also times to be serious.

LEAVING OFF GETTING EVEN

"We have come to ... do to him as he did to us." "I merely did to them what they did to me."

—Judges 15:10–11

O h boy, what a mess. When the Philistines cheated to answer Samson's riddle, he got even by killing thirty Philistines. Then Samson's father-in-law gave away Samson's wife. Samson got revenge by burning down the Philistines' wheat fields. Did it stop there? No. The Philistines got back at Samson by killing his wife. Then Samson got revenge by slaughtering a bunch of Philistines. Then the Philistines sent out an army to capture Samson ...

That's the thing about getting even. Rarely do people ever call it quits. If some kid trips you so that you fall in the mud, and the next day you see an opening and you push him down, he usually doesn't laugh and say, "Okay, we're even," and stop. No, now he wants re-revenge. He'll get you again—only harder next time—and things keep on until it becomes a vendetta.

Normally the rule God wants us to live by is: "Do not say, 'I'll do to him as he has done to me; I'll pay that man back for what he did'" (Proverbs 24:29). Samson's was a special case—God wanted Samson to fight to free the Israelites from the Philistines. But take note that God knew the revenge factor would play a role in starting the war. And human nature hasn't changed since Samson's time—if you try to get back at someone, the cycle will just keep going.

Vendettas go on and on and don't stop, so break out of the revenge cycle now. You do that by letting go and choosing to make peace with the past.

TAKING RESPONSIBILITY

If a fire breaks out and spreads into thornbushes so that it burns ... standing grain or the whole field, the one who started the fire must make restitution.

—Exodus 22:6

Sometimes the Israelites would get careless with their cooking fires, or throw away hot oven ashes, and next thing you know the thornbush hedges around their land caught fire—and if it was the dry season they popped and crackled and burned like crazy. If their neighbor's crop caught fire too, they had to "make restitution" (res-ti-too-shun), meaning pay for damages.

Most people live in towns or cities today, and the big danger isn't hedges burning and catching wheat fields on fire. Being careless with matches causes fires, sure, but carelessness causes other kinds of accidents too: for example, a friend lends us a computer game and we leave it laying around until the CD gets scratched, or he lends us his baseball and it drops down a sewer drain.

We can't just say, "It wasn't our fault," or "We didn't mean to do that," even if we didn't mean to. If we wreck someone's belonging or lose it, but he forgives us or his parents have mercy and say we don't have to pay, well and fine. But if we're asked to make restitution, then we must use our own money to replace what was damaged or lost.

Saying we're sorry is a beginning, and sometimes that's enough. But sometimes it's not enough. When it's not, we need to do whatever we can to make things right.

DUMPING ANGER

Get rid of all bitterness, rage and anger, brawling and slander ... Be kind and compassionate to one another, forgiving each other just as in Christ God forgave you.

—Ephesians 4:31–32

God's idea of a "real man" is different than what you see in movies where some guy trash-talks his opponent while slugging the daylights out of him. God's ideal is not an angry guy full of rage (violent anger). Nor does he want you to slander (speak evil of others) or go wild brawling (fighting noisily). He says to get rid of all that.

You might have a quick temper and think you just can't help it: you're gonna blow up no matter what. Sure, it's easy to let your emotions go and rage like a wounded bear, but that usually just gets people angry with you. Hurt them and they'll figure out ways to get back at you and turn others against you as well. It doesn't pan out in the end if you go through life angry.

You can get rid of anger. Decide ahead of time that you'll control yourself. Pray and ask God to give you love and patience then bite your tongue. No, you shouldn't just stand by calmly if some little kid is being beat up. There's a time to step in and take action. But there's no sense lashing out in anger if someone simply makes a dumb mistake.

And notice the end of that verse, the most important part of it. We should do this not only because it will make our lives easier, but because it is part of becoming the people Christ calls us to be.

A DEAL TO AVOID

"It's no good, it's no good!" says the buyer; then off he goes and boasts about his purchase.
— Proverbs 20:14

Solomon described how a buyer had spent time chiseling a seller down, lying to him that his merchandise was no good, it was broken, it was old, it was cheap, or whatever. But as it turned out, the buyer was lying to the seller. He knew the merchandise was good and that he was getting a bargain. Yeah, but he got it by swindling the seller and ripping him off.

Some people have this idea: "Listen, if some kid is stupid enough to let me talk him out of his toy, he deserves to lose it." The idea being, a clever person has a right to rip off a not-so-clever person and take advantage of him. If you can persuade a kid to sell you his collectible toy cheap, go for it! A deal's a deal, and he shouldn't whine to get it back later. Right?

Wrong. If a kid knows what something's worth but he's giving you a low price because he doesn't want it anymore or he likes you, that's one thing. But a man of God doesn't cheat someone in a trade or a sale then go off laughing how he cheated the guy. Don't say something's not worth much or that it's no good when you know it is good.

If you treat others honestly and fairly, you won't be able to walk off boasting that you ripped them off, but you can walk off knowing that you acted as Christ would act.

LISTEN TO YOUR FOLKS

Listen to your father, who gave you life, and do not despise your mother when she is old.

— Proverbs 23:22

In Israelite society, boys knew that when they were young, they were supposed to listen to their parents. That was a no-brainer. As long as they lived at home, they had to mind mom and dad. But what about when they grew up and were living on their own? They no longer had to do everything their parents said, true, but they still had to honor them and to listen respectfully to their advice.

When you've grown up—or while you're growing up—you'll often be tempted to ignore dad or despise mom's advice. To despise means to look down on something, to not pay attention to something because you don't think it's worth much. Lots of kids ignore their parents because they figure, "They're old. They're behind the times. No one does things that way anymore or dresses that way or cuts their hair that way."

God knew that it'd sometimes be hard for growing boys to listen to their parents and respect what they say. He knew that you'd sometimes get frustrated with them and want to let what they say roll off your brain like water off a duck's back. God saw it coming, so he made sure to tell you to listen and to keep a respectful attitude.

No matter how big you're growing or how old your parents are getting, love them, respect them and listen to them.

GHOSTS ON THE LOOSE?

When they saw him walking on the lake, they thought he was a ghost. They cried out, because they all saw him and were terrified.

—Mark 6:49–50

In Bible times, people thought that when someone died their spirit went down into the earth. Some superstitious people worried that unhappy spirits could come back to cause trouble. When Jesus' disciples were crossing the Sea of Galilee and they saw Jesus walking on the waves, they were sure he was a ghost. They were wrong. When Jesus showed up after he had been crucified, again they thought they were seeing a ghost. Again they were wrong (Luke 24:37–39).

Some people today believe that after a person dies, his or her spirit wanders around and seeks revenge or maybe haunts houses. So if the wind slams a door or the cat steps on a squeaky floorboard, they let out a gasp, thinking it's a ghost. The Bible warns that if God's people disobey him, they'll end up so jittery that they'll be spooked by a rustling leaf and run when no one's even chasing (Leviticus 26:36).

The Bible does not teach that people's spirits wander around like spooks after they die. When Christians die, their spirits go to heaven. When the unsaved die, they go to hell. (Didn't know that? Hey, check out Luke 16:22–23.) The only kind of spirits that go around causing trouble are evil spirits—demons—and you can command them to leave in Jesus' name.

Believe in the Bible and trust in the power of the name of Jesus, and you won't need to fear creaking floorboards, slamming windows, and fluttering leaves.

BADLY MISTAKEN THINKING

Jesus replied, "Are you not in error because you do not know the Scriptures or the power of God?... You are badly mistaken!"
—Mark 12:24, 27

Jesus taught that one day God would raise peoples' bodies back to life. The righteous will live with God forever; the evil will end up in the other place. Now, some religious leaders called Sadducees (sad-you-sees) didn't believe in the resurrection. They thought that once a person died, that was it—no heaven, no hell. Jesus said they were mistaken because they didn't know what the Bible taught.

A lot of people today have badly mistaken ideas because they don't read the Bible. They just guess what it says, and they guess wrong—or else they get their ideas from TV shows and movies. Here are some common errors: Everyone goes to heaven. People turn into angels when they die. After a short stay in heaven, you reincarnate and come back to earth. Witches have "magical powers" from God.

If you don't want to end up with weird, mistaken ideas rattling around in your head like an out-of-control pinball machine, sit down and read the Bible.

KEEP YOUR COOL

"I your servant had two sons. They got into a fight with each other in the field, and no one was there to separate them. One struck the other and killed him."

—2 Samuel 14:6

One day a woman from Tekoa showed up in King David's palace with a story from Joab. She told David a parable, saying that she was a widow with two sons. One day her boys were out in the field and began arguing. Then they began fighting. Since no one was there to pull them apart, the fight got out of hand, and next thing you know, somebody was dead.

Ever get in a fight with your brother or sister? First you start by arguing. When no one backs off, next thing you know you're yelling at him or her. Then what? Do you start swinging your fists? Do you shove him backwards? Of course, you don't mean to really hurt him, but if there's no adult there, how far will things go?

No one is saying that you should like it if your sister is bugging you or if your brother grabs the seat you wanted to sit in. What matters is what you do about it. Taking the law into your own hands can seriously hurt someone. It's not easy, but it pays to keep your cool. That way—even if there are no adults around—you can work things out.

Control your words and your fists and you won't have to worry about accidentally injuring a family member or a friend.

NOT LIMITED BY CIRCUMSTANCES

"Jephthah the Gileadite was a mighty warrior. His father was Gilead; his mother was a prostitute."

—Judges 11:1

Jephthah was the son of Gilead and a prostitute. It must've been tough for Jephthah when he was growing up. His stepbrothers even kicked him out of the house because they didn't want to share their inheritance with him. On top of that, the city rulers told him to split. Jephthah went to Tob where he became a mighty warrior. Years later, when Ammonites began attacking his people, folks stopped trash talking Jephthah's mom and started saying what a great guy Jephthah was.

Sometimes kids will talk down about other kids' parents. Maybe they made dumb mistakes in the past. Or maybe your dad doesn't have a glamorous job or doesn't earn enough to take you to Disneyland. Perhaps your parents aren't as fun as other kids' parents. Or maybe it's just that as you get older, you start thinking it's cool to dis your parents.

Your parents may not be perfect, but they deserve your respect. Work with what you've got and go from there. You are where you are right now, but you don't have to be limited by your circumstances. Whatever your parents did or didn't do, it's up to you to make the most of your life. Where do you want to go?

God has a plan for your life, so pray and ask him to lead you into it. Then work hard to make it happen. And honor your parents in the meantime.

DEVOTION 300

LISTENING TO WISE ADVICE

Moses listened to his father-in-law and did everything he said.
—Exodus 18:24

God had just used Moses to send earth-shaking plagues on the kingdom of Egypt. Moses was now leader of a nation of two to three million Israelites. He was the greatest prophet on the planet. Why did he need to listen to anybody but God? Why listen to some guy who wasn't even an Israelite? Why? Because Moses realized that God had given wisdom to other men too.

Honestly now, you have to admit that sometimes pride gets in the way and it's hard to listen to others, even when they're older and know more than you do. You want to be independent, you figure you know enough and don't need to listen to anyone. But unless you're trying to sleep in a noisy room or go swimming, stuffing earplugs in your ears is a bad idea.

If you're building a tree-fort, it's not good to ignore the advice of a carpenter, right? Sure, if you're itching to start a project it's hard to hold yourself back when Mr. Sawdust advises you to stop, re-figure things and then go at it. You don't want to wait. But it pays to respect an older man and listen to him, particularly if he's been around the block and knows a thing or two.

If Moses, as smart and as close to God as he was, was humble enough to listen to his father-in-law and follow his advice, you should take the time to listen to wise men too.

RESPECTING PEOPLE'S PROPERTY

"What are you doing here and who gave you permission to cut out a grave for yourself here ...?"

—Isaiah 22:16

Okay, this is a strange one. In King Hezekiah's day, a non-Israelite named Shebna was in charge of the royal palace. Shebna had a high position, yeah, but not high enough to be buried with the kings of Judah. But Shebna decided to honor himself by cutting out his own grave among the tombs of the famous kings. The prophet Isaiah asked him, "Who gave you permission?"

Now, there's probably no danger of you digging a grave in your neighbor's flower garden. Or if your goldfish dies—say you accidentally unplugged the air-bubble thing—you probably won't try burying him under a brick at the Washington Monument. But what about trespassing on your neighbor's lawn? What about sneaking through some fence and dirt biking on private property?

Always respect fences. Think of them as de-fences. They're there for a reason—mainly to keep people off private property. Even if a whole dump truck full of kids go to some vacant lot and rock out playing baseball, or they're running all over the place inside an old house screaming like howler monkeys, or skateboarding down city sidewalks—unless you know you have permission, don't go there. Trespassing means you think you are above the rules, better than others who are expected to obey.

Always ask permission before doing things on other people's property. That way if anyone walks up and asks, "Who gave you permission?" you'll have a good answer.

DEVOTION 302

LOVE YOURSELF? PROVE IT!

He who gets wisdom loves his own soul; he who cherishes understanding
prospers.

—Proverbs 19:8

For some guys, reading and learning and getting wisdom
are a drag. School is booorring. They'd rather run off and
join the circus, go rafting down the Mississippi with Tom
Sawyer, or sail the Caribbean with a shipload of pirates—or at
least do that on video games. Anything but school. Anything but
reading the Bible and gaining godly wisdom.

But guess what? The Bible says that getting an education
proves you love yourself. How so? If you want to prove you love
yourself, isn't it easier to just take five scoops of ice cream or
spend all day at the swimming pool? Isn't that self-love at
its finest?

No, that's all wrong. The way to prove you fear the Lord and
love yourself is to get wisdom and understanding. Here's how it
works: if you study hard in school, you'll get a better education,
and you'll likely end up in a career that suits your God-given
talents. You'll "prosper," or do well in life, and have true wisdom
about practical situations.

Go for wisdom. Get understanding. Do the education thing,
even if it's kind of boring at times. It proves you love yourself.

BAD BOY'S GOOD ADVICE

Now go out and encourage your men ... If you don't go out, not a man will be left with you by nightfall.
—2 Samuel 19:7

When Absalom's army attacked David, David's men risked their lives to defend him, and Absalom died in the battle. Was David relieved? No. He loved Absalom so much that he wouldn't stop crying. David's men felt awful, like they'd done something wrong. General Joab often did stupid stuff, but this time he wisely warned David he'd better get out there and thank his men or they'd all leave. Fortunately, David listened and the kingdom was saved.

There are kids you don't like to listen to, right? Some of them hassle you all the time, so you don't want to say they're right even if they are right. Others are constantly doing stuff you think is dumb, so you've made up your mind that they aren't right about anything. Other kids like to lecture you and—even though they're usually right—they're so annoying that it's no fun listening to them.

If someone explains why you're wrong about something, don't tell yourself, "I can't admit he's right." It's foolish to be stubborn and refuse good advice. Remember Balaam: he refused to listen to his donkey, and it nearly cost his life! And hey, if David was willing to listen to a mess of a messenger like Joab, you're wise to do the same.

Even if someone's way of saying stuff stinks, it's still worth listening to him if he happens to be right.

FEELING DUMB?

I am the most ignorant of men; I do not have a man's understanding. I have not learned wisdom, nor have I knowledge of the Holy One.

—Proverbs 30:2–3

One day a dude named Agur was having a chat with his pals Ithiel and Ucal, and he told them, "I am the most ignorant of men; I do not have a man's understanding." You notice they didn't argue, "C'mon, Agur! Don't be so hard on yourself. You're not that dumb." Well, they should've! Agur may not have been highly educated, but he was smart about important stuff in life.

Ever feel dumb? That can happen if you compare yourself to kids with different talents than yours. When you hear some girl say she loves math, do you think, "Are you out of your mind?" You struggle to get a C or a C+, and she's pulling in A's like the stuff was easy? Things like that can discourage you. Maybe you start complaining how dumb you are. Don't.

You can't be smart about everything. And just because some kid outshines you in math or science or history doesn't mean she's all that and more. Thank God for the smarts God has given you. Think about the stuff you're quick at—and not just school subjects. Of course, while you're at it, work hard to bring up your grades. But if you're already doing your best, don't beat yourself up.

Like Agur, you may feel you have not "learned wisdom," but God has made you smart in your own way. And anyone, whether they're a genius or not, can gain "knowledge of the Holy One"—God!

GROWING OUT OF ELEMENTARY GRADES

You need someone to teach you the elementary truths of God's word all over again.... Let us leave the elementary teachings about Christ and go on to maturity, not laying again the foundation.
—Hebrews 5:12; 6:1

B ack in the days of the early church, some teachers wanted Christians to learn new things and move on to the next grade. Problem was, many people still hadn't gotten the elementary lessons. They were still struggling to get the basic, foundational truths down—like why they should love others, why they needed to repent for their sins, or why Christians should be baptized.

It's like if you invite a friend over to play a video game, and to your surprise the guy has no clue which buttons are for "jump" or "attack." He can't even make the character run right or left. His character is stuck against some wall, his little feet are flying, but he's not getting anywhere. Your friend doesn't have the foundations of the game. You need to teach him the basics so he can move on to the next level and actually play the game.

If you're a Christian, it's important to learn the basics about your faith so you'll know what you believe about Jesus and why you believe it. Then you'll know how to live. So how do you learn the basics? Well, listen during Sunday school. Grab a Bible storybook. Best of all, read your Bible and think about what it's saying. If you come to a part you don't understand, ask someone who knows.

God wants you to learn the basics so that you can move from the elementary teachings to other stuff you need to know. Do you have the basics down?

KEEP AT IT! DON'T STOP PRAYING!

Elijah was a man just like us. He prayed earnestly that it would not rain, and it did not rain on the land for three and a half years. Again he prayed, and the heavens gave rain.

—James 5:17 – 18

E lijah bent down to the ground and put his face between his knees and prayed for rain wholeheartedly. (You don't have to be that flexible to pray, by the way.) Six times he sent his servant to go see if there were any rain clouds. Six times the guy returned and said, "Nothing." Elijah kept at it, and finally the servant came back with news of a cloud. Next thing you know there was a gully-washer!

Have you been praying for something but it hasn't happened yet—like you need to earn money to buy a bike? Or maybe you're sick, or someone close to you is sick? If the answer takes a while, you sometimes get discouraged and give up, right? You wonder why God doesn't answer. Maybe you ask yourself, "Doesn't God care?"

We're so impatient. We're used to doing a drive-through, not even getting out of the car. We put in our order and pick it up a few minutes later. We get so many things in life immediately that it's hard to wait. But don't give up if your prayers aren't answered right away. God heard you, but he's not a fast-food chef.

Since the prophet "Elijah was a man just like us," and God answered his prayers, that means we can pray earnestly too, and we can get miraculous answers. Keep praying!

WATER BUFFALOS, BUTTERFLIES, AND YOU

"In his hand is the life of every creature and the breath of all mankind."
—Job 12:10

T hink how much power God has and how much he cares
for us! All life on earth, from each big muddy water buffalo
to every tiny butterfly—including all six and a half billion
people on this planet—are in the palm of God's hand. God
decides when every bit of life is born, and he decides the
moment it will die. God is totally in charge of life.

People like to think they're independent and don't need
God. Some say, "Sure I believe God exists, but I'm not going to
worship him." Yet God created this whole world and everything
in it. Look at the beautiful world he created. God created
the complicated web of life and all the systems that work so
amazingly together. God created your mind that allows you to
understand and appreciate what he has done. He's the one who
gives you life and breath each day. Do you need God? Yes, you
do. Of course you should worship him! How can you not be in
awe of such a wonderful God!

The sooner we realize how much he cares for us and how
much we need him, the better off we'll be. Not even one tiny
sparrow dies unless it's God's will, so he's surely looking after
you. Though God has created a big and complicated world, he
loves us and knows about everything that happens to us.

Every day you live is a gift from God. Does he care for you?
Yes. Is he close to you? He sure is! Your breath is in his hands.

DOING STUFF NOW

Do not withhold good from those who deserve it, when it is in your power
to act. Do not say to your neighbor, "Come back later; I'll give it tomorrow" — when you now have it with you.

—Proverbs 3:27 – 28

Pretty straightforward, huh? If it's within your power to do
something, do it. In fact, don't just do it if you can do it, but
do it right away. Don't put off your neighbor for one day. If
someone deserves good, and you have the goods, don't withhold
that good thing from him for even twenty-four hours.

Of course, it doesn't always feel convenient to do something
right away. You may be in the middle of a TV show and not want
to look for the item. Or maybe your room's a mess and it'll take
time to find anything there. But if someone's come out of his
way to pick up a video game or book that you said you'd lend
him, and you send him away without it, that's wasting his time.

If someone's asking to borrow something and you have what
he needs, roll your body off the couch, dig it out from wherever
it's buried and hand it to him. Or if you've promised to bring
something to school to lend it to someone, don't put it off. Do
what you say you'll do and do it when you say you'll do it. Be a
man of your word.

If someone deserves something good, do good to him. If
someone needs help today and you're able to help him today,
do it today.

THE COURAGE TO CONFESS

When a man or woman wrongs another in any way, and so is unfaithful to the Lord, that person is guilty and must confess the sin he has committed.
— Numbers 5:6 – 7

In Bible days, people sometimes did sneaky stuff and the person they wronged never knew whodunit. For example, a guy might sow weeds in his neighbor's wheat field or let his ox out of its pen. Or a woman might gossip about her neighbor or kick over her water jug. When the person's conscience got to them it wasn't enough to think, "I feel bad." The wrong they had done wasn't just a mistake. It was "unfaithfulness to the Lord." They had to confess to the person they had wronged.

Some common sneaky stuff kids do today is to lie about someone and tell others bad things about him. Or maybe the story's true but it's embarrassing (like when some kid didn't make it to the bathroom on time), and they tell it to hurt him. And of course it's wrong to steal his eraser or pencil just to cause him grief and watch him waste time looking for it.

If you wrong someone in any way, you feel guilty because you are guilty. You have been unfaithful to the Lord's will for you. The thing to do is to be honest and confess that you were the one who did it and then try to make things right. Go to the person you've wronged and try to fix things. Don't try to hide it or cover it, especially if the one you hurt is still hurting.

It's great if you never hurt anyone, but we can't always say that. We do hurt people, and when we do, it takes courage to confess it.

BUTTING IN

Because you shove with flank and shoulder, butting all the weak sheep with your horns until you have driven them away, I will save my flock.

—Ezekiel 34:21 – 22

In the book of Ezekiel, God talked about how badly the rich, powerful Israelites treated their fellow countrymen. He compared them to big, fat sheep that butted the weak, skinny sheep aside so they could get to the front of the food line. In fact, they didn't just butt with their horns. They shoulder checked and even body-blocked with their flanks (sides).

If you're more powerful than other kids either because of your size or because you're more popular than they are, you may be tempted to push them around to get what you want. Some kids bully others just for the fun of it.

That's not how God wants men, or even boys, to act. When you push others around, it hurts them and forces them to do without. Do that often enough and God will see to it that you get slowed down—and it might hurt. God cares for weaker kids and he'll protect them from bullies who shove them around. Make sure you're not one of those bullies.

God is gentle with the weak and he wants you to use your strength to make sure that smaller kids are treated fairly. A man of God never uses his strength just to get his own way.

WILLING BUT WEAK

"Watch and pray so that you will not fall into temptation. The spirit is willing, but the body is weak."

—Matthew 26:41

J esus said these words in the Garden of Gethsemane just before he was arrested, taken away, and crucified. When Jesus had warned Peter that this was coming, Peter had boasted that he was willing to go to prison and even die for Jesus. Peter's spirit was willing. He wanted to be all-out for Jesus. But when he was tested, he washed out. When the soldiers arrested Jesus, Peter took off running.

You've probably had moments like that. You want to do what's right, but sometimes you fail. Like if your mom can't figure out how to block a channel, so you promise not to watch it. But then you get tempted and click to it anyway. And of course, your mom walks into the room right then, catches you like a deer in the headlights, and takes away your privileges.

You know what your weaknesses are, so avoid them. Like King Solomon said, "Do not set foot on the path of the wicked ... avoid it, do not travel on it; turn from it" (Proverbs 4:14–15). Don't even get near things that tempt you. If certain kids are always tempting you to do wrong stuff, stay away from them. If certain shows are off-limits, don't even peek at them.

Avoid temptation. And if you can't avoid it, pray for God's strength to resist it. He can give you the willpower to do what's right.

IS IT WORTH GETTING INTO?

A gentle answer turns away wrath, but a harsh word stirs up anger.
—Proverbs 15:1

The Proverbs of Solomon contain some commonsense stuff. You've heard that Solomon was the wisest man who ever lived, right? So you may wonder why such a brilliant guy wasted his time saying simple stuff like, "harsh words stir up anger." Who doesn't know that? Well, look around. Listen to guys arguing. It appears that millions of people don't know that.

Sometimes when a kid is angry he's just looking for a fight. He's frustrated and full of wrath and wants to fight with anyone who's dumb enough to fight him. If you allow your pride to take control and think, "Nobody talks to me that way!" and answer back with an insult, you're playing into his hands and next thing you know you're fighting over nothing. Either that or he stomps off, plotting how to hurt you.

But if, when some kid comes at you angry, you decide, "This isn't worth getting into," and you answer back calmly, it's hard for him to get mad at you or stay mad at you. Answering gently doesn't mean letting some hothead push you around. It doesn't mean bowing down to him or being weak. It just means staying cool and not getting suckered into fighting.

If you can stay calm and avoid speaking proud, harsh words, you can step over trouble just like you'd step over a pile of doggie dung. It's just not worth getting into.

WHEN SEWER WATER'S FLYING

But among you there should not even be a hint of sexual immorality ...
Nor should there be obscenity, foolish talk, or coarse joking.
— Ephesians 5:3 – 4

Sexual immorality is completely out for a man of God. Don't even have a hint of it in your life. It should also come as no surprise that obscenity (filthy talk) and coarse joking (dirty jokes) are out of line too. So is foolish talk. Now, in case you worry that this means you can't even tell a silly joke, foolish talk is not just goofy humor; it's seriously empty, worthless talk.

It's normal for tween boys to be curious about the differences between boy's and girl's bodies and to want to be informed about sex. It's an important part of life, after all, and God intended men and women to enjoy sex within marriage. But the problem comes when immature kids make obscene, crude jokes about it. So what can you do?

If a friend's making sick jokes, tell him he's out of line. Maybe he'll stop. If some kid insists on telling crude jokes, walk away. You wouldn't just stand there soaking it in if some dog swam in the sewer then shook himself, totally drenching you, right? Well, don't stand around listening if some kid's telling filthy jokes. And avoid internet sites or shows that treat sex like a cheap joke.

Some things are just wrong—like laughing about someone's physical handicap or telling racial jokes. It's the same with telling crude jokes about girls.

GOD ISN'T JUST LIKE YOU

"I am God, your God.... You thought I was altogether like you."
—Psalm 50:7, 21

Back in Old Testament times, many Israelites preferred to worship idols of false gods and goddesses that looked like tiny clay humans. And they gave these "gods" personalities. They quarreled, were selfish, and liked all the sinful stuff that selfish humans liked. In other words, the people liked gods who were just like them. Go figure!

So is the eternal, unchanging God just like you? No way. The Lord of heaven and earth is who he is. He is God. The trouble is that lots of people don't like how the Bible describes God. For example, they don't think he should judge them for their sins. So what do they do? They say he doesn't mind their sin. They "remake" God. By the time they're done, they've invented a God who's a lot like them and who approves of the things they like.

Only problem is that's not God. That's a cheap imitation. God does not look like the reflection in your mirror. He is not "altogether like you." If he were just like you, he wouldn't be God. Want a good idea of what the Lord is like? Read your Bible. God is exactly who he is and—like it or not—no amount of wishful thinking will change him.

God is the unchanging, eternally existing Lord of heaven and earth. You can't control him. You can't give him a makeover. All you can do is worship and obey him.

A DROP IN THE BUCKET

The nations are like a drop in a bucket; they are regarded as dust ... they are regarded by him as worthless and less than nothing.
—Isaiah 40:15, 17

God is so big that we can't even imagine how huge he is. He's bigger than the universe itself. Solomon said that "the heavens, even the highest heavens, cannot contain him" (2 Chronicles 2:6). God is bigger than a gazillion galaxies put together. No yardstick can even begin to measure God. And he's not just immense size-wise. He's also all-powerful, and his understanding is infinite.

No wonder that, compared to God, even powerful nations like the United States seem like a drop in the bucket. Even large countries like Australia are regarded as dust. And you gotta wonder, if great nations are like worthless specks of dust, what about you? Um ... I guess that'd make you smaller than a microbe on a dust speck. Okaaay, next question: If you're so microscopic, why would God care for you?

As nothing as people are—as tiny and less-than-dust sized as we happen to be—God cares for us. He loves us so much that he created this whole world just for us to live on. (It's big to us, at least!) He loves people so much that he sent his only Son, Jesus, to come down to this dusty, peewee-sized planet and live among us microbes ... er, people.

The nations may be a drop in the bucket. They may be worthless dust. But eensy-teeny people are worth a great deal! You are very valuable to God.

YOU KNOW WHAT I'M TALKING ABOUT

"The king is familiar with these things, and I can speak freely to him. I am convinced that none of this has escaped his notice, because it was not done in a corner."

—Acts 26:26

When Paul was talking to King Agrippa about Jesus, Paul said he was glad that he could speak freely to the king. He didn't have to stop and explain who Jesus was, what he had done, or that he had died on the cross. Paul didn't have to remind Agrippa that when Jesus died, "darkness came over the whole land" for three hours (Mark 15:33). The king knew all these things. Everyone in Israel did. Jesus had been headline news.

Lots of people today might be clueless about Jesus, but back in those days everybody in Israel knew who he was. No one denied that Jesus had actually lived. ("Hello! What planet are you from?") No one questioned that Pontius Pilate had crucified Jesus. No one denied that Jesus' tomb was empty. These were well-known facts.

This is the cool thing: Christianity is based on facts. Jesus lived and died and came back to life in real time in real history.

FEASTING WITH THE FAMOUS

Many will come from the east and the west, and will take their places at the feast with Abraham, Isaac and Jacob in the kingdom of heaven.
— Matthew 8:11

I n Jesus' day, the Jews believed that God would one day raise all the Israelites back to life, and the righteous would enjoy eternal life in God's kingdom. Part of their reward was that they'd sit down at huge tables and enjoy a fantastic feast. But Jesus said that there wouldn't just be Jews at the feast — but also non-Israelites from all over the world.

Ever been invited to a dinner with a famous celebrity, like maybe a sports hero or someone else you really admire? The food is great, the company's great, and you're having a great time! Or hey, even if it's not a banquet, maybe it's a great feast like Thanksgiving or Christmas, or a family reunion or picnic, and you get to enjoy mouth-watering food and spend time with long-lost cousins.

One of the very cool things about heaven is that we'll be reunited forever with saved loved ones. On top of that, tons of amazing Christians who have lived for the past two thousand years will be there. And we'll also be sitting down to eat with Abraham and Isaac and Jacob and other men and women straight out of the pages of the Bible.

One day, every believer who has ever lived will be invited to a great feast (Revelation 19:9) Make sure you believe in Jesus so that there's a place reserved for you!

RILED ABOUT RABBLE RUBBISH

The rabble with them began to crave other food, and again the Israelites started wailing and said, "If only we had meat to eat!"
—Numbers 11:4

When the Israelites left Egypt, many other people (non-Israelites and Egyptians) left Egypt with them. When they were out in the barren desert, God did a miracle and gave the Israelites manna to eat day after day. It was heavenly food, but the rabble (the rebellious crowd) got tired of it real quick. They hated manna and longed for other kinds of food.

If you've ever spent time with a rebellious kid or some guy with an attitude, you know it doesn't take long before he gets tired of good video games and craves other entertainment, like violent games and R-rated videos. He thinks Christian books are dumb and Christian videos are lame. He's loud about his opinions and he tries to get you dissatisfied with things that have Christian values.

The solution is to not rub shoulders with the rabble if you can help it. Just like the manna in the desert was the daily food of the Israelites, the Bible and Christian books and devotionals are your spiritual food. If other kids get bored with Christian stuff, that's their problem. Let them go. But don't let them make their problem your problem.

When the rebellious rabble try to get you riled up and dissatisfied, let them know that the manna is here to stay and that they can take it or leave it.

MEDDLING AND INTERFERENCE

Like one who seizes a dog by the ears is a passer-by who meddles in a quarrel not his own.
—Proverbs 26:17

I f you grab a dog by the ears, guess what he'll do? He'll bite you, of course! Or if his teeth can't reach you, he'll howl like crazy. Bottom line: you have no business grabbing Rover's ears. It's the same thing if you're walking by, see two people quarreling and butt in and give your opinion. That's called meddling (interfering) and you'll likely suffer for it.

Do you know what "interference" is when you're playing hockey? It's when you grab or bump a player from the other team—and he doesn't even have the puck. Do that and you get a penalty. Interference happens in regular life too: you see two kids arguing and you jump in uninvited. Don't. People don't like it when you butt in on quarrels. They were mad at each other, but they may get mad at you.

If you're really, really interested in an argument and it's really your concern, first stop and listen to what they're saying. Understand the issues before you start talking. Of course, if two people are quarreling furiously and getting madder and madder and calling each other names, that's different. If they're your friends, try to calm them down. If they're not friends, stay completely clear.

It can sometimes be a fine line knowing when to give your opinion and when not to. But if it's none of your business, well, it's a thick line. Don't cross it.

USE YOUR GOOD REP

"Ahikam son of Shaphan supported Jeremiah, and so he was not handed over to the people to be put to death."
—Jeremiah 26:24

The prophet Jeremiah preached an unpopular message, and the priests and false prophets hated him for it. One day they managed to get their grubby hands on him and decided to do him in. They would've too, except that Ahikam and some other guys spoke up for Jeremiah. Now, Ahikam wasn't Mr. Muscles. He wasn't a soldier. He was just an official, probably a secretary like his dad. But he was respected, so he used his rep to protect Jeremiah.

What do you do if you see someone picking on a little kid—teasing him, knocking his books down, or actually pushing him around? You don't want to get in a fight, right? But what do you do? Just walk on by and not get involved?

If there are no adults around, there are some things you can try. If you know the bully, then tell him to stop. If you're well known and have a rep, step in and tell him to cut it out. Remind him how lame it is for him to pick on little kids. Hopefully he'll listen to you. Of course, if he's hurting the kid, you have to do more—and tell an adult.

Avoid fights if you can. But if you have any kind of reputation, or say-so, use it to stop kids from hurting or harassing other kids. That's why God gave you a rep.

FEEL OTHERS' PAIN

"He feels but the pain of his own body and mourns only for himself."
—Job 14:22

We feel the pain of our own bodies, that's for sure. God designed us so that if we're cut and bleeding, we can feel it and do something about it before all the blood drains out of us. Or if we're sick, we feel it and get some rest. In his book *The Gift of Pain*, Dr. Paul Brand explains that pain is actually God's "gift" to us. Okaaay.

Newborn babies think only of themselves. If little Sweet Pea has a diaper rash, he could care less if you just broke your leg in a bungee jump. He cares only about his own pain. He's wailing like a cat with his tail stuck in an electrical circuit. Don't laugh. A lot of tween boys are the same. Mom has a pounding headache, but will they help set the table or carry the laundry basket for her? Nah.

God put your pain nerves in your body. He doesn't expect you to feel when someone else has pain. But he did happen to supply everyone with mouths and ears, so if someone tells you he's in pain, then you know it. And if you care for that person, you want to do something to help him.

One of the surest signs that you're growing up into a man of God is when you start thinking of other people.

A PUPIL'S PUPILS OPEN

At the end of your life you will groan ... "I would not obey my teachers or listen to my instructors. I have come to the brink of utter ruin."

—Proverbs 5:11–14

That does happen, you know. Kids who don't pay attention to their studies or don't obey their teachers and don't work in school often end up doing low-paying jobs like pulling the guts out of dead chickens all day long. And if they're still not serious then, they've got real trouble! They end up on the brink of ruin and wish they could go back to school again and do it right this time around.

You don't have to wait till the end of your life for this reap-what-you-sow principle to kick in. If you don't listen to your teachers, you'll fail math, English, and history. Fail enough subjects, and you'll have to take the whole grade over. What a waste of a year! Or refuse to listen to your instructors—whether it's a swimming instructor or a piano teacher—and you just blew your time and your parents' money.

No one's expecting you to be perfect. What has been known to work, however, is to listen to your instructors and teachers and make an effort. Sure, you'll mess up sometimes—we all do—but as long as you're trying to learn, you'll get the most out of what the teacher says.

If you don't wanna groan later on the road to ruin, apply yourself now. Take advantage of your opportunities to study and tune in to your teachers.

PAYING ATTENTION IN SCHOOL

"For in him we live and move and have our being." As some of your own poets have said, "We are his offspring.'"
—Acts 17:28

When Paul was preaching the gospel to the Greeks of Athens, he had to talk about God in a way they could understand and relate to. So in the sentence above, he quoted lines from two well-known Greek poets, Epimenides and Aratus. Another time, Paul recited lines from a comedy written by Menander (1 Corinthians 15:33). When Greek kids went to school in those days, they had to study Greek poets and play-wrights, and obviously Paul was paying attention.

When you're sitting in English class bored out of your skull learning about some poets or writers, you may wonder, "Who cares?" Or maybe you're in history class and the teacher's making you memorize the year the Revolutionary War began—and you wonder, "Why on earth do I need to know this?" Or maybe you listen and memorize facts just long enough to write your test paper—then forget them all afterward.

That kind of "learning" isn't really learning. It's some kind of bizarre mental gymnastics, but it's not how to get the most out of class time. You should study stuff to actually learn. Sure, some information is more important than other stuff, but you never know when the "unimportant" facts will come in handy—and not just to answer some trivia question, either.

You may not see the use of some things you study in school right now, but tune in when you're in class. Those facts may be more valuable than you realize.

GETTING A SECOND OPINION

Make plans by seeking advice; if you wage war, obtain guidance.
—Proverbs 20:18

When Solomon said, "Make plans by seeking advice," he meant get lots of good advice from people who've been there, done that, and lived to tell the tale. Then finalize your plans. When he says, "If you wage war, obtain guidance," he isn't talking about a snowball battle. He's advising kings not to just send soldiers charging into battle without a plan, but to first sit down with wise old warriors and let them explain how to do things.

When you have to do something you've never done before—like planning a camping trip or dogsledding across Antarctica—seek advice. Don't say, "Man, this is such a no-brainer, I'm going to just do it." You could end up fighting mosquitoes while you set up a tent in a swamp in the pouring rain at midnight. Or your dog team could be ambushed by giant killer penguins at the South Pole. (Just kidding!)

Other people may have experience to share; they've done it before and know what to do and what not to do. They can help you figure out the best way to do things. (Or they may warn you not to try it at all.) They may know how to put up a tent so it doesn't fill up with thirsty mosquitoes and sink in the swamp. Or they may know where to buy sled dogs.

Even if you've done something before, hey, situations change, so check things out each time.

IT PAYS TO LISTEN

If you have anything to say, answer me ... But if not, then listen to me;
be silent, and I will teach you wisdom.

—Job 33:32–33

When Job suffered a disaster, his friends took turns trying to figure out why God had let such bad things happen to him. The first three pals basically told Job, "God's punishing you." Finally it was Elihu's turn, and fortunately, Elihu was wiser. Now, Job had argued back to the other three guys, and Elihu had heard all of Job's explanations. Elihu was willing to listen if Job had anything new to say, but he also wanted Job to pay attention when he was talking.

You've probably noticed that it bugs your teacher or coach—or even your friends—if they're trying to teach you something or explain something and you keep interrupting, saying, "Yeah, yeah. I know that. I know. I know." If someone's trying to explain something to you, one of the surest signs that you're not listening—and not wanting to listen—is if you're talking back.

If you have something to say or need to explain something, by all means say it. But when your parents have let you say your piece, then open your ears to what they have to say. Even if you already know some of what they're telling you, respect them by listening. They'll probably say something you really need to hear.

There is a time to talk and explain your side of things. But when it's time to listen, then listen. You'll learn stuff and end up wiser.

BUILDING MUSCLES

"Five times I received ... the forty lashes minus one. Three times I was beaten with rods, once I was stoned."

—2 Corinthians 11:24–25

When the apostle Paul went around preaching the gospel, a lot of people loved him. His message got some people so mad, however, that they beat him. Fortunately, Paul was in top physical shape. He took lickings that most men wouldn't have survived and kept on ticking. There were so many whip marks and bruises on his back and arms and legs that Paul couldn't pick one out and tell you where it came from.

That's why the army puts soldiers through boot camp when they join; they want soldiers to be in top shape for when they fight. That's the same reason that you have physical education in your school. Teachers know that kids need gym class to be in shape and healthy. Besides that, physical exercise helps you think more clearly.

Most likely you won't get battered with stones and beaten like Paul, but the Christian life can still be hard. When you do good stuff—like helping some lady from your church move or cleaning up some older folks' yards—you have to be in shape. You're probably too young to be working out in the gym, but another way to get muscles is to faithfully do your chores.

Paul said, "Endure hardness with us like a good soldier of Christ Jesus" (2 Timothy 2:3). To endure hard times, you need hard muscles. To get those you need to exercise.

THANK GOD FOR MONEY

"You may say to yourself, 'My power and the strength of my hands have produced this wealth for me.' But remember the Lord your God, for it is he who gives you the ability to produce wealth."

—Deuteronomy 8:17–18

God was just about to bring the Israelites into Canaan and give them a rich land full of fruit and grain and luxury stuff like olive oil and honey. Oh yeah, and he was throwing in mines full of iron and copper. All God asked was that when their flocks and herds and wealth increased, they remembered to thank him. After all, he was the one giving them this rich land and the strength to make it produce.

God tells you to work because hard work earns money. But if you start getting the idea that it's your strength alone that brings in cash, remember who gave you strength and health in the first place. Or if you get paid for doing chores, thank God that your family has a house where you can do chores, and that your parents have jobs so they can earn money to pay you.

That's why Christians give money to church. You give part of your earnings back to God to acknowledge that he's the one giving you everything in the first place. If you're thankful to God for your blessings, you show it in a way that counts.

Take a moment to thank God for your health, your strength, and the fact that you either get an allowance or can earn money.

THE GREEN-EYED MONSTER

Do not fret because of evil men or be envious of the wicked, for the evil man has no future hope, and the lamp of the wicked will be snuffed out.
—Proverbs 24:19–20

In Bible times, most Israelites were poor farmers. There were some good rich people, but some of them had become rich by oppressing and cheating the poor. Meanwhile, many poor people envied the fine clothing, great food and life of luxury of the proud rich. Sure, the wicked were enjoying life for the moment, but as Solomon warned here, "the evil man has no future hope" (Proverbs 24:20).

When your parents struggle to find the money to buy you a bike and your allowance isn't big enough to buy a new computer game, but you see movie stars with all that their hearts can desire or drug lords traveling around the world in private jets and living on their own islands, it can be tempting to envy them. Or you cry, "Life isn't fair!"

No, life isn't always fair … at the moment. But it will be fair in the long run. The ungodly may have luxury now, all the designer clothes and newest high-tech toys, but if they don't have God they have "no future hope"—and their final destination … well, it isn't good. Whereas you may miss a few luxuries in this life, if you love Jesus, you'll inherit heaven.

It's insane envying the cool crowd and trying to keep up with them. And in the end, only the way of the cross promises the real results we desire.

WITNESSING AND ALLIGATORS

"Go into all the world and preach the good news to all creation."
—Mark 16:15

Jesus' disciples were enthusiastic about the fact that Jesus had died to save them from sin. Why? Because Jesus hadn't stayed dead! He was resurrected. He conquered death itself, and by doing this, he proved that he could give eternal life to everyone who believed in him. Then Jesus told his disciples to go into all the world and preach this good news to everyone. Thousands of Christians got excited, because it is terrifically good news.

Think about it like this: if you discovered a brand new TV show and it had the coolest characters with awesome graphics and action, but none of your friends knew about it, you'd be excited to tell them what channel it was on and what time it ran, right? Or if some kid was giving away free baby alligators, you'd tell all your friends about it, right? Well, your friends don't really need an alligator, but they do need Jesus.

The word gospel means "good news," and in Jesus' day, Christians obeyed Jesus and preached the good news. Christians are still doing it today. Maybe your church has missionaries in far-away nations. But you know what? Even Hometown, U.S.A., is part of "all the world," and people in your city need to hear about Jesus too, right? So tell them!

You don't have to be a Bible expert or a missionary to tell others about Jesus! You don't have to go to a far-away country. Tell your friends what you know or invite them to church.

BALANCED MEALS

"Now I urge you to take some food. You need it to survive."
—Acts 27:34

One time a ship carrying 276 passengers, including the apostle Paul, was sailing across the Mediterranean Sea. Suddenly a hurricane-force wind came roaring down on them. For fourteen days the storm blocked out the sun, battering them violently in total darkness. The passengers were terrified. They vomited up everything in their guts. They stopped eating and gave up hope. But Paul knew that they were about to crash on the rocks and needed the strength to swim to land, so he said, "Eat."

You probably aren't on a storm-tossed ship, screaming and puking into a hurricane, but the lesson still applies—you need to eat. You can't build muscles and stay healthy if you skip breakfast half the time, only snack on a granola bar at lunch, and pick at your dinner. Maybe you're not that picky, but do you only go for the starch and meat and skip your veggies?

You need your meat—no beef about that—but you need fruits and vegetables just as much. Remember Daniel and his pals who were shipped off to Babylon? They ate only vegetables and did fine. So chow down on the carrots and peas and corn. Gobble the cukes. Savor the salad. You need the stuff. Doesn't taste so great? At least eat some! Your body is screaming for the vitamins they contain.

TAKING CARE OF YOUR TEMPLE

"Don't you know that you yourself are God's temple ...? If anyone destroys God's temple, God will destroy him."
—1 Corinthians 3:16–17

A couple thousand years ago, the Israelites traveled to a special building—the temple in Jerusalem—to worship God. Since God dwelled there, people who entered the temple had to make sure that they were right with God before stepping inside. Then Jesus came along and announced that the day of stone temples was done and sent his Holy Spirit into the hearts of all believers! Now you are God's temple. Makes you want to be right with God all the time, huh?

Since the Holy Spirit lives inside you, take care of yourself. If you don't, you'll pay the price. That doesn't mean God's going to write your name on a lightning bolt and zap you with a million volts. He doesn't have to. God designed your body so that if you take care of it, it'll usually last a long time. But abuse it by smoking, and you're liable to get cancer. Take drugs—marijuana or crystal meth or whatever—and you'll mess up your body and your brain.

If you want to be healthy and strong for a long time, don't smoke or take drugs. That way you can be mountain biking as an old man instead of lying in the hospital. You can be scuba diving instead of sitting in a drug rehab center.

If you want to do your best and enjoy life to the fullest, keep your mind and your body clean. It's better than self-destructing.

MUSTARD AND MULBERRY MIRACLES

"If you have faith as small as a mustard seed, you can say to this mulberry tree, 'Be uprooted and planted in the sea,' and it will obey you."
—Luke 17:6

One day, Jesus' disciples asked him to increase their faith. They knew they didn't have great faith. But Jesus told them that even if they had a little faith, it could accomplish great things. The mustard seed was a very tiny seed, yet when it grew up, it became huge. Just like a tiny seed grows into something mighty, just a bit of faith can do great things.

Maybe you feel like your faith isn't strong, so you don't bother to pray. But Jesus' advice applies to you too. Do you need an obnoxious kid to leave you alone? Do you need a better memory for homework—or even to find your homework? Pray. God can do great things. Just don't pray for things God never meant for you to have—like your own flying saucer. It isn't always easy to know if you are being greedy or out of line in what you ask for. Pray for things that your heart tells you are best and ask if it's his will for you to have those things. Now, very few people have the faith to command a mulberry tree to rip its roots out of the ground and drop itself into the sea. But do you get what Jesus was saying? God can do astonishing miracles. (After all, he created the world and the entire universe out of nothing.) You just have to pray and believe that he'll answer you.

If mulberry miracles are possible, then surely God can do less dramatic miracles for you. Even if you think your faith isn't super great, pray.

FUN TRIVIA VERSUS WORTHLESS IDOLS

"They followed worthless idols and became worthless themselves."
—Jeremiah 2:5

Back in Jeremiah's day, many people turned their backs on God—the one who gave them life and blessed them with good things—and began praying to dead idols. Now, since those stone statues couldn't answer prayer, they were useless. The people's prayers to them were worthless. Since they were living their lives to please worthless idols, the people's lives ended up being worthless.

This might make you worry. "Wait a second. Lots of stuff I'm interested in—like collecting stamps or cartoon books or baseball cards—don't really have spiritual value, but I'm interested in them. They entertain me! I think they're cool!" Does God want you to give up your hobbies? If it doesn't have spiritual value and doesn't draw you closer to God, is it a worthless idol?

You can enjoy trivia and collect cartoon books and stuff. And music and videos are fun. God gave you a brain and a personality so you can use them. He doesn't want you to make any of those things the center of your life. Don't follow worthless stuff that takes you away from God. Love God and you'll have a truly worthwhile life.

JUNKING JUNK, POUNDING IDOLS

He tore down the altars and the Asherah poles and crushed the idols to powder and cut to pieces all the incense altars throughout Israel.

—2 Chronicles 34:7

Josiah was a young king who wanted to do what was right in God's eyes. Many Jews had stopped worshiping God and were bowing down to idols of the demon gods, Baal and Asherah. So Josiah started a spiritual revolution. He tore down the altars of Baal. He smashed the wooden carvings of Asherah. He hammered the stone idols to pieces and then pounded the pieces to powder.

There probably aren't any stone idols of Baal in your town, but lots of things can be like idols. This does not mean you should grab a sledgehammer and go after your neighbor's lawn ornaments. You are not responsible for other people's yards, so leave the gnomes alone. What you are responsible for is cleaning up any idols in your own life.

Look around your bedroom. Check under your mattress. Check out your walls. See any bad stuff you need to get rid of? Now, just because you like something a lot doesn't mean that it has become an idol. You can have posters of music stars or sports stars on your wall. The problem comes when they stand for values that are against God and your faith. Then you gotta send them packing.

Josiah broke the idols to pieces and then crushed them to dust to show that he was serious about getting rid of idols. No one worships dust, right? If you have junk to junk, junk it today.

COMMONSENSE SOLUTIONS

My men will haul them down from Lebanon to the sea, and I will float them in rafts by sea to the place you specify.
—1 Kings 5:9

King Solomon needed thousands of tons of cedar wood to build the temple of God. Cedar trees grew in King Hiram's land in the mountains of Lebanon. So Hiram said he'd have his men chop down the trees, drag them to the sea, and float them to some port in Israel. You notice Hiram didn't try to drag those monster logs a hundred miles overland from Tyre to Jerusalem. It was far easier to float those supersized suckers down the coast!

Sometimes what seem like totally huge problems and obstacles have simple solutions. Say you need to do your homework, but none of your pencils have a point and your pencil sharpener has vanished. Since you can't do your homework, you might as well goof off, right? Or what if you can't find your swimming trunks? Do you miss out on a swim?

Don't give up easily. Think of simple solutions. Your official sharpener might have evaporated, but there are other ways to get your pencil up and running. Like, you could ask your dad to sharpen it with a kitchen knife. (Don't try this yourself.) It's primitive, but it works. Lost your trunks? Wear your gym shorts. Again, primitive, but so what?

Work smarter, not harder. Solutions don't need to be things of beauty to work. They just need to work.

BUCKLE DOWN AND DO IT

Those who are wayward in spirit will gain understanding; those who complain will accept instruction.

—Isaiah 29:24

When someone is wayward it means they've wandered off the way and gone astray. Think of a field trip. Your class hikes to a fish farm, but you leave the path to chase a skunk through the woods. You are wayward, dude! You won't pass Go, you won't collect $200, and you won't learn anything about fish. (True, you'll learn a lot about how skunks defend themselves.) Wayward can also be a lazy kid doing whatever he can to get out of homework.

It's great that "those who complain will accept instruction," but right now these dudes are groaning and complaining and not accepting instruction. The reason they're complaining (besides the fact that it's a habit) is they have the idea that if they complain enough, they'll get out of cleaning their room or doing their homework or brushing their teeth. That's not how things work in the real world.

A big part of growing up is when you realize that, like it or not, there are things you have to do—so you do them without mumbling every step of the way. And since most wayward wandering, murmuring complainers eventually do buckle down and do what they're supposed to (because they can't get out of it), they might as well smarten up and stop complaining now.

When you stop chasing skunks through the woods, buckle down and get busy learning—that's when you gain understanding.

TESTED WITH HARD QUESTIONS

When the queen of Sheba heard about the fame of Solomon ... she came to test him with hard questions ... Solomon answered all her questions.
—1 Kings 10:1, 3

These verses don't mean that the queen of Sheba gave Solomon a killer math test. No, she did a lot of deep thinking and wasn't satisfied with the answers her wise men gave, so she was saving up a list of tough questions. When she heard how wise Solomon was, she hopped on her camel and rode a thousand miles north to Jerusalem to quiz him. Some of her questions must've been humdingers. No sweat. Solomon had the answers.

Ms. Sheba wasn't asking Solomon trivia questions, either. She was asking deep stuff like, "Why are we on earth?" and "Why do good people die?" (the kind of questions people still ask today). Well, as smart as Solomon was, an even wiser person came along—Jesus! Luke 11:31 says, "The Queen of the South ... came from the ends of the earth to listen to Solomon's wisdom, and now one greater than Solomon is here."

Solomon's answers to the queen's questions are lost, but, fortunately, some guy with a pen was handy when Jesus was talking, so his wisdom was written down and is recorded in the Gospels. This is great news when you consider that Jesus answered the very toughest questions of all. That's why it's important to read the Gospels.

It's cool to ask hard, deep questions. That's how you get answers. And there are answers. Check out the Bible today.

ODD OLD WORDS

They read from the Book of the Law of God, making it clear and giving the meaning so that the people could understand what was being read.
— **Nehemiah 8:8**

One day a huge crowd of Jews gathered, and a teacher named Ezra brought out the law of Moses, stood up on a platform, and began reading. But soon people began giving Ezra puzzled looks. See, the Hebrew Scriptures were nearly eight hundred years old! Many Jews spoke mostly Aramaic by then and didn't understand old Hebrew words. So Ezra first read the text very clearly, then he paused and explained the difficult words.

This still happens today. If you have a four-hundred-year-old King James version of the Bible and you read, "The rent is made worse" (Mark 2:21), you'd think it was talking about a greedy landlord, right? Wrong. It means the rip in the clothing just got bigger. Or if it talks about "earthquakes, in divers places" (Matthew 24:7), it doesn't mean quakes in the sea where divers dive. It means earthquakes in different places.

The great thing about newer translations is that they're written in modern English. Still, even with everyday English, you might not understand some words, right? You may hit a word and not understand what it means. Grab a dictionary or ask someone to explain. Don't just wing it.

If you really want to understand the Bible, start with the four Gospels in the New Testament. They're interesting and very easy to understand.

CRAFTY, WINDY TALK

We will no longer be infants ... blown here and there by every wind of teaching and by the cunning craftiness of men in their deceitful scheming.
—Ephesians 4:14

Infants will swallow just about any tale. Literally. You see toddlers chewing away on storybooks all the time. Even young kids don't really know what the Bible's about. They just listen to what adults tell them and believe them. That's great if those telling the stories are honest, good-hearted people doing their best to follow Jesus.

But what if someone's got some weird ideas, and they're cunning and crafty and can pass them off as truth? Then you're in trouble. You can get "blown here and there by every wind of teaching." It's like the big bad wolf's at the door, and your house is made of straw instead of solid bricks. You and the house both get blown away by wolfy's bad-breath tornado. You end up rolling around like a tumbleweed.

Don't wanna be blown here and there by wolfy windbags? Read the Bible for yourself so you know what it says. Start by driving slowly through the Gospels. There are lots of cool, important facts in Matthew, Mark, Luke, and John. Then if someone comes along and tries to blow you away with a deceitful, wild tale, you can pipe up and say, "Hey! The Bible doesn't say that!"

Don't be a toddler and just chew on the book. Read your Bible and get some solid truth inside you. Then you won't be blown away when the blowhards blow.

IT'S NOT LUCK

"Joseph is no more and Simeon is no more, and now you want to take Benjamin. Everything is against me!"
—**Genesis 42:36**

You can understand poor old Jacob thinking that everything was against him. As far as he knew, his son Joseph was dead, his son Simeon was in prison, and now he risked losing his youngest son, Benjamin. But the truth was, Joseph was alive, Simeon was fine, and Ben was in no danger. This wasn't a case of "bad luck," or everything being against him. We know from the rest of the story that God was in control and working things out to Jacob's benefit—although it certainly didn't seem that way to him.

Ever had a string of bad stuff happen and you say, "I'm having bad luck"? Some kids try to get good luck and keep away bad luck by carrying around lucky charms or lucky pennies. Is God okay with that?

No, we know he's not. He said he was against magic charms (Ezekiel 13:20). God wants people to know that he is in control of their destiny, not lucky charms. And even if God allows tough things to happen, it's for a good purpose. Or if bad stuff is happening because you're disobeying God, then repent, start obeying, and pray—and God can turn things around!

When it seems like everything is against you, remember: it has nothing to do with luck. God is the one who's in control of your life.

WHY THE GOSPELS WERE WRITTEN

These are written that you may believe that Jesus is the Christ, the Son of God, and that by believing you might have life in his name.
—John 20:31

After Jesus died, he showed himself to his disciples and gave them many proofs that he had come back to life. For example, Thomas said he wouldn't believe it was really Jesus unless he put his finger in the holes where the nails had been. Jesus showed up and said, "Put your finger here; see my hands." That convinced Thomas, and because this story was written down it can encourage our faith as well. (See John 20:24–28.)

You may wonder why it's so important to read your Bible regularly, or to spend time each day reading devotional books. You might think, "I've heard these stories in Sunday school. I know them. Why read them again?" Or you may wonder, "I already believe in Jesus, so I already have eternal life. So do I really need to read the Bible?"

You not only need eternal life, but reading and believing God's Word gives you the spiritual strength to face the troubles of this life also. Jesus said, "I have come that they may have life, and have it to the full" (John 10:10). Why struggle along in your own strength? Live life to the full! Besides, the purpose of reading devotions is to devote yourself to God, and that starts by getting his Word deep in your heart.

The Bible is full of amazing stories and miracles. Read it today and let God's Holy Spirit fill your heart with faith.

RULING NATIONS - OUR DESTINY

To him who overcomes and does my will to the end, I will give authority over the nations.

— Revelation 2:26

Jesus knew that Christians would be constantly tempted to compromise and disobey and live selfishly, so he made a terrific promise: If his followers were faithful to overcome their sins and do what was right, he would greatly reward them. The most faithful would be given authority over entire nations. To have authority means Christians will "reign on the earth" (Revelation 5:10). And of course, there'll be rulers under them who govern states and cities and towns.

Have you ever watched news on TV and been discouraged about what a mess the world is in? Have you ever wished that judges and governors and rulers would start treating people fairly and do what was right? Have you ever wished honest people could rule the world for a while? Well, one day that's going to happen. After Jesus returns, he will set up his kingdom on earth and pick godly people to run every part of this planet.

God's kingdom won't be like those games where you're the king of the castle and you get to boss all the other kids around and make them tie your shoes and be your slaves. Christians will rule, yes, but Jesus said that if you want to be a ruler, you have to first learn how to serve people and care about them (Mark 10:42–44). You govern others well by doing what's best for them.

ZONED OUT AND DISTRACTED

While your servant was busy here and there, the man disappeared.
—1 Kings 20:40

One time a prophet dressed up like a soldier to tell King Ahab a story. He basically said, "I was in the thick of battle when someone brought me this super-important prisoner and said, 'Drop everything and guard this prisoner! Don't let him escape! If he goes missing, you're dead!'" Well, sure enough, the soldier got busy with this and that, he took his eyes off the prisoner, and the man slipped away.

What about you? How easily do you zone out and get sidetracked? Your mom tells you to clean your room before dinner, but as you're picking up your books you get sucked into reading a comic. Or you're taking your dirty clothes to the laundry, but on your way you see your broken skateboard so you get busy fixing it. Next thing you know, it's dinnertime, your laundry's heaped in the hall, and your room's still a disaster.

If you allow yourself to get distracted, there'll be consequences. You really want to avoid consequences if you can—and you can! If you know that you're easily distracted, determine to get a grip on this problem and overcome it. That's half the battle right there. When you're given a responsibility or told to do something, stay focused. Discipline yourself. Remind yourself that there will be consequences if you don't.

The zone-out stuff may be interesting. But it you want to avoid trouble, don't allow it to derail you from what you're supposed to do.

TRIVIA AND JUNK INFORMATION

All the Athenians and the foreigners who lived there spent their time doing nothing but talking about and listening to the latest ideas.
—Acts 17:21

The guys in Athens, Greece, really wanted to be on top of stuff! Anything new that blew into town, they had to check it out. These guys liked to just sit around all day blabbing about new ideas—not necessarily important stuff, either. They were into trivia. They were junk-information junkies. They sure liked to talk and show off what they knew.

Now, if you're into baseball and love memorizing lists of batting averages, go for it! If you love Star Trek and want to be a trekkie, trek on! (Just don't set your brain to stunned.) But if that's all you do—like, if you do nothing but that—you are tripped off, dude! You can get into trivia so much that you miss living life itself.

Don't forget to comb your hair, do your homework, and live a life beyond TV and baseball cards. Get outside and breathe some fresh air! Go out and actually play baseball. Your hobby will still be waiting for you. The joystick will still be hooked up to the game box. But in the meantime, break out of your zombie state and live!

It's okay to be fascinated by trivia and keen to learn new stats and facts, but whatever you're into, you gotta take breaks from it and come up for air.

GETTING GROUNDED BY GOD

Jonah was inside the fish three days and three nights. From inside the fish Jonah prayed to the Lord his God.
—Jonah 1:17; 2:1

You know the story: Jonah disobeyed God and ran, so God had a monster fish swallow him. Jonah spent days sloshing back and forth in saliva, gagging and groaning—and probably barfing too. Do you know what happens to a chunk of meat in a fish's stomach? It gets digested. Next thing Jonah knew, gallons of digestive juice and stomach acids were pouring down at him. Acid? You know that's gotta sting!

Have you ever disobeyed God and ended up swallowed by a giant fish? Not likely. But maybe you were disrespectful to your parents and were sent to your room. Or you fooled around with the wrong crowd, doing the wrong things, and you were grounded for a week.

It's important to obey your parents, but you should determine to please God as well. God doesn't like to punish you or take away privileges in your life, and as long as you obey him, he doesn't need to. But if he needs to, God definitely will "ground" you in some way to get your attention. He wants to help you see that you need to obey.

When Jonah repented, God forgave him and gave him another chance. The monster fish puked him onto dry land. So the next time you're having some time out, try praying for God's forgiveness. God heard Jonah from a fish's gut. He can hear you too.

TAKE TIME TO CHEW

"I have treasured the words of his mouth more than my daily bread."
—Job 23:12

Job was an old, super wealthy wise man who lived a long time ago in the desert kingdom of Uz. In fact, he lived so long ago that only the first bit of the Bible existed—the book of Genesis. Yet Job treasured that one book more than all his jewels and gold and camels and land. He treasured it more than his daily bread, because bread kept him alive physically, but God's Word gave spiritual life.

You've got to eat good food to stay strong and healthy. But while you're chewing your cereal, remember that God's words are even more important. So take time to read your Bible. While you're munching your lunch, remember to snack on a Scripture "power bar." Just a few verses can pack a lot of energy. When you sit down to dig into dinner, be thankful for the Bible.

Jesus said to pray, "Give us today our daily bread," but he also said, "Man does not live on bread alone, but on every word that comes from the mouth of God" (Matthew 4:4; 6:11). You need food to live, but can't stuff your face with sandwiches and think that's all you need. You need to feed yourself spiritually. If you've never read the Bible on your own, start reading it today.

Job's Bible had only one book in it, yet Job considered it his greatest treasure—more important than food. You have the whole Bible—an entire banquet. Dig in!

FALSE KNOWLEDGE

Turn away from godless chatter and the opposing ideas of what is falsely called knowledge.

—1 Timothy 6:20

G reeks in New Testament times were big into education and learning, which was great! Some Greeks were really deep thinkers. Pythagoras, for example, is said to have discovered the Pythagorean theorem—a complicated math formula. He also decided that the world was round two thousand years before Magellan thought of it. But some Greeks took this deep-thinking stuff too far. They dreamed up complicated theories about God and creation and called their guesses "secret knowledge."

There are lots of theories and guesswork falsely called knowledge today too. People earn a lot of money writing wild books about the Bible and what it "really" means and what "really" happened. They write complex theories about how Jesus was never crucified, how he never died, etc. The gospels tell it like it was, yet some people try to explain it all sideways and say that it means something totally different.

In recent years, many people have invented "opposing ideas" to avoid believing the simple, straightforward message of the Bible. The apostle Paul said that such ideas were about as intelligent as "godless chatter," and he said to turn away from them. By the way, if you wanna know what chatter is, picture a budgie bird on steroids that chirps and chatters all day long and simply will not shut up.

If you want real knowledge, read the Bible and accept it at face value. Turn away from the chattering false knowledge people invent to oppose God's Word.

REASONABLE FAITH

"I am not insane, most excellent Festus," Paul replied. "What I am saying is true and reasonable."
—Acts 26:25

When the apostle Paul was explaining his faith to the Roman governor Festus, things were going fine until Paul talked about Jesus coming back to life from the dead. Festus nearly jumped out of his throne. "You are out of your mind, Paul!" he shouted. "Your great learning is driving you insane!" Paul denied being bonkers and insisted that what he was saying was true. It really happened. Not only that, but Christianity is reasonable—it all makes sense.

Some skeptics joke that you have to leave your brains at the door to believe in God. "You gotta take the Bible by faith," they say, "because it makes no sense." Oh, man! Way, waaaay out to lunch! That is simply not so. Christianity is the most reasonable faith of all. The Bible isn't a bunch of fluffy poetry and myths like most religions. Bible characters were real people who lived on earth in real time.

Archaeologists are scientists who dig in the earth to learn about ancient people and civilizations. One thing they've discovered time and time again is that the Bible is right! They've dug up tons of tablets and evidence in Israel and other places that prove the events the Bible described really happened and its facts are true and reasonable.

Don't leave your brains at the door when reading the Bible. You'll need them to examine the solid facts your faith is built upon.

WHEN GOD ANSWERS NO

"I had it in my heart to build a house ... and I made plans to build it. But God said to me, 'You are not to build a house for my Name'"
— 1 Chronicles 28:2 – 3

King David wanted to build a temple for God and when he asked God's prophet Nathan about it, Nathan thought a second then answered, "Whatever you have in mind, go ahead and do it, for the Lord is with you" (2 Samuel 7:3). Oh yeah! That's the kind of answer we like. But that night when Nathan prayed about it, God told him no, David was not to build a temple.

Sometimes your requests to God seem perfectly reasonable—like asking God to make your plans work out, or asking him to supply the money for summer camp. You think, "Well, I'm doing my best to obey God, so of course he's going to give me a yes answer." But you pray, and God either doesn't do it, or else he does something different than you expected. What do you make of that?

Sometimes it's just not the right time for whatever you're praying for. Or maybe, even if what you want is a good thing, God knows that it wouldn't be the best for you. In King David's case, God had other plans for David and made him some terrific promises, so David was okay with not building the temple. Solomon built it instead.

Remember, God is God. He's in charge. He doesn't have to answer yes to everything you desire, but he will do what's best for you.

DEVOTION 350

LISTENING TO GOD'S BREATHING

All Scripture is God-breathed and is useful for teaching, rebuking, correcting and training in righteousness.
—2 Timothy 3:16

Scripture means the "writings of the Old Testament." It also means the gospels about Jesus and the letters of the apostles in the New Testament. God inspired it all. God's breath, his Holy Spirit, fills every page. That's why you should let the Bible teach you what's right, rebuke you when you sin, correct you when you make mistakes, and train you how to live a godly life.

Lots of books today have good advice. The book that tells you how to program your new TV comes with good advice—what you can understand of it. Once in a while, even cartoon books have some good lessons in them. Come to think of it, even kids' TV shows have at least one good moral per show—usually something like, "Be nice to others." You can learn how to be a better person from many different books—fiction and nonfiction.

So is the Bible like other books? Was it just written by people to teach other people some practical information about life? No. People can give messed-up advice. The Bible gives solid, guiding truths. Men wrote it, but God's Holy Spirit inspired them to write it—from the first verse in Genesis that says God created the world to the last verses in Revelation that promise Jesus is coming back.

You want to know what God thinks about something? Read the Bible. Want to obey God and do what's right? Obey the Scriptures. God's Spirit inspired—breathed into—them.

CAN YOU WAIT A MINUTE?

"Pharaoh sent for Joseph.... When he had shaved and changed his clothes, he came before Pharaoh."
— Genesis 41:14

Joseph was falsely accused and ended up in prison in Egypt. Now, Egyptian men were all clean-shaven and Joseph *knew* that, but after years in prison, it seems he gave up caring how he looked. He just let his beard grow. Then one day Pharaoh had a dream that no one could explain so he sent a messenger to bring Joseph to interpret it. Suddenly Joseph was scrambling to clean up.

You know that you should shower and comb your hair and wear clean, unwrinkled clothes. Like your mom tells you, "Be presentable." You also know that you should brush the cereal off your teeth. Yet lots of times, you may not bother. "Who cares?" you figure. You're not out to impress anyone, so what's the big deal about how you look or smell?

But bump into someone you want to make a good impression on and suddenly you care a *lot* about how you look and smell—and there you stand, with spaghetti dangling from your molars, your hair tangled, and wearing a jam- and pasta-stained shirt. Hey, God even said that the high priest had to comb his hair (Leviticus 21:10).

Make yourself presentable before you dash out the door. Joseph was called to see Pharaoh immediately, but he still took the time to change his clothes and shave first.

DON'T STAND THERE WITH YOUR MOUTH OPEN

"Always be prepared to give an answer to everyone who asks you to give the reason for the hope that you have."
—1 Peter 3:15

You don't have to stand on a box on a street corner to tell others about Jesus. Live honestly, show concern for others and let them know you're a Christian and kids will come to you to ask you *why* you believe. They may ask sincerely or they may ask half-mockingly, surprised that you'd believe the Bible—but either way, be prepared to answer.

Some Christians can't really "give the reason" why they have hope that Jesus will give them eternal life. Why? Because they don't spend time *reading* the Bible. They tune out in church. It's like knowing you have a big test coming up but not bothering to open the text book and study, or not listening to the teacher explain the answers.

You need to be able to explain *why* you have hope—stuff like: (a) Jesus died and came back to life, so you can trust him to give *you* eternal life too; (b) God answers prayer; (c) archaeology proves the Bible was right time and time again, and can be trusted; and (d) science shows that life is so complex and amazing that there has to be an intelligent Creator.

To be able to explain why you believe, you need to know *what* you believe. Read the Bible. Ask your pastors and parents for good answers. Then you can explain to others.

YOUR FAITH, GOD'S WILL AND POWER

"If we ask for anything according to his will, he hears us. And if we know that he hears us — whatever we ask — we know that we have what we asked of him."
— 1 John 5:14 – 15

When two blind men asked Jesus to give them sight, he asked if they believed he had the power to do it. When they said, "Yes," Jesus replied, "According to your faith will it be done to you." They *did* have enough faith, because suddenly they could see! (Matthew 9:27 – 30)

Some people get the idea that faith is *the* main thing. As long as they have faith, they can ask God for anything. If they want perfect health or a yacht or their own candy store they put in their order with God then sternly remind him: "You *promised* I'd get *whatever* I asked for! So keep your word!" They even get angry at God if he doesn't answer.

But faith isn't everything. You have to humbly remember that God is the Lord God Almighty, Creator of the Universe, not some genii who shows up at a snap of your fingers to grant your wishes. When you pray to God, you must pray for things that are "according to *his* will." True, God can give you just about anything ... if it's his will.

Have faith when you pray. Believe God will give you what you want and need — but also remember to say, "If it be *your* will."

LIVING IN JESUS

"So then, just as you received Christ Jesus as Lord, continue to live in him, rooted and built up in him, strengthened in the faith as you were taught."
— Colossians 2:6 – 7

When you become a Christian, you're doing more than just believing that Jesus died to save you. You're also stating that he's your Lord and Master. Your brother or sister may not be the boss of you, but Jesus definitely is. He's the Son of God, he rules the entire universe, and you're a dot on a little planet called Earth. Just so you have that straight.

Now, this verse is saying that after you receive Jesus and become saved, you need to continue to remember that Jesus is Lord. He didn't change, after all. He's still the Son of God. He's still ruling the universe. And what does it mean to you personally when you realize Jesus is Lord? Well, it means that you will obey him and follow his teachings. How do you do that?

You need to continue to "live in him." Sink your roots deep down into Jesus. Stay plugged into Jesus and his power. Read the Bible. That way you'll not only be spiritually strong but you'll know what you believe and you'll clue into how he wants you to live.

Live in Jesus. He said in John 15:4, "Remain in me, and I will remain in you." And when you do that, Jesus gives you the power to live the Christian life.

CONTROLLING THE TRAFFIC

"He who guards his lips guards his life, but he who speaks rashly will come to ruin."
— **Proverbs 13:3**

T o "guard your lips" does *not* mean to avoid getting kissed. Long ago, cities had stone walls around them and the only way to leave or enter the city was through narrow gates. Armed guards stood in the gates and if they didn't think you had a good reason for entering the city—or for leaving it—they stopped you right there. (See Jeremiah 37:12–13.)

When you're upset or have a strong opinion about some subject, or if some mouthy kid challenges you or says you don't know a thing, you can be tempted to speak rashly—to blurt out whatever comes to mind. But as you probably already know, that can cause you a heap of trouble. Angry words stir up anger in others, and thoughtless comments can ruin even good friendships.

The solution is to be like a guard and stop the words about to go out the gate of your lips. Check them out. Question whether they need to be said or not. If you have trouble doing that, ask *God* to help you. Even King David had to pray, "Set a guard over my mouth, O Lord; keep watch over the door of my lips" (Psalm 141:3).

If you control the traffic going out of your mouth, you'll avoid offending good friends and stop a lot of angry traffic from coming back at you.

STOP NON-STOP QUARRELS

I plead with Euodia and I plead with Syntyche to agree with each other in the Lord.

—Philippians 4:2

E uodia and Syntyche were two ladies in the city of Philippi. They were Christians and as Paul said, "these women ... have contended at my side in the cause of the gospel" (Philippians 4:3). To "contend" means to fight or argue. They had argued *for* the gospel, yet now they were arguing *with* each other. We don't even know what they were quarreling about, just that Paul had to finally step in and urge them to stop.

Maybe you and your brother are always arguing over whose turn it is on the computer, or whose turn it is to do the dishes. Or maybe you have a sister who bugs you, and you constantly quarrel like cats and dogs. Or maybe you've had a falling out with a good friend and now you disagree with each other just to be disagreeable.

It's natural to disagree with others from time to time. Even the occasional argument is bound to happen. But to keep quarreling on and on is not good. Remember the things that unite you. They're more important than the petty things that divide you. Your brother or your sister are *family*—and if you're both Christians, they're your brother or sister in the Lord—so "agree in the Lord."

Jesus said to love others as much as you love yourself (Matthew 22:39), and if you do that, it'll be easier to stop quarreling with them.

ANGELS FREEZING TONGUES

"How will this be?" Mary asked the angel.
— Luke 1:34

W hen the angel Gabriel told Mary she'd have a baby, she asked, "How will this be?" So Gabriel explained. But when Gabriel told Zechariah that his wife would have a baby and Zech asked, "How can I be sure of this?" (Luke 1:18), the angel struck him dumb! For nine months! Are angels tougher on boys than girls? No. It was all in their attitudes. See, Mary believed; she just had a question. Zech didn't believe.

If you don't understand something in the Bible, it's okay to ask questions. If you wonder how God parted the Red Sea, ask your parents. They may tell you that God performed a miracle. Maybe you already knew that, but you wanted to know the mechanics of it. So ask someone else. Check it out with your youth group leader or read a Bible question-and-answer book. They may be able to tell you that the sea spread apart because "all that night the Lord drove the sea back with a strong east wind" (Exodus 14:21). Whoa! That was some wind!

There are commonsense answers to most Bible questions. Sure, sometimes God's power will be way beyond our under-standing. Why not? He's God. He invented matter and energy, and he can make them do some mind-bending stuff. Just about all we can say is, "It's a miracle." But you can *ask*. God won't strike you with lightning, and the angel Gabriel won't freeze your tongue.

DEVOTION 358

THE OTHER SIDE OF THE STORY

The first to present his case seems right, till another comes forward and questions him.

—Proverbs 18:17

In ancient Israel, just like today, when people had disputes they dragged the matter to court. Since each guy was convinced he was right, he passionately argued that such-and-such belonged to him, or that some accident was the other guy's fault. Guy Number One could be pretty convincing. But when it was Guy Number Two's turn to talk, he'd bring up all the details that Guy One had deliberately left out.

Ever get in a fight with your brother and then go running to your mom saying, "He hit me!"? So your mom calls your brother into the kitchen and she's ready to send him to his room or the dungeons. But when your brother limps into the kitchen he asks, "Did you tell Mom you kicked me first?" (Oh, yeah ... *that* little detail.)

There's usually more than one side to a story. Listen to all sides before you make up your mind. And if you're telling your side, make sure to tell not only the truth but the *whole* truth.

RULE NUMBER FIVE

Children, obey your parents in the Lord, for this is right. "Honor your father and mother."

—Ephesians 6:1 – 2

God gave adults authority over their children and thought that it was so important for kids to honor their parents that rule number five of the Ten Commandments reads: "Honor your father and mother" (Exodus 20:12). Then, to make sure we understood what *honor* means, the apostle Paul told us that the most sure-fire way to honor our parents is to obey them.

When I hear "obey your parents" I usually first think about little kids who don't have a clue what they're supposed to do, so they have to be told. As a thirteen-year-old I thought Rule Five didn't apply so much, because I already *knew* I was supposed to do my homework, clean my room, feed the dog, yadda yadda. No one needed to tell me what to do.

Well, the point isn't whether I know what to do. It isn't whether I *don't* know what to do and have to be told. The point is that we honor our parents by obeying them. Now, God knows that as we get older we start figuring out how to do things differently than our parents do them. Fine, if we can get mom and dad to sign off on it, cool. Just letting them have the final word is just so *hard*.

Why obey our parents? Because it's right. It's not only right but it's *so* right that God chiseled it into the Ten Commandments along with the other nine.

KEEPING PROMISES

The chief cupbearer, however, did not remember Joseph; he forgot him.

—Genesis 40:23

One time Joseph was falsely accused and ended up in prison in Egypt. When Pharaoh's cupbearer—the guy who served Pharaoh wine—landed in prison too, Joseph did him a huge favor by interpreting his dream. When the cupbearer was released and headed back to his job, Joseph said, "Mention me to Pharaoh and get me out of this prison." But the cupbearer forgot. Joseph sat in prison two more years.

Being spacey and forgetful is bad enough when you forget your homework or your lunch—and you're the only one that suffers. It's worse when your forgetfulness causes others to suffer, like if your dad's on top of a ladder in the rain and sends you into the house to get a hammer ... and you forget. No joke. People often forget to do what they're asked.

If you promise to be there to help someone or if you're asked to pass on an important message, remember to do it. If you know that you have a habit of getting tripped off and forgetting, try this: tell yourself, "Dad sent me to get a hammer. If I forget, he'll be standing in the rain at the top of a ladder, getting soaked and cold." Reminding yourself that others are depending on you will help you remember.

Keep your promises and do what you said you would do. It's an important part of being a man of God.

HAPPY CELEBRATION TIME

The Israelites who were present in Jerusalem celebrated the Feast of Unleavened Bread for seven days with great rejoicing.
— 2 Chronicles 30:21

The Israelites had so much fun worshiping God at this seven-day Feast, in fact, that they agreed to celebrate the festival seven *more* days. Keep the party going! It was fun, but things were disorganized. For example: they started celebrating the Feast a month behind schedule, tons of people showed up totally unprepared, and all kinds of unexpected strangers showed up.

Ever been to a cookout like that? Or ever attended a family reunion where people showed up late and unprepared? Like they brought hot dogs and buns, but no ketchup? Or there was soda pop but it was warm and there were only five cups for fifty people? Someone remembered to bring a barbeque but the gas bottle ran out after fifteen minutes, yadda yadda. What do you do? Do you join Aunt Bertha in complaining, "This is a *nightmare*"?

Nah. That's life. Stuff happens. You've just got to enjoy the party for what it is, not complain that you have to stand in line waiting for a cup when you're thirsty. Talk to your long-lost cousin while you're waiting. After all, that's the *reason* for get-togethers and reunions: to meet family members you haven't seen in a long time.

The Israelites attending the Feast in Jerusalem were totally disorganized, but they had a great time! That's the main thing, after all.

DESPERATELY THIRSTY DUDES

O God, you are my God, earnestly I seek you; my soul thirsts for you ...
in a dry and weary land where there is no water.

—Psalm 63:1

Before David became king, the army of old King Saul chased David all around the deserts of Judah. David wanted a cool, refreshing drink, and longed to relax in the shade, but it wasn't safe to camp near a well. He had to stay out in dry, dusty, dangerous places. That's when it dawned on him that he needed God just as much as water.

Have you ever been "dying of thirst"? Ever been on an all-day hike when everyone forgot to bring water? Or ever staggered up to a soda pop machine, nearly wild with thirst, and then realize that you have no change? Being thirsty doesn't just mean you *want* a drink. "Thirsty" gets to the point where cool liquid is all you can think of. Doctors say that people should glug down about six to eight glasses of water a day to stay healthy. We often don't do that so we get sick, have headaches, etc.

It's the same with our relationship with God. We should tank up on God's Spirit. But what do we do instead? We skip prayer time, miss Bible reading, and end up weak and confused. David was thirsty for God, and we are too: we just need to realize it.

Feel a thirst for God? Don't stagger around a dusty desert like a thirsty camel. Make a run for God's well, let down the bucket, and have a good, cool drink.

KEEP IT FLOWING

"When Samson drank, his strength returned and he revived."
—Judges 15:19

E ven Samson the Strong lost his strength when he hadn't drunk water in a while. He'd just finished wasting one thousand Philistines, and then he staggered among the piles of corpses, muttering, "Must I now die of thirst?" (No one answered; they were all dead.) Fortunately, God showed him a water spring, and Samson lay on the ground and chugged the cool stuff down. You thought Samson's strength was only from his long hair? Hey, the guy had to *drink water* to keep his strength up too.

Most people today don't drink nearly enough water. If all you're getting is a glass of milk in the morning, a juice box at lunch, and a glass of water at dinner, you're not even halfway there! Your body can get dehydrated (dried out)—and then you're in trouble. You can get headaches, or worse.

Want to avoid grief? Drink six to eight glasses of liquid a day. Sure, you'll be peeing more, but God designed your urine to carry poisonous wastes out of your body. Drink too little water, and the golden stream nearly dries up. By the way, make most of your liquid intake *water*. Drink that much soda pop and you'll have a sugar buzz. They'll be peeling you off the ceiling.

The Bible does not say, "Thou shalt drink water," but common sense tells you that you need to keep your tank full.

NOT BEATING THE AIR

"I do not fight like a man beating the air."
—1 Corinthians 9:26

Boxing is a lot tamer now than it used to be. The Greeks and Romans held boxing competitions, only back then boxers didn't wear gloves. They used bare fists. Worse yet, they wrapped hard leather around their hands to cause *extra* cutting damage. Paul obviously spent time watching boxers training and beating the air. See, no one had thought to invent punching bags yet, so Romans were big into shadowboxing.

A boxer has to practice to be prepared, but when it comes time to fight, practice is over; now all his skills are put to the test. It's the same with any sport. In basketball, for example, you practice dribbling and shooting the ball through the hoop. But when you're out on the court, and the crowds are going wild in the stands, you've got to take what you've learned, slip through the other team's defenses, and make things happen.

Paul used boxing as a symbol of a man of God battling against wicked spiritual forces and said he wasn't just shadow-boxing. Even though the forces fighting you are invisible, they're real! You're not just beating the air.

In whatever you do, if you want to excel, you have to practice. But when the real deal comes, it's showtime. No more beating the air. Now the goal is to connect.

FESTERING INFECTION

"He went to him and bandaged his wounds, pouring on oil and wine."
— Luke 10:34

Remember the story of the Good Samaritan? A Jew was journeying to Jericho when robbers jumped him, grabbed his clothes, beat him up, and left him dying in the dirt. A Samaritan saw the guy lying there and though he didn't know about germs, he *did* know that wounds had to be cleaned. So Good Sam used wine as antiseptic, then poured oil on the wounds, and wrapped them up to keep out the dirt. Smart thinking!

Boys are usually a lot more rough-and-tumble than girls. You're going to get more than your share of bumps, cuts, scrapes, and bruises. And since so many accidents happen outside in the dirt, germs swarm onto you like Viking raiders, feasting and festering. They breed like crazy, and next thing you know a zillion of them are causing an infection. There are deadly, dastardly diseases in the dirt, so the lick-and-spit trick just isn't good enough.

You don't want to be like a little toddler who needs a bandage on every tiny scratch. On the other hand, don't try to prove you're tough by refusing to get a wound looked after — especially if dirt has gotten into it. And let your mom pour on the antiseptic even if it stings. It's for your own good.

Germs can make you sick. Stop those little losers dead in their tracks. And remember the soldier's motto: take care of your wounded.

ALL FOR YOU

"Then Pilate took Jesus and had him flogged. The soldiers twisted together a crown of thorns and put it on his head."

—John 19:1–2

After Pilate ordered Jesus to be flogged, the Roman soldiers beat Jesus with a cat-o'-nine-tails. This was a whip made of nine knotted cords. Jesus' back and legs and arms were cut wide open. Jesus lost so much blood it left him weak. As if that wasn't enough, the soldiers shoved a "crown" of sharp thorns down onto his head.

Ever gone into a thorn bush and slashed your legs? Ever sliced your finger or stepped on a nail? It can hurt so badly that it makes you scream. Jesus knows what it's like to suffer terrible pain—stuff far worse than anything you've been through. His flesh was ripped open again and again.

Jesus suffered all this for you—even before he was crucified on the cross! Why did he do it? He didn't have to. He had a choice and he could have avoided it. He suffered because he loved you, and because he loved you, he wanted to make you a child of God so that you could live in heaven forever. It doesn't get any better than that!

You can invite Jesus to come into your heart right now and make him Lord of your life. If you've already done that, then thank him that he's already given you eternal life.

OLD TESTAMENT

Genesis

6:5	103
6:15–16	119
11:31	102
13:8	80
21:14	139
25:11	43
27:15	133
27:27	133
28:20–21	278
29:2, 10	142
36:24	157
39:6	83
40:23	366
41:14	357
42:7	146
42:36	346
44:33	116
45:5	161
45:24	161
49:14–15	162

Exodus

14:21	363
18:17	193
18:24	306
20:12	291, 365
20:17	51
22:6	298
23:2	27
23:5	179
31:3	129
33:20	195
34:29	289

Leviticus

13:47	71
14:35	21
15:13	88
15:16	244
19:16	16
19:17	108
19:17–18	49
19:32	41
19:33–34	57

Numbers

5:6–7	315
11:4	324
15:39	67

Deuteronomy

6:6–7	250
7:26	164
8:17–18	333
11:10	113
22:1, 3	177
29:5	218
34:7	65

Joshua

10:7, 9	66
11:18	115
14:12	98

Judges

5:18	165
6:13	196
8:20	241

11:1	305
13:9	40
13:12	189
14:6	22
15:10–11	297
15:19	367
20:15	258

1 Samuel

2:23, 25	224
2:26	64
13:13	138
14:29	30

2 Samuel

3:39	215
5:6, 8	153
7:3	355
9:3	286
14:6	304
14:25	10
14:30	226
16:6–7	145
17:7–8	163
19:7	309
19:43; 20:2	23
21:15	201
23:20	187

1 Kings

4:30	233
5:9	341
10:1, 3	343
12:8	160
19:21b	175

20:26	90
20:40	349
20:43	50
21:4	50

2 Kings

3:4–5	174
3:11	243
4:1	152
6:17	173
7:2	212
10:15	176
14:10	48

1 Chronicles

1:40	71
5:7–8	79
7:24	169
8:40	14
27:30	120
28:2–3	355
28:9	17
28:11–12	290

2 Chronicles

2:6	321
14:6	73
15:5	73
26:5, 16	270
26:16	203
30:21	367
32:8	186
34:7	340
34:33	223

Ezra

2:62	69
6:1–2	237

Nehemiah

3:5	78
4:3	109
4:10	248
4:14	188
5:9, 11	274
6:9	248
8:8	344
8:10	154

Job

1:9	86
8:8–9	117
12:7–8	35
12:10	313
14:22	327
16:4b–5	245
19:17	219
21:7	144
23:12	352
29:25	149
30:2	63
31:1	149
32:11–12	156
33:32–33	331
38:31–33	182
41:5	99

Psalms

4:8	55
8:3–4	267
19:9	255
23:4	55
26:12	251
31:10	282
31:24	282
34:7	106
39:5–6	227
50:7, 21	320

63:1	368
78:19–20	82
84:5, 7	87
91:11	106
101:3	164
104:21–22	24
107:27–28	96
119:11	125, 250
119:18	288
133:1	28
139:4	17
139:14	220
141:3	367
147:5	130
149:1	252

Proverbs

1:5	236
1:8–9	291
1:10, 15	185
2:4–6	12
3:5	268
3:6	54
3:27–28	314
4:14–15	317
5:11–14	328
6:6	35
6:6, 9	75
9:8	15
10:1	159
10:19; 17:28	126
13:3	361
13:20	26
15:1	318
17:9	111
17:14	225
17:17	205
17:22	154
18:13	128, 156
18:17	148, 364

19:8	308
19:21	36
19:22; 20:6	42
20:4	132
20:14	300
20:18	330
20:29	74
23:22	301
24:19–20	334
24:20	334
24:29	297
25:16	89
25:19	181
25:20	112
26:13	216
26:17	325
27:6	287
29:11	20
30:2–3	310

Ecclesiastes

3:1, 4	296
4:12	61
8:5–6	151
9:11	85
10:10	33
11:9	134

Isaiah

2:6	240
8:19	257
12:2	55
19:14	140
22:16	307
29:12	91
29:24	342
35:3	76
40:15, 17	321
47:13–14	191
61:5	208

Jeremiah

2:5	339
2:13	105
9:23, 24	13
12:5	260
26:24	326
29:13	96
33:3	268
35:6	171
36:17–18	34

Ezekiel

34:21–22	316

Daniel

1:17	32
9:2	234

Hosea

7:14	96

Obadiah

4	38
12	262

Jonah

1:17; 2:1	351

Micah

7:18	254

Zechariah

8:3, 5	272

Malachi

3:6	254

NEW TESTAMENT

Matthew

4:4; 6:11	352
4:9	136
4:10	136
5:24	58
5:39	202
6:15	95
6:19–20	56
6:28, 32	271
7:1–2	247
7:6	275
7:9–11	280
8:11	323
11:29	94, 281
12:34–35	206
18:21–35	95
21:28, 30	143
23:6	198
24:6	172
24:7	344
25:40	285
26:41	317

Mark

1:1	71
1:8	230
2:21	344
6:49–50	302
7:4	243
9:30–31	281
12:24, 27	303
13:26–27	137
15:33	322

16:15	335

Luke

1:3	101
1:18	363
1:34	363
6:22–23	229
6:48	284
8:28	121
10:34	371
11:31	343
14:28	68
15:29–30	60
17:6	338
17:15–16	147
24:11	209

John

2:23	122
3:3	72
7:15	183
8:31–32	231
10:10	347
14:2	293
14:6	19
14:9–10	195
14:26	288
19:1–2	372
19:36–37	266
20:31	347

Acts

1:8	11
2:31–32	9
2:38	230
4:12	19
4:13	37
7:22	29, 44
7:26	144

8:30	45
10:28	59
10:34–35	59
11:2–4	128
17:21	350
17:28	329
18:24	192
19:9–10	235
19:19	81
20:7, 9, 11	200
20:9	283
24:16	25
26:25	354
26:26	322
27:34	336

Romans

1:20	8
6:4	230
10:9	19
10:17	124
12:2	52
12:8	155
12:16	178
12:19	210
13:5	84
13:12	123
16:3–4	259
16:18	204
16:19	207

1 Corinthians

1:20	190
3:16–17	337
8:16	46
9:14	276
9:24	249
9:25	62, 107
9:26	269, 370
10:20	253

11:1	170
12:4, 7	53
13:11	127
14:20	127
15:32	100, 263
15:51–52	292

2 Corinthians

1:8	100
4:17	294
5:10	238
6:14	184
8:13	213
9:7	276
10:5	104, 168
11:24–25	332

Galatians

3:28	39
4:6	280
5:7	277
5:15	118

Ephesians

3:16–17	279
4:14	345
4:29	131
4:31–32	299
5:3–4	319
6:1–2	365
6:7–8	273

Philippians

2:3, 4	214
3:8	264
3:20–21	292
4:2	362
4:3	362

4:6	97
4:8	295
4:13	260

Colossians

1:15	195
2:6-7	360

1 Thessalonians

4:3	232
5:17, 18	18

1 Timothy

1:7	208
4:7-8	217
4:12	7
5:1-2	222
6:20	353

2 Timothy

1:15	261
1:17	246
2:3	332
2:5	47
2:22	135, 166
2:23	242
2:24	118
3:7	92
3:15	167
3:16	356
4:3-4	256
4:10	166
4:13, 21	199

Titus

3:2	110

Hebrews

5:12; 6:1	311
10:22	239
10:25	288
11:3	211
11:25	77
12:1	269
13:2	31
13:5	261

James

1:5	32
1:19	20
1:23-24	70
2:8-9	180
4:7	265
5:17-18	312

1 Peter

1:3-4	107
3:15	358
4:4	158
4:8	111
4:9	155
5:7	97
5:8-9	265

2 Peter

1:16	194
2:12	150

1 John

2:16	221
3:17	197
5:14-15	359

Revelation

1:3	93
1:5-6	94
2:26	348
3:20	279
5:10	348
21:23	293

Abraham, 43, 80, 139, 242, 323
adoption, 280
alcohol, 90, 140
angels
    as our guardians, 55, 106, 173
    not aliens, 208
    other occurrences, 31, 40, 137, 189, 209, 242, 249, 303, 363
anger management, 20, 50, 110, 154, 225, 226, 299, 318, 361
baptism, 230
becoming an overcomer, 98, 263, 348, 349
being adopted by God, 280
being content, 48
being different for good reasons, 28, 37, 39, 53, 120, 178
being worthy of trust, 83, 101
believing in Jesus, 72, 124, 238, 263, 280, 294, 323, 347
boy/girl relationships, 149
boy/girl roles, 39, 40, 169, 222, 259, 371
breakfast, 30, 127, 338
building family unity, 28, 78, 116, 286, 362
building trust with family, 28, 43, 78, 116, 286, 362
building trust with others, 146, 193, 287
bullies, 111, 145, 188, 274, 326
bullying, 48, 109, 316
cars, 14, 183
cheating, 16, 47, 176, 297, 300, 334
Christmas, 26, 107, 323
chores, 83, 87, 134, 143, 273, 284, 332, 333
church
    early 178, 228, 230, 311
    your 87, 140, 155, 176, 184, 197, 222, 252, 276, 332, 335
    other occurrences, 78, 132, 207, 230, 251, 259, 333, 358
clothes, 56, 133, 218, 271, 334
cleaning
    your body, 88, 243, 282, 337
    your cat's litter box, 67, 273

your clothes, 21, 133, 218, 349, 357

your hands, 243

your room, 75, 83, 93, 263

other occurrences, 273, 282, 284, 371

competing, 47, 48, 62, 107, 214, 249, 370

computers, 26, 29, 38, 61, 103, 190, 362

conscience, 25, 84, 239, 315

cross, 9, 92, 95, 167, 204, 231, 266, 322, 334, 372

crucifixion, 101, 194, 209, 266, 302, 317, 322, 353, 372

David, 17, 23, 120, 145, 163, 187, 215, 226, 251, 266, 286, 288, 304, 355, 361

drugs, 185, 207, 337

excellence vs. perfection, 7, 85, 170, 328

facing illness, 86, 154, 199, 205, 282, 312, 371

faith

the Christian, 53, 105

in God, 248, 257; great, 338

in Jesus, 12, 81, 124, 277

little, 257, 338

strong, 248

other occurrences, 7, 77, 98, 101, 135, 167, 191, 210, 211, 265, 278, 294, 311, 340, 347, 354, 359, 360

family

history, 69, 79

life, 73, 171, 186, 296, 367

traditions, 14

unity, 28, 78, 116, 286, 362

food, 30, 63, 64, 65, 75, 89, 131, 336, 352

forgiveness

asking for, 17, 72, 161, 239, 351

giving, 95, 104, 111, 161

other occurrences, 238, 254, 266, 298

friendship, 110, 111, 191, 286, 361

getting along with family, 118, 304, 362

getting along with others, 23, 110, 118, 161, 242

girls, 39, 40, 149, 169, 222, 259, 371
goals and dreams, 36, 119, 217, 264, 294, 370
God's help, 32, 36, 98, 100
gospels, 71, 124, 195, 233, 343, 344, 345, 347, 353, 356
grades, 30, 310
grandparents, 41, 103, 122, 162
greed, 51, 136, 137, 338
heaven
    good deeds rewarded in, 107, 238, 249, 294
    how to get in, 19, 81
    Jesus' return from 137
    other occurrences, 85, 293, 302, 323, 334, 372
Holy Spirit
    and the Bible, 288, 356
    in our hearts, 11, 72, 230, 285, 289, 337, 347
    power of the, 11, 22, 28, 94, 129
    other occurrences, 125, 281, 290
honesty, 18, 315, 358
hope, 124, 137, 197, 212, 216, 282, 334, 336, 358
integrity, 83, 101
internet use, 26, 61, 79, 101, 116, 158, 164, 237, 319
Isaac, 43, 133, 323
Jacob, 133, 142, 162, 278, 323, 346
Job, 41, 63, 86, 99, 114, 141, 149, 156, 219, 220, 245, 260, 331, 352
joking
    dirty, 131, 319
    dumb, 222
    good, 109
    hurtful, 109
    other occurrences, 7, 42, 57, 68, 126, 191, 200, 296, 354
Joseph, 83, 116, 146, 161, 346, 357, 366
keeping a promise, 143, 165, 314, 317, 366
love
    for enemies, 254
    for God, 46, 136, 170, 183, 227, 233, 249, 263, 339
    of God, 197, 202, 273
    for others, 46, 49, 57, 150, 165, 170, 180, 190, 214, 311, 362
    other occurrences, 41, 42, 58, 111, 116, 122, 135, 138, 144, 147, 198,
232, 238, 247, 255, 259, 262, 299, 301, 308, 334, 350
loyalty to friends, 286
material possessions, 51, 111, 136, 179, 197, 274

military, 76, 115, 169, 176, 332
moods, 50, 152, 216
Moses, 29, 40, 44, 65, 77, 82, 88, 98, 129, 144, 183, 184, 193, 195, 254, 277, 289, 306, 344
moving, 43
music choices, 252, 253, 339
Noah, 92, 103, 119
overcoming fear, 55, 76, 96, 97, 98, 231, 289, 302
parents
    and favoritism, 60
    honoring your, 159, 200, 241, 291, 301, 305
    listening to your, 93, 117, 160, 166, 291, 301
    obeying your, 50, 73, 143, 159, 200, 224, 241, 250, 273, 351, 365
peer pressure, 26, 27, 176
playing fair, 60, 80, 85
pornography, 158, 176, 221
practicing, 85, 129, 258, 370
punishment, 42, 84, 121, 145, 210, 218, 224, 262, 263, 331, 351
racism, 59, 147
religion, 81, 105, 184, 354
resurrection, 9, 263, 303
rewards, 12, 56, 107, 273, 294
rules, 16, 47, 62, 84, 110, 167, 171, 221, 241, 283, 307
salvation, 19, 55, 167, 197
saying no, 45, 90
science, 37, 44, 98, 116, 154, 192, 211, 248, 268, 310, 358
self-control, 20, 50, 232, 265
setting goals, 264
sex, 149, 158, 166, 221, 222, 232, 244, 319
sibling relationships
    and favoritism, 60
    getting along, 28, 95, 144, 198, 222, 304, 362
    other occurrences, 108, 139, 188, 210, 215, 223, 245, 283, 364
smoking, 64, 135, 337
Solomon, 12, 33, 75, 85, 134, 154, 156, 169, 185, 233, 290, 317, 318, 321, 330, 334, 341, 343, 355
sports, 29, 47, 62, 66, 74, 98, 129, 206, 214, 217, 270, 272, 323, 340, 370
stealing, 16, 25, 196
taking responsibility, 101, 298, 340
telling the truth, 18, 315, 358
thoughtfulness toward others, 25, 131, 150, 214, 285

toys, 51, 56, 80, 114, 136, 177, 186, 197, 215, 216, 283, 292, 334
trusting God, 55, 82, 113, 154, 210, 248, 268
trustworthiness, 83, 101
turning failure into success, 317
turning hardship into success, 163
TV
    shows, 206, 252, 295, 303, 314, 335, 356
    watching, 29, 71, 117, 162, 206
    other occurrences, 9, 23, 25, 91, 103, 153, 172, 221, 264, 269, 303, 348, 350
unbelievers, 184, 221, 254
video games
    complex, 117
    dark, 207
    good, 324
    playing, 61, 139, 164, 165, 241
    violent, 206
    other occurrences, 69, 103, 166, 236, 308
what's on our mind, 20, 206, 295
working together, 7, 47, 113, 135, 259
working together as a family, 28, 78, 116, 286, 362

We want to hear from you. Please send your comments
about this book to us in care of zreview@zondervan.com. Thank you.